UGC

University Grants Commission

NET/SET (JRF & LS)

Conducted By NTA

Teaching & Research Aptitude

General Paper I

17 Years' (2004-2020) Solved Papers

G K Publications (P) Ltd

Title : UGC 2021 : NET/SET (JRF & LS) :
Teaching & Research Aptitude General Paper I-17 Years' Solved Papers 2004-2020

Language : English

Editor's Name : Meenakshi Ramesh

Typeset & Published by :

Career Launcher Infrastructure (P) Ltd.

A-45, Mohan Cooperative Industrial Area, Near Mohan Estate Metro Station, New Delhi - 110044

Marketed by :

G.K. Publications (P) Ltd.

Plot No. 9A, Sector-27A, Mathura Road, Faridabad, Haryana-121003

ISBN : **978-93-90820-93-1**

Printer's Details : Made in India, New Delhi.

For product information :

Visit ***www.gkpublications.com*** or email to ***gkp@gkpublications.com***

Preface

UGC NET is a national level exam meant for scrutinizing the expert of the knowledge required for holding the position of lecturers and research fellows at Indian universities & colleges. This exam being conducted twice in a year has a huge group of candidates appearing for it every year, thus increasing the complexity level of the exam.

Cracking coveted and highly competitive examination like UGC NET is no cake walk. However, you can certainly guarantee yourself a smooth journey if you start early and plan it well. GKP provides a wide range of content for the UGC NET exam preparation in the form of Study Guides and Solved Papers for all three papers as per the exam pattern.

The Study Guides include comprehensive theory with a rich collection of questions in every chapter as per the syllabus. These books are completely designed as per the latest pattern by qualified subject matter experts, which can be used as a quick reference for every topic of the syllabus. The theory is presented in a crisp and lucid manner for an apt preparation, followed by questions that are up to the exam level and can help you solve most of the questions in the exam.

Once you are thorough with the entire concept and had moved on to the practicing phase, there is no better way to practice than to pick up the previous year papers of the exam. Therefore, as a serious aspirant, you must prefer the Solved Papers book which is a compilation of previous years papers. It is suggested to repeatedly solve all the questions in this book unless you have acquired the full marks in all of these papers.

Rigorous practice is required to crack an exam like UGC NET and it is our wish that this book will go a long way in ensuring that you get the same.

We hope this little effort of ours will be helpful in achieving your dreams. If you have any suggestions on improvement of this book, you can write to us at gkp@gkpublications.com.

All the Best!

Team GKP

Contents

Solved Paper 2020 (September)
Paper I

GENERAL APTITUDE

Directions for questions 1 to 5: Study the data in the given table and answer the questions that follow.

The table below provides data on the percentage (%) distribution of job vacancies in IT companies situated in various Indian cities in the year 2009 and 2019. In the year 2009, the total number of vacancies was 5.4 lakhs and in the year 2019, it was 8.6 lakhs.

City	Percentage (%) of Job Vacancies	
	2009	**2019**
Bangalore	15	22
Hyderabad	10	8
Pune	12	6
Mumbai	10	18
Chennai	8	10
NCR	21	20
Other cities	24	16

1. If the number of vacancies in the city of Pune is 48000 in the year 2019 and the percentage distribution is the same as given in the table, then what is the number of vacancies available in NCR in 2019?

(a) 1.2 lakhs
(b) 1.32 lakhs
(c) 1.48 lakhs
(d) 1.6 lakhs

2. What is the approximate percentage rise seen in vacancies available in the city of Hyderabad from 2009 to 2019?

(a) 21.8% (b) 23.23%
(c) 26.23% (d) 27.41%

3. What is the difference between the number of vacancies available in the city of Bangalore in the year 2019 and 2009?

(a) 108200 (b) 113120
(c) 118400 (d) 96400

4. What is the average number of vacancies available in the city of Hyderabad in the year 2009 and 2019?

(a) 41080 (b) 42740
(c) 58610 (d) 61400

5. What is the total number of vacancies available in the city of Chennai in 2009 and in that of Mumbai in the year 2019?

(a) 2.16 lakhs (b) 2.04 lakhs
(c) 1.98 lakhs (d) 1.92 lakhs

6. Given below are two statements

Statement I: Action research is cyclic in so far as it involves 'Plan-Act-Observe-Reflect' cycle

Statement II: The purpose of Action research is to develop a theory to explain causal relationship among variables

In light of the above statements, choose the ***most appropriate*** answer from the options given below

(a) Both Statement I and Statement II are correct
(b) Both Statement I and Statement II are incorrect
(c) Statement I is correct but Statement II is incorrect
(d) Statement I is incorrect but Statement 11 is correct

7. What type of device is a joystick?

(a) Input (b) Output
(c) Memory (d) Processor

8. The positive impact of communication depends upon

A. Acceptance of barriers

B. Planning

C. Sudden expression

D. Media selection

E. Use of language

Choose the correct answer from the options given below:

(a) A, Band D only

(b) B, D and E only

(c) C, D and E only

(d) A, D and E only

9. Which of the following committees/ commissions in their report recommended that science Education and Research should receive high priority to accelerate national economy?

(a) Acharya Narendra Dev Committee

(b) Mudaliyar Commission

(c) Radhakrishnan Commission

(d) Kothari Commission

10. Information is

(a) Raw data

(b) Processed data

(c) Redundant data

(d) Always ordinal data

11. In the statement 'the hill has smoke because it has fire', which type of fallacy may be identified?

(a) Asidha (b) Sadharana

(c) Asadharana (d) Vyapyatvasidha

12. If the word HEART is written as SQPMZ, then EARTH can be written as

(a) QPMSZ (b) QPMZS

(c) QMPSZ (d) QMPZS

13. Which of the following is an application software?

(a) Android (b) iOS

(c) Linux (d) MS Word

14. According to the classification of Ministry of New and Renewable Energy and Central Electricity Authority of India, small hydro power plants have capacity in the range

(a) 1-25 MW (b) 100-1000 kW

(c) 1-50 MW (d) 1-100 kW

15. Match **List I** with **List II**

List I	List II
A. Software	I. Step by step procedure to solve a problem
B. Hardware	II. Raw facts and figures
C. Algorithm	III. Hard Disk
D. Data	IV. Linux

Choose the correct answer from the options given below:

(a) A - Ill, B - I, C - II, D - IV

(b) A - Ill, B - II, C - I, D - IV

(c) A - IV, B - I, C - II, D - Il l

(d) A - IV, B - Ill, C - I, D - II

16. "A university teacher plans to study the performance of students in implementing specific projects in terms of their creativity level".

Which method of research will be appropriate to use in this context?

(a) Historical method

(b) Descriptive survey method

(c) Experimental method

(d) Ex post facto method

17. All knowable objects are nameable;

The pot is a knowable object;

Therefore, the pot is nameable

The above is an example of which type of inference?

(a) Kevalãnvayi

(b) Kevalavyãti reki

(c) Anvaya Vyatireki

(d) Shesavat

18. In the sequence

10KL13, 15PQ18, 19TU22, __

What will be last place?

(a) 22VW23 (b) 22VW24

(c) 23XY25 (d) 23XY26

19. Identify the correct sequence in increasing order of the carbon content per unit mass of the following reservoirs of carbon in terrestrial environment

A. Plants

B. Peat

C. Soil organic matter

D. Fossil fuels

Choose the correct answer from the options given below

(a) B, A,C, D

(b) A, C, B, D

(c) B, C, D, A

(d) B, AD, C

20. Match List I with List II

List I

Example

A. Addressing the nation over national TV network

B. Conducting a workshop for a select number of teachers

C. Internal conversation with fellow workers

D. Recollection of past events

List II

Type of communication

I. Horizontal communication

II. Intra-personal communication

III. Mass communication

IV. Group communication

Choose the **correct** answer from the options given below:

(a) A - I, B - II, C - III, D - IV

(b) A - II, B - III, C - IV, D - I

(c) A - III, B - IV, C - I, D - II

(d) A - IV, B - I, C - II, D - III

21. 'NEAT' an MHRD scheme, aims at

(a) Better learning outcomes in higher education

(b) Facilitating medical entrance examination

(c) Better financial resource management

(d) Promoting 'SWATCHH' campuses under Swatchh Bharat Abhiyan

22. Which of the following constitutes the 'ability' (can do) component for describing the competence of a teacher?

A. Confidence in performing teaching task

B. Knowledge of the subject being taught

C. Skill in analysing the learning tasks

D. Experience in handling learning task related situations

E. Commitment to organizing teaching-learning tasks

Choose the correct answer from the options given below:

(a) B, C and D only

(b) A, B and C only

(c) A, C and D only

(c) C, D and E only

23. Given below are two statements, one is labelled as Assertion A and the other is labelled as Reason R

Assertion A: Lakes are less pro ne to getting polluted than rivers

Reason R: Water in lakes gets replaced through natural processes

In light of the above statements, choose the most appropriate answer from the options given below

(a) Both A and R are correct and R is the correct explanation of A

(b) Both A and R are correct but R is NOT the correct explanation of A

(c) A is correct but R is not correct

(d) A is not correct but R is correct

24. Given below are two statements

Statement I: Maximum performance tests are designed to assess the upper limits of the examinee's knowledge and abilities

Statement II: Typical response tests are designed to measure the behaviour and characteristics of examinees

In light of the above statements, choose the most appropriate answer from the options given below

(a) Both Statement I and Statement II are correct

(b) Both Statement I and Statement II are incorrect

(c) Statement I is correct but Statement II is incorrect

(d) Statement I is incorrect but Statement 11 is correct

25. When reflective level teaching and learning are successful, students emerge with

A. A strong logical basis to retain the information

B. An enlarged store of tested insights of a generalized character

C. A firm relational structure in the items of information

D. An enhanced ability to develop and solve problems on their own

E. Seeing relationship and tool use of a fact

Choose the correct answer from the options given below:

(a) A and B only

(b) B and D only

(c) C and D only

(d) D and E only

26. Under Millenium Development Goal 5, maternal mortality ratio between 1990 and 20 15 was to be reduced by

(a) 50% (b) 75%

(c) 66% (d) 40%

27. A model of teaching is a description of

(a) Teacher behaviour including teacher and student talk

(b) Learning environment including teaching behaviour

(c) Learner-behaviour including personality characteristics

(d) Subject matter including its logical structure

28. Which of the following numbers are non-prime?

A. 11

B. 13

C. 19

D. 21

E. 15

Choose the correct answer from the options given below:

(a) A and E only (b) B and C only

(c) C and E only (d) D and E only

29. Find the odd number in the following series

644, 328, 164, 84, 44, 24, 14

(a) 44 (b) 84

(c) 164 (d) 328

30. Kavita sold a mobile phone at the price of Rs. 1950 and made a loss of 25%. At what price will she have to sell it to get a profit of 30%?

(a) Rs. 2600/- (b) Rs. 2780/-

(c) Rs. 3000/- (d) Rs. 3380/-

31. The chronological sequence in the development of communication system is

A. Emergence of language

B. Cave paintings

C. Interpersonal communication (verbal)

D. Appearance of printing technology

E. Telecommunication system

Choose the correct answer from the options given below

(a) A, B, C, E, D (b) B, E. D, C, A

(c) C, D, E, A, B (d) B, A, C, D, E

32. Given below are two statements, one is labelled as Assertion A and the other is labelled as Reason R

Assertion A: Universality of communication makes education vital and vibrant

Reason R: Semiotic narration does not lend itself credence to make it an efficient mode of teaching

In light of the above statements, choose the most appropriate answer from the options given below

(a) Both A and R are correct and R is the correct explanation of A

(b) Both A and R are correct but R is NOT the correct explanation of A

(c) A is correct but R is not correct

(d) A is not correct but R is correct

33. A predatory journal is the one whose publishers

(a) Publish for a fee with substandard or no peer reviewing

(b) The publishers of journals have acquired the publishers of journals in similar disciplinary domains

(c) Publish without a fee but with proper reviewing

(d) Insist on charging a fee for publishing after the manuscript has been accepted for publication with proper reviewing and editing

34. Match List I with List II

List I	List II
A. Web browser	I. Hard Disk
B. Operating system	II. Chrome
C. Secondary memory	III. MS-Word
D. Application software	IV. DOS

Choose the correct answer from the options given below:

(a) A - III, B - II, C - I, D - IV

(b) A - II, B - IV, C - I, D - III

(c) A - III, B - I, C - II, D - IV

(d) A - III, B - I, C - IV, D - II

35. A research scholar while writing his/her thesis uses ICT at various stages of research conducted. He/she justifies the conceptual errors in interpreting results attributing the same to the specific ICT devices. This will be labelled as

(a) Technical incompetence

(b) Research design's inadequacy

(c) Moral and ethical lapse

(d) Human error

36. Shifting technologies and communication institutions contribute to

(a) System integration

(b) Temporal dis integration

(c) Psychological disintegration

(d) Spatial integration

37. Which of the following features of research are associated with qualitative-inquiring?

A. Actual settings as the direct source of data

B. Data collection under controlled conditions

C. Concern with process rather than simply with outcomes

D. Establishing relationships and explaining the causes of changes

E. Concerned with what are called participant perspectives

Choose the correct answer from the options given below:

(a) A, C and D only

(b) A, C and E only

(c) B, C and D only

(d) C, D and E only

38. Consider the following three expressions

A. $35 \div 0.07$

B. $2.5 \div 0.0005$

C. $136.09 \div 43.9$

What is the correct descending order for the simplified values of A, B and C?

Choose the correct answer from the options given below

(a) B > A > C (b) C > A > B

(c) C > B > A (d) B > C > A

39. The first National Sports University (a Central Government University) is in the state of

(a) Haryana

(b) Manipur

(c) Arunachal Pradesh

(d) Punjab

40. Given below are two statements, one is labelled as Assertion A and the other is labelled as Reason R

Assertion A: Global emissions of carbon dioxide stagnated during the years 2014-2016

Reason R: Strong energy efficiency improvement measures and low carbon technologies were deployed during 2014-2016

In light of the above statements, choose the most appropriate answer from the options given below

(a) Both A and R are correct and R is the correct explanation of A

(b) Both A and R are correct but R is NOT the correct explanation of A

(c) A is correct but R is not correct

(d) A is not correct but R is correct

41. In which level of teaching, the activities of structuring, guiding and closely supervising the students' behavior predominate?

(a) Autonomous development level

(b) Reflective level

(c) Understanding level

(d) Memory level

42. Given below are two statements

Statement I: If the ratio of the speeds of A and B is a : b, then the ratio of the times taken by them to cover the same distance is b : a

Statement II: Suppose two men are moving in the same direction at u m/s and v m/s respectively, where u > v, then their relative speed is (u + v) m/s

In light of the above statements, choose the most appropriate answer from the options given below

(a) Both Statement I and Statement II are true

(b) Both Statement I and Statement II are false

(c) Statement I is correct but Statement II is false

(d) Statement I is incorrect but Statement II is true

43. Match List I with List II

List I Pairs	List II Pairs of analogies
A. Newspaper - Press	I. Thirst - Water
B. Dog - Kennel	II. Cow - Calf
C. Hen - Chick	III. Cloth - Mill
D. Darkness - Lamp	IV. Mouse - Hole

Choose the correct answer from the options given below

(a) A - II, B - IV, C - I, D - III

(b) A - III, B - IV, C - II, D - I

(c) A - IV, B - II, C - I, D - III

(d) A - I, B - III, C - II, D - IV

44. Identify the characteristics of a good research hypothesis from the following

A. Amenable to empirical verification

B. Conceptual clarity in defining the variables

C. Plausibility of relationships postulated

D. Accessibility in terms of researcher's resources

E. Extent of its non-refutability

Choose the correct answer from the options given below:

(a) B, C and D only (b) A B and D only

(c) C, D and E only (d) A B and C only

45. India's first National Policy on Education was a sequel to the recommendations of which of the following committee/ commissions?

(a) Kothari Commission

(b) Mudaliyar Commission

(c) Ramamurti Review Committee

(d) Radhakrishnan Commission

Directions for questions 46 to 50: Read the given passage carefully and answer the questions that follow

The ceremonial use of slogans and catchwords in educational discussions raises the suspicion of a tenuous linkage between thought and action. As stock phrases multiply and the talk begins to take on an idealistic ring, the wary listener might well begin to wonder whether the lip service paid to these concepts is connected with what actually goes on in classrooms. It is difficult in this day and age to be opposed to democracy, creativity, and innovation in education, but how are these attractive words related to the more mundane business of teaching practice? The answer, of course, is that the two are often not related - a fact that accounts for one of the most frequently recurring complaints among today's educators: the all-too-obvious gap between theory (i.e., educational talk) on the one hand and practice on the other.

The dissonance between what teachers say, or at least what their leaders say, and what they do takes many forms and has several important consequences. For some, it lays the groundwork for the development of a cynical outlook towards the admonitions of idealists and the advocates of new and supposedly revolutionary practices. This cynicism, which grows out of a prior sense of disillusionment, strikes many young teachers as they begin to appreciate the unrealistic quality of several of the expectations aroused during the period of their professional training. Teaching as actually experienced and as described in textbooks and college courses often turns out to be to quite different states of affairs. The result is that college instructors of education and other outsiders begin to be looked upon with suspicion by many practitioners. Even the testimony of fellow teachers may be viewed suspiciously when it conflicts with the listener's own experience in the classroom.

46. What is the sequel of lack of congruence between saying and doing as evident in teacher behavior?

(a) Opposition to revolutionary practices

(b) Lays ground for frequent complaints

(c) Emergence of disillusionment among teachers

(d) Support to the admonition of idealists

47. The passage analyses

(a) The linkage between language and discussions

(b) The schism between theory and actual practice of teaching

(c) The need to the use of high brow language in educational discussions

(d) The importance of idealism in education

48. How are the idealistic concepts related to the routine practices in education?

(a) They intertwine theory and practice

(b) They make classroom teaching innovative

(c) They make the business of education highly profitable

(d) They lead to the identification of gap between theory and practice

49. Why do young teachers appreciate the unrealistic quality of expectations?

(a) Because of the cynical attitude among teachers

(b) Because of the testimonial given by fellow teachers

(c) Because of their professional training

(d) Because of their own experience in teaching

50. The use of stock phrases in educational discussions has tended to reveal

(a) The linkage between thought and action

(b) The difference between saying and doing in classroom contexts

(c) The ceremonial importance of slogans

(d) The idealistic ring of talks

ANSWERS

1. (4)	**2.** (4)	**3.** (1)	**4.** (4)	**5.** (3)	**6.** (3)	**7.** (1)	**8.** (2)	**9.** (4)	**10.** (2)
11. (4)	**12.** (2)	**13.** (4)	**14.** (1)	**15.** (4)	**16.** (4)	**17.** (1)	**18.** (4)	**19.** (1)	**20.** (3)
21. (1)	**22.** (1)	**23.** (4)	**24.** (1)	**25.** (2)	**26.** (2)	**27.** (2)	**28.** (4)	**29.** (4)	**30.** (4)
31. (4)	**32.** (3)	**33.** (1)	**34.** (2)	**35.** (1)	**36.** (1)	**37.** (2)	**38.** (1)	**39.** (2)	**40.** (1)
41. (4)	**42.** (3)	**43.** (2)	**44.** (4)	**45.** (1)	**46.** (3)	**47.** (2)	**48.** (4)	**49.** (1)	**50.** (2)

Solved Paper 2019 (December)
Paper-I

1. In the two sets given below. Set I provides levels of teaching while Set II gives their focus of concern :

Set I (Levels of Teaching)	Set II (Focus of concern)
(a) Autonomous	(i) Problem raising and development problem solving level
(b) Memory level	(ii) Affects and Feelings
(c) Understanding	(iii) Recall of facts and level informations
(d) Reflective level	(iv) Seeings of relationship among facts and their examples
	(v) Peer learning

Select correct answer from the options given below:

(1) (a)-(i), (b)-(ii), (c)-(iv), (d)-(v)

(2) (a)-(i), (b)-(iv), (c)-(iii), (d)-(ii)

(3) (a)-(ii), (b)-(iii), (c)-(iv), (d)-(i)

(4) (a)-(v), (b)-(iv), (c)-(iii), (d)-(ii)

2. In the context of classroom teaching, the foundation on which a warm and nurturing relationship with learners can be built is called :

(1) Probing (2) Teacher Affect

(3) Structuring (4) Feedback

3. From the list of learning outcomes indicated below, identify those which are said to be high level outcomes :

(a) Learning of facts and rules

(b) Showing the ability to analyse and synthesize

(c) Awareness, responding and valuing

(d) Imitation, manipulation and precision

(e) Articulation and naturalization

(f) Organization and characterization

Select correct answer from the options given below :

(1) (b), (e) and (f)

(2) (a), (b) and (c)

(3) (b), (c) and (d)

(4) (a), (c) and (f)

4. Which one of the following sequences correctly reflects the evolution of educational technology support in higher education?

(1) Programmed learning material, text, book support, online and modular material

(2) Text book supplementation, programmed learning material, modular material and online methods

(3) Modular material, programmed learning, online and text book supplementation

(4) Online methods, modular material, text-book supplementation and programmed learning material

5. Match the two sets given below in which Set I mentions levels of measurement and Set II their properties :

Set I (Levels of measurement)	Set II (Properties)
(a) Nominal	(i) Classification, order, equal units and absolute zero
(b) Ordinal	(ii) Classification, order and equal units
(c) Interval	(iii) Classification
(d) Ratio	(iv) Classification and order

Select correct answer from the options given below

(1) (a)-(i), (b)-(ii), (c)-(iii), (d)-(iv)
(2) (a)-(ii), (b)-(iii), (c)-(iv), (d)-(i)
(3) (a)-(iii), (b)-(i), (c)-(ii), (d)-(iv)
(4) -(iii), (b)-(iv), (c)-(ii), (d)-(i)

6. Identify the tests from the list given below, which are maximum performance tests in the context of research :

(a) Personality tests
(b) Projective personality tests
(c) Achievement tests
(d) Attitude tests
(e) Intelligence tests
(f) Aptitude tests

Choose correct answer from the options given below:

(1) (a), (b) and (c) (2) (b), (c) and (e)
(3) (c), (e) and (f) (4) (a), (d) and (f)

7. Which of the following research is cyclic in nature?

(1) Fundamental research
(2) Applied research
(3) Action research
(4) Evaluative research

8. In which of the following sampling methods employed in research, the units comprising the sample are given equal and independent chance?

(1) Stage sampling
(2) Cluster sampling
(3) Dimensional sampling
(4) Snowball sampling

9. The issue of research ethics becomes relevant in which of the following stages of research?

(a) Problem selection
(b) Hypothesis formulation
(c) Hypothesis testing
(d) Data analysis and interpretation
(e) Defining of research population

Select correct answer from the following options:

(1) (a) and (b)
(b) (c) and (d)
(3) (b) and (e)
(4) (c) and (e)

10. In which type of qualitative research designs, individual stories to describe the lives of people are explored?

(1) Ethnography
(2) Grounded theory research
(3) Symbolic interaction
(4) Narrative research

11. Mini-summaries at the end of each class is called

(1) Verbal break-up
(2) Cliched conclusion
(3) Verbal signposting
(4) Staggered conclusion

12. Micro expressions, as part of classroom communication, are

(1) negative
(2) positive
(3) manipulative
(4) fleeting

13. Which of the following are essential for good classroom communication?

(a) Over emphasis on certain words

(b) Use of gobbledygook

(c) Proper employment of redundancy

(d) Immediacy of feedback

(e) Non-verbal cues

(f) Sidelining student criticism

Choose the correct option from the following :

(1) (a), (b) and (c) (2) (b), (c) and (f)

(3) (c), (d) and (e) (4) (d), (e) and (f)

14. Pitch of the teacher's voice in the classroom is described as

(1) Linguistic

(2) Paralinguistic

(3) Non-linguistic

(4) Macro-linguistic

15. Given below are two statements - One is labelled as Assertion (A) and the other is labelled as Reason (R).

Assertion (A): If a teacher wants to improve his or her abilities as an effective classroom communicator, he or she should first understand the students.

Reasons (R) :The ability to understand students and intended listening are disjointed propositions.

In the light of the above two statements, choose the correct option from the following :

(1) Both (A) and (R) are true and (R) is the correct explanation of (A)

(2) Both (A) and (R) are true, but (R) is not the correctexplanation of (A)

(3) (A) is true, but (R) is false

(4) (A) is false, but (R) is true

16. What is the missing term in the series given below?

2, 4, 6, 12, 10, 36, 14, ?, 18, 324...

(1) 50 (2) 72

(3) 108 (4) 18

17. Apoorav is son of Madhu. Vinod is brother of Madhu's husband. How is Apoorav related to Vinod?

(1) Uncle (2) Brother

(3) Nephew (4) Cousin

18. In a certain code "ENGLAND" is written as "ULSNYLV". Using the same code. "IRELAND" will be written as

(1) HQUNYLV (2) QHUNYLV

(3) QUHNYLV (4) HUQNYLV

19. The ratio of two numbers a and b is 3 : 7. After adding 9 to each number, the ratio becomes 9 : 17. The numbers a and b are :

(1) (6, 14) (3) (9, 21)

(3) (15, 35) (4) (18, 42)

20. The next term in the series

AT, EQ, IN, OK, ... is

(1) UH (3) UP

(3) US (4) UU

21. "Everyone is going to the party. You should go too." This inference commits which kind of fallacy?

(1) Ad Populum

(2) Equivocation

(3) Ad Verecundiam

(4) Ad Ignorantiam

22. "All students cleared their examination" and "Few students did not clear their examination".

This is an instance of ______.

(1) Contradictories

(3) Superaltern

(2) Subaltern

(4) Contraries

23. Product of two consecutive integers is divisible by 2. Therefore 4 × 5 (=20) is divisible by 2.

This is an example of which type of Reasoning?

(1) Abductive (2) Informal

(3) Inductive (4) Deductive

24. The distinction between laukika and alaukika is made with reference to which one of the following pramanas ?

(1) Anumāna (Inference)

(2) Upamāna (Comparison)

(3) Pratyaksa (Perception)

(4) S'abda (Verbal testimony)

25. 'Some students are sincere' is an example of which preposition?

(1) Universal Affirmative

(2) Universal Negation

(3) Particular Affirmative

(4) Particular Negation

Q. No. 26-30

The following table gives the percentage of marks obtained by five students in five subjects Maximum marks in each subject are given in the parenthesis below the subject name.

Student	Percentage (%) Marks obtained				
	Maths (100)	Chemistry (150)	Physics (150)	English (100)	Physical Education (100)
A	90	80	95	80	90
B	80	75	90	70	80
C	100	95	95	85	95
D	75	70	60	65	60
E	60	50	65	50	70

26. The aggregate of marks obtained by E is :

(1) 252.5 (2) 251.5

(3) 353.5 (4) 352.5

27. What is the difference between aggregate marks obtained by A and C?

(1) 40.5 (2) 41.5

(3) 42.5 (4) 43.5

28. In which subject, the students have obtained lowest average (%) percentage of marks?

(1) Chemistry

(2) Physics

(3) English

(4) Physical Education

29. The aggregate percentage of marks obtained by C are :

(1) 92.20% (2) 94.17%

(3) 95.21% (4) 91.17%

30. What is the average percentage of marks obtained by the students in Chemistry?

(1) 74%

(2) 79%

(3) 80%

(4) 81%

31. Which of the following is a programming language?

(1) Deep learning

(2) Machine learning

(3) Artificial Intelligence

(4) Python

32. Match List I with List II.

List I	List II
(a) WWW	(i) Volatile memory
(b) JAVA	(ii) Non-volatile memory
(c) RAM	(iii) World Wide Web
(d) ROM	(iv) Programming language

Choose the correct option from the following :

(1) (a)-(i), (b)-(ii), (c)-(iii), (d)-(iv)

(2) (a)-(ii), (b)-(iii), (c)-(iv), (d)-(i)

(3) (a)-(iii), (b)-(iv), (c)-(i), (d)-(ii)

(4) (a)-(iv), (b)-(i), (c)-(ii), (d)-(iii)

33. Which description is appropriate among the following for 'E-Governance'?

(1) To engage, enable and empower the citizens

(2) To provide fair and unbiased services to the citizens

(3) To provide technology driven governance

(4) To ensure people's faith in E-Commerce application

34. Which of the following is a search engine?

(1) Internet

(2) Bing

(3) Skype

(4) Acrobat Reader

35. Given below are two statements - One is labelled as Assertion (A) and other is labelled as Reason (R) :

Assertion (A) :The internet is a collection of interconnected computer networks, linked by transmission medium such as copper wires, fibre-optic cables, wireless connections etc.

Reasons (R) :World Wide Web is a collection of interconnected documents.

In the right of the above two statements, choose the correct answer :

(1) Both (A) and (R) are true, and (R) is the correctexplanation of (A)

(2) Both (A) and (R) are true, but (R) is not correctexplanation of (A)

(3) (A) is true, but (R) is false

(4) (A) is false, but (R) is true

36. Identify the Sustainable Development Goals from the list given below :

(i) Zero Hunger

(ii) Quality Education

(iii) Universal Primary Education

(iv) Clean Water and Sanitation

(v) Green Agriculture

(vi) Climate Action

Select correct answer from the options given below :

(1) (i), (ii), (iii) and (iv)

(2) (ii), (iii), (iv) and (v)

(3) (iii), (iv), (v) and (i)

(4) (i), (ii), (iv) and (vi)

37. Match the following two sets. Set I lists the names of states, while Set II indicates state specific missions.

Set I	Set II
(a) Andhra Pradesh	(i) Mukhva Mantri Jal Swavalamban Abhiyan
(b) Gujarat	(ii) Jalyukt Shivar Abhiyan
(c) Maharashtra	(iii) Neeti Samrakshana Udyamam
(d) Rajasthan	(iv) Sujalam Sufalam Jal Abhiyan

Select correct answer from the options given below :

(1) (a)-(i), (b)-(ii), (c)-(iii), (d)-(iv)

(2) (a)-(iv), (b)-(iii), (c)-(ii), (d)-(i)

(3) (a)-(ii), (b)-(i), (c)-(iv), (d)-(iii)

(4) (a)-(iii), (b)-(iv), (c)-(ii), (d)-(i)

38. Average noise levels in heavy traffic zones in major cities in India are generally in which of the following ranges of noise levels?

(1) 31-40 dBA
(2) 41-50 dBA
(3) 70-95 dBA
(4) 110-120 dBA

39. The Montreal Protocol refers to

(1) Cooperation among UN member countries to combat climate change

(2) Phasing out the consumption and production of ozone depleting substances

(3) Ensuring environmental sustainability

(4) Safeguarding societal quality of life worldwide

40. In which category Cochin International Airport has been conferred, the UN's Champion of the Earth Award?

(1) Policy Leadership

(2) Entrepreneurial Vision

(3) Science and Innovation

(4) Inspiration and Action

41. Which of the following modes of admission was prevalent in Nalanda University in ancient times?

(1) Entrance Examination

(2) Interview

(3) Good Academic Credentials

(4) Peer Discussion

42. What are the current challenges in the field of higher education in India?

(i) Expansion

(ii) Equity

(iii) Funds

(iv) Examination Reforms

(v) Excellence

(vi) Entrance Examinations

Select correct answer from the options given below :

(1) (i), (ii) and (vi) (2) (ii), (iii) and (iv)

(3) (iii), (iv) and (vi) (4) (i), (ii) and (v)

43. Which of the following emphasized that education needs to be managed in an atmosphere of utmost intellectual rigour, seriousness of purpose and of freedom essential for innovation and creativity?

(1) National Policy on Education-1968

(2) National Policy on Education-1986

(3) NITI Aayog-Three Year Action Agenda (2017-18 to 2019-20)

(4) Draft National Education Policy—2019

44. From the following, identify the organisation that provides a common platform to all universities including institutions of national importance :

(1) University Grants Commission

(2) Association of Indian Universities

(3) Distance Education Council

(4) Indian Institute of Advanced Study

45. Creation of World-Class Universities requires :

(i) Autonomous governance

(ii) Focused funding

(iii) Control over evaluation mechanism

(iv) Independent outcomes

(v) Appointment of staff by the State Machinery

Select correct answer from the option given below:

(1) (i), (ii) and (v) (2) (ii), (iii) and (v)

(3) (iii), (iv) and (v) (4) (i), (ii) and (iv)

Read the following passage carefully and answer questions from 46-50.

Intra-industry trade arises in order to take advantage of important economies of scale in production. That is. international competition forces each firm or plant in industrial countries to produce only one. or at most a few. varieties and styles of the same product rather than many different varieties and styles. This is crucial in keeping unit costs low. With few varieties and styles, more specialised and faster machinery can be developed for a continuous operation and a longer production run. The nation then imports other varieties and styles from other nations. Intra-industry trade benefits consumers because of the wider range of choices, i.e.. the greater variety of differentiated products, available at the lower prices made possible by economies of scale in production. Because of this, large welfare gains arise from the ability of consumers to greatly increase the variety of goods that they can purchase through trade. The importance of intra-industry trade became apparent when tariffs and other obstructions to the flow of trade among members of the European Union, or common market were removed in 1958. It was found that volume of trade surged but most of the increase involved the exchange of differentiated products within each broad industrial classification.

46. The impact of international competition on intra-industry trade can be seen in

(1) the availability of wide varieties of products

(2) the limited varieties of the same product

(3) adverse effect on industrial production

(4) restrictive advantages of production

47. Mass production of a few varieties of products will result in

(1) low cost of unit

(2) advantage to industrial economies of scale

(3) benefits to the customers of important economies

(4) increased cost of production

48. Development and use of specialised machinery will lead to

(1) more varieties of products

(2) decreased consumer welfare

(3) import of varieties of product

(4) hindered intra-industry trade

49. Lower product price means

(1) continued production run

(2) absence of choice

(3) increase in trade information exchange

(4) increased consumer purchasing power

50. What was the consequence of removal of barriers to the flow of trade in European Union?

(1) Sluggish intra-industry trade

(2) Flow of uniform products

(3) Spurt in trade volume among member states

(4) Emphasis on differentiated products

ANSWERS

1. (3)	**2.** (2)	**3.** (1)	**4.** (2)	**5.** (4)	**6.** (3)	**7.** (3)	**8.** (2)	**9.** (2)	**10.** (4)
11. (3)	**12.** (4)	**13.** (3)	**14.** (2)	**15.** (3)	**16.** (3)	**17.** (3)	**18.** (2)	**19.** (4)	**20.** (1)
21. (1)	**22.** (1)	**23.** (4)	**24.** (3)	**25.** (3)	**26.** (4)	**27.** (3)	**28.** (3)	**29.** (2)	**30.** (1)
31. (4)	**32.** (3)	**33.** (1,2,3)	**34.** (2)	**35.** (2)	**36.** (4)	**37.** (4)	**38.** (3)	**39.** (2)	**40.** (2)
41. (1)	**42.** (4)	**43.** (2)	**44.** (2)	**45.** (4)	**46.** (2)	**47.** (1)	**48.** (3)	**49.** (4)	**50.** (3)

Solved Paper 2019 (June)
Paper-I

1. A shift in attitude in respondents between two points during data collection is called

(1) Reactive effect
(2) Maturation effect
(3) Regression effect
(4) Conditioning effect

2. The time-frame in which a study explores a situation or problem is also called the

(1) Reference period
(2) Age
(3) Longitudinal
(4) Retrospective time

3. The major characteristic of correlation analysis is to seek out

(1) Differences among variables
(2) Variations among variables
(3) Association among variables
(4) Regression among variables

4. Which of the learner characteristics will influence his/her perspective in a course of study?

i) Learner's commitment
ii) Parents interest in the learner
(iii) Prior knowledge of the learner
(iv) Skill of the learner in the concerned area
(v) Family size of the learner
(vi) Socio-economic background of the family to which the learner belongs

Choose the correct answer from the options given below:

(1) (i) (iii) and (iv) (2) (i), (ii) and (Iii)
(3) (iii), (iv) and (v) (4) (iv), (v) and (vi)

5. The performance of a student is compared with another student in which type of testing?

(1) Criterion referenced testing
(2) Diagnostic testing
(3) Summative testing
(4) Norm-referenced testing

6. From the list given below identify those which are called Non-probability sampling procedures':

(i) Simple random sampling
(ii) Dimensional sampling
(iii) Snowball sampling
(iv) Cluster sampling
(v) Quota sampling
(vi) Stratified sampling

Choose the correct option

(1) (i), (ii) and (iii)
(2) (ii), (iv) and (v)
(3) (i), (iii) and (v)
(4) (ii), (iii) and (v)

7. The conceptual framework in which a research is conducted is called a

(1) Synopsis of research
(2) Research design
(3) Research hypothesis
(4) Research paradigm

8. Which of the following is an example of a maximum performance test?

(1) Personality tests
(2) Projective personality tests
(3) Aptitude tests
(4) Interest and attitude scales

9. Which of the strategies in the list given below will be associated with direct teaching?

(i) Providing examples and explanation

(ii) Promoting inquiry

(iii) Focussing on concepts

(iv) Giving review and recapitulation

(v) Oering practice and feedback

(vi) Problem raising and problem-solving

Choose the correct answer from the options given below:

(1) (i), (ii) and (iii) (2) (ii), (iii) and (iv)

(3) (i), (iv) and (v) (4) (iv) (v) and (vi)

10. From the list given below identify those questions which are called process rather than content based questions?

(i) Convergent questions

(ii) Divergent questions

(iii) Fact based questions

(iv) Concept based questions

(v) Open questions

(vi) Closed questions.

Choose the correct answer from the options given below:

(1) (i), (ii) and (iii) (2) (ii), (iii) and (M

(3) (iv), (v) and (vi) (4) (ii), (iii) and (v)

Geography seeks to understand the physical and human organization of the surface of the Earth. In the field of geography, inter-related themes are frequently seen. These are scale, pattern and process. Scale is defined as the level of structure on organisation at which a phenomenon is studied. Pattern is defined as the variation observed in a phenomenon studied at a particular scale. The third theme, process, further connects the first two. Process is defined as the description of how the factors that aect a phenomenon act to product a pattern at a particular scale. For instance, when a passenger on an aircraft looks out of the window, the View changes according to the scale. At the global scale when the aircraft maintains its height, he can see the chunks of clouds in all their pattern, the sun or the moon, as per the time. When the aircraft loses a little height, passengers can see the land and water masses in their dierentcolours and the shape of land masses. At the continental scale, the passengers can see the shapes of the land features and how they are distributed. The pattern emerges as the variation of land and water and the proportion of each. Looking carefully, passengers can note how each land mass aligns with the others and how each mountain bears the signs of the process through which it emerged.

The processes in a geography change in a regular and repetitive manner. One instance of this is the annual solar cycle of the sun and the earth. Most systems in nature display time cycles that are organised in a rhythm of their own as these time cycles and natural processes are always active, the environment of the earth is always in a state of dynamism. This environmental change is not only the result of natural process but also the result of human activity. Physical geography works towards understanding the interaction between man and nature and also the results of this interaction in order to manage global climate change better.

11. The time cycles of the system of nature follow their own

(1) Path

(2) Rhythm

(3) Process

(4) Cycle

12. The view seen by a passenger looking out of the window of an aircraft; will be affected by the

(1) Process

(2) Pattern

(3) Scale

(4) Rhythm

13. Physical geography studies the results of the interaction between man and nature in order to

(1) Understand global climate change

(2) Study the impact of man's activities on nature

(3) Address the issue of global climate change

(4) Reduce man-animal conflict

14. In geography, pattern studies the variation observed in a phenomenon at

(1) A particular scale (2) Any scale

(3) Every scale (4) Most scales

15. The alignment of landmass with other elements can be seen by a passenger on a flight on a

(1) Global scale

(2) Continental scale

(3) Local scale

(4) Time scale

16. Match Set 'A' with Set 'B'.

	A (Media)		B (Transmission/
(a)	Audio	(i)	Bandwidth
(b)	Advertising	(ii)	Linear communication
(c)	Internet	(iii)	Non personal Communication
(d)	Newspaper	(iv)	Frequency modulation

Choose the correct answer from the options given below:

	a	b	c	d
(1)	iii	iv	ii	i
(2)	i	ii	iii	iv
(3)	iv	iii	i	ii
(4)	ii	i	iv	iii

17. When subject and predicate of both the premises are the same but they differ in quality only, it is known as

(1) Contradictories (2) Contraries

(3) Subaltern (4) Super altern

18. Which of the following fractions is the result of the sum of an integer and its reciprocal?

(1) 15/8 (2) 26/5

(3) 36/7 (4) 37/5

19. Mass media do not have pre-determined functions for everyone and people use them the way they like. This is suggestive of the fact that,

(1) Audiences are active

(2) Content is of little significance

(3) Content lacks plurality

(4) Audiences are homogeneous

20. If proposition 'All republics are grateful' is taken to be true then which of the following propositions can be false?

(i) Republics are not grateful

(ii) Some republics are not grateful

(iii) No republics are grateful

(iv) Some republics are grateful

Select the correct answer from the options given below:

(1) (i) only (2) (ii) only

(3) (i), (ii) and (iii) (4) (ii) and (iii)

21. Sanjay sold an article at a loss of 25%. If the selling price had been increased by Rs. 175, there would have been a gain of 10%. What was the cost price of the article?

(1) Rs. 350 (2) Rs. 400

(3) Rs. 500 (4) Rs. 750

22. A communication process can be considered complete when

(1) The sender transmits the message

(2) The message enters the channel

(3) The message leaves the channel

(4) The receiver understands the message

23. A customer writes to a bank, 'Kindly send me a statement of my transactions in my savings bank account 'A' during the last three months". In terms of communication it will be called

(1) Input

(2) Message

(3) Output

(4) Feedback

24. A train leaves Agra at 5 am and reaches Delhi at 9 am. Another train leaves Delhi at 7 am and reaches Agra at 10:30 a.m. At what time do the two trains cross each other?

(1) 6:36 am (2) 6:56 am

(3) 7 am (4) 7:56 am

25. The proposition 'No red is black is equivalent to which of the following propositions?

(i) No black is red

(ii) All red are black

(iii)Some red are not black

(iv) Red is not black

Select the correct answer from the options given below:

(1) (i), (ii), (iii) and (iv)

(2) (iii) only

(3) (1) and (iv)

(4) (iv) only

26. Given below are two premises with four conclusions drawn from them. Which of the following conclusions could be validly drawn from the premises?

Premises:

(i) Some bags are tables

(1i) All bags are chairs.

Conclusions:

(a) Some tables are chairs

(b) No chair is tablewww.netugc.com

(c) Some chairs are bags

(d) Some bags are not tables

Select the correct answer from the options given below:

(1) (a) and (c) (2) (b), (c) and (d)

(3) (a) and (d) (4) (b) only

27. The average of 35 raw scores is 18. The average of first seventeen of them is 14 and that of last seventeen is 20. Find the eighteenth raw score.

(1) 42 (2) 46

(3) 52 (4) 56

28. Identify the reasoning in the following argument: Pre-active stage of classroom teaching is important just as pre-learning preparation stage of communication'

(1) Hypothetical (2) Deductive

(3) Inductive (4) Analogical

29. In the context of communication, usual sequence is

(1) Language -> Communication -> Society -> Civilization

(2) Communication -> Society -> Language -> Civilization

(3) Communication -> Language -> Society -> Civilization

(4) Language -> Society -> Communication -> Civilization

30. If REASON is coded as 5 and GOVERNMENT as 9, than what is the code for ACCIDENT?

(1) 6 (2) 7

(3) 8 (4) 9

Consider the following table that shows expenditures of a company (in lakh rupees) per annum over the given years. Answer the questions based on the data contained in the table:

	Item of expenditure				
Year	Salary	Transport	Bonus	Interest on Loans	Taxes
2008	150	90	2.00	20.0	80
2009	180	100	2.50	30.5	95
2010	200	110	2.75	35.5	105
2011	240	115	3.00	40.0	85
2012	250	125	3.25	42.5	100

31. The approximate ratio between the total expenditure on taxes for all the years and the total expenditure on transport for all the years is

(1) 31 : 40 (2) 25: 36

(3) 27 : 30 (4) 31 : 36

32. The total amount of bonus paid by the company during the given period is approximately what percent of the total amount of salary paid during this period?

(1) 0.9% (2) 1.3%
(3) 1.6% (4) 2.0%

33. Total expenditure of all the items in 2008 was approximately what percent of the total expenditure in 2012?

(1) 66% (2) 69%
(3) 72% (4) 75%

34. The approximate ratio between the total expenditure of the company in the year 2008 and the total expenditure of the company in the year 2009 is

(1) 57: 75 (2) 52: 68
(3) 57 : 68 (4) 68 : 57

35. What is the average amount of interest per year which the company had to pay (in Rupees) during this period?

(1) 30.5 Lakh (2) 32.7 Lakh
(3) 33.7 Lakh (4) 35.5 Lakh

36. Which of the following statements represent the main functions of UGC?

(i) Recognition of institutions
(ii) Maintenance of quality and standards
(iii) Appointment of Vice Chancellor
(iv) Giving grants to institutions
(v) Making state governments responsible for educational development

Choose the correct answer from the options given below:

(1) (i), (ii) and (iii) (2) (i), (iii) and (iv)
(3) (i), (ii) and (iv) (4) (ii), (iii) and (v)

37. The main aim of the faculty recharge scheme of UGC was to

(1) Address the shortage of faculty in higher education institution
(2) Upgrade the teaching skills of the faculty
(3) Upgrade the research infrastructure for the faculty in colleges and universities
(4) Strengthen the academia - industry linkage

38. Which of the following is an online store house of all academic awards like certificates, diplomas, degrees marksheetsetc?

(1) SWAYAM
(2) National Digital Library
(3) National Academic Library
(4) National Academic Depository

39. The convenient place to store contact information for quick retrieval in e-mail is

(1) Address box (2) Message box
(3) Address book (4) Message book

40. Montreal protocol aims at

(1) Reduction in emissions of green house gases
(2) Phasing out ozone depleting substances
(3) Prohibiting transboundary movement of hazardous waste
(4) Enhancing cooperation among UN member states for peaceful uses of nuclear energy

41. SMTP is an acronym for

(1) Simple Mail Transport Protocol
(2) Simple Mail Terminal Protocol
(3) Simple Mail Transfer Protocol
(4) Simple Mail Transition Protocol

42. In large parts of Eastern India, the ground water is contaminated by

(1) Arsenic (2) Lead
(3) Mercury (4) Nickel

43. Taj Mahal is mainly threatened by the deleterious effects of

(1) Sulphur dioxide (2) Chlorine
(3) Oxygen (4) Hydrogen

44. Two statements are given

Statement I: Earthquake 'A' is 5 on Richter scale and Earthquake 'B' is 8 on the same scale. Earthquake 'B' has 1000 times the wave amplitude compared to 'A'.www.netugc.com

Statement II: The energy released in 'B' is three times that of 'A'

Choose the correct option:

(1) Statement I is correct and Statement II is incorrect

(2) Statement I and II are correct

(3) Statement II is correct and I is incorrect

(4) Statement I and II are incorrect

45. A computer has main memory of 960 KBytes. What is the exact number of bytes contained in this memory?

(1) 960×8 (2) 960×1000

(3) 960×1024 (4) $960 \times 1024 \times 1024$

46. Name the scheme which facilitates academic and research collaboration between Indian Institution and the best institution in the world

(1) ICSSR - IMPRESS

(2) Sta Development Scheme

(3) SPARC

(4) Institutional Development Scheme

47. Which of the following file format is not a video file format?

(1) AW

(2) .MOV

(3) .MP4

(4) .JPEG

48. For the day to day administration of University, which of the following bodies is responsible?

(1) Senate

(2) Syndicate/ Executive council

(3) Student council

(4) Academic council

49. Efficiency of electrical power generation is least amongst the following sources of energy in case of

(1) Solar

(2) Wind

(3) Geothermal

(4) Nuclear

50. Which of the following is a non-conventional learning programme in higher education?

(1) Swayam

(2) Face-to-face teaching-learning

(3) Tutorial class

(4) Seminar

ANSWERS

1. (3)	**2.** (1)	**3.** (3)	**4.** (1)	**5.** (4)	**6.** (4)	**7.** (2)	**8.** (3)	**9.** (3)	**10.** (4)
11. (2)	**12.** (3)	**13.** (3)	**14.** (1)	**15.** (2)	**16.** (3)	**17.** (2)	**18.** (2)	**19.** (1)	**20.** (3)
21. (3)	**22.** (4)	**23.** (2)	**24.** (4)	**25.** (3)	**26.** (1)	**27.** (3)	**28.** (4)	**29.** (3)	**30.** (2)
31. (4)	**32.** (2)	**33.** (1)	**34.** (3)	**35.** (3)	**36.** (3)	**37.** (1)	**38.** (4)	**39.** (3)	**40.** (2)
41. (3)	**42.** (1)	**43.** (1)	**44.** (1)	**45.** (3)	**46.** (3)	**47.** (4)	**48.** (2)	**49.** (3)	**50.** (1)

Paper-I

Note : This paper consists of **Fifty (50)** objective type questions of **Two (2)** marks each. All questions are **compulsory**.

50 Q x 2 M = 100 Marks

1. Which of the following set of statements best describes the nature and objectives of teaching? Indicate your answer by selecting from the code.

(a) Teaching and learning are integrally related.

(b) There is no difference between teaching and training.

(c) Concern of all teaching is to ensure some kind of transformation in students.

(d) All good teaching is formal in nature.

(e) A teacher is a senior person.

(f) Teaching is a social act whereas learning is a personal act.

Code :

(1) (a), (b) and (d) (2) (b), (c) and (e)

(3) (a), (c) and (f) (4) (d), (e) and (f)

2. Which of the following learner characteristics is highly related to effectiveness of teaching?

(1) Prior experience of the learner

(2) Educational status of the parents of the learner

(3) Peer groups of the learner

(4) Family size from which the learner comes.

3. In the two sets given below Set - I indicates methods of teaching while Set - II provides the basic requirements for success/effectiveness. Match the two sets and indicate your answer by choosing from the code :

Set - I (Method of teaching)

(a) Lecturing

(b) Discussion in groups

(c) Brainstorming

(d) Programmed Instructional

Set - II (Basic requirements for success/ effectiveness)

(i) Small step presentation with feedback provided

(ii) Production of large number of ideas

(iii) Content delivery in a lucid language

(iv) Use of teaching-aids procedure

(v) Theme based interaction among participants

Code :

	(a)	(b)	(c)	(d)
(1)	(i)	(ii)	(iii)	(iv)
(2)	(ii)	(iii)	(iv)	(v)
(3)	(iii)	(v)	(ii)	(i)
(4)	(iv)	(ii)	(i)	(iii)

4. From the list of evaluation procedures given below identify those which will be called 'formative evaluation'. Indicate your answer by choosing from the code :

(a) A teacher awards grades to students after having transacted the course work.

(b) During interaction with students in the classroom, the teacher provides corrective feedback.

(c) The teacher gives marks to students on a unit test.

(d) The teacher clarifies the doubts of students in the class itself.

(e) The overall performance of a students is reported to parents at every three months interval.

(f) The learner's motivation is raised by the teacher through a question-answer session.

Code :

(1) (a), (b) and (c)

(2) (b), (c) and (d)

(3) (a), (c) and (e)

(4) (b), (d) and (f)

5. Assertion (A) : All teaching should aim at ensuring learning.

Reason (R) : All learning results from teaching.

Choose the **correct** answer from the following code :

(1) Both **(A)** and **(R)** are true, and **(R)** is the correct explanation of **(A)**.

(2) Both **(A)** and **(R)** are true, but **(R)** is not the correct explanation of **(A)**.

(3) **(A)** is true, but **(R)** is false.

(4) **(A)** is false, but **(R)** is true.

6. There are two sets given below, their characteristics.

Match the **Set - I** specifies the types of research, while **Set - II** indicates two and give your answer by selecting the appropriate code.

Set-I (Research types)

(a) Fundamental research

(b) Applied research

(c) Action research

(d) Evaluative research

Set-II (Characteristics)

(i) Finding out the extent of perceived impact of an intervention

(ii) Developing an effective explanation through theory building

(iii) Improving an existing situation through use of interventions

(iv) Exploring the possibility of a theory for use in various situations

(v) Enriching technological resources

Code :

	(a)	(b)	(c)	(d)
(1)	(ii)	(iv)	(iii)	(i)
(2)	(v)	(iv)	(iii)	(ii)
(3)	(i)	(ii)	(iii)	(iv)
(4)	(ii)	(iii)	(iv)	(v)

7. Which of the sets of activities best indicate the cyclic nature of action research strategy?

(1) Reflect, Observe, Plan, Act

(2) Observe, Act, Reflect, Plan

(3) Act, Plan, Observe, Reflect

(4) Plan, Act, Observe, Reflect

8. Which of the following sequences of research steps is nearer to scientific method ?

(1) Suggested solution of the problem, Deducing the consequences of the solution, Perceiving the problem situation, Location of the difficulty and testing the solutions.

(2) Perceiving the problem situation, Locating the actual problem and its definition, Hypothesizing, Deducing the consequences of the suggested solution and Testing the hypothesis in action.

(3) Defining a problem, Identifying the causes of the problem, Defining a population, Drawing a sample, Collecting data and Analysing results.

(4) Identifying the causal factors, Defining the problem, Developing a hypothesis, Selecting a sample, Collecting data and arriving at generalizations and Conclusions.

9. The problem of 'research ethics' is concerned with which aspect of research activities ?

(1) Following the prescribed format of a thesis

(2) Data analysis through qualitative or quantitative techniques

(3) Defining the population of research

(4) Evidence based research reporting

10. In which of the following activities, potential for nurturing creative and critical thinking is relatively greater ?

(1) Preparing research summary

(2) Presenting a seminar paper

(3) Participation in research conference

(4) Participation in a workshop

Read the following passage carefully and answer questions from 11 to 15 :

If India has to develop her internal strengths, the nation has to focus on the technological imperatives, keeping in mind three dynamic dimensions : the people, the overall economy and the strategic interests. These technological imperatives also take into account a 'fourth' dimension, time, an offshoot of modern day dynamism in business, trade, and technology that leads to continually shifting targets. We believe that technological strengths are especially crucial in dealing with this fourth dimension underlying continuous change in the aspirations of the people, the economy in the global context, and the strategic interests. The progress of technology lies at the heart of human history. Technological strengths are the key to creating more productive employment in an increasingly competitive market place and to continually upgrade human skills. Without a pervasive use of technologies, we cannot achieve overall development of our people in the years to come. The direct linkages of technology to the nation's strategic strengths are becoming more and more clear, especially since 1990s. India's own strength in a number of core areas still puts it in a position of reasonable strength in geo-political context. Any nation aspiring to become a developed one needs to have strengths in various strategic technologies and also the ability to continually upgrade them through its own creative strengths. For people-oriented actions as well, whether for the creation of large scale productive employment or for ensuring nutritional and health security for people, or for better living conditions, technology is the only vital input. The absence of greater technological impetus could lead to lower productivity and wastage of precious natural resources. Activities with low productivity or low value addition, in the final analysis hurt the poorest most. The technological imperatives to lift our people to a new life, and to a life they are entitled to is important. India, aspiring to become a major economic power in terms of trade and increase in GDP, cannot succeed on the strength of turnkey projects designed and built abroad or only through large-scale imports of plant machinery, equipment and know how. Even while being alive to the short-term realities, medium and long-term strategies to develop core technological strengths within our industry are vital for envisioning a developed India.

11. According to the above passage, which of the following are indicative of the fourth dimension?

(a) Aspirations of people

(b) Modern day dynamism

(c) Economy in the global context

(d) Strategic interests

Code :

(1) (a), (b) and (c) only

(2) (b), (c) and (d) only

(3) (a), (c) and (d) only

(4) (a), (b) and (d) only

12. More productive employment demands :

(1) Pervasive use of technology

(2) Limiting competitive market place

(3) Geo-political considerations

(4) Large industries

13. Absence of technology would lead to :

(a) Less pollution

(b) Wastage of precious natural resources

(c) Low value addition

(d) Hurting the poorest most

Code :

(1) (a), (b) and (c) only

(2) (b), (c) and (d) only

(3) (a), (b) and (d) only

(4) (a), (c) and (d) only

14. The advantage of technological inputs would result in :

(1) Unbridled technological growth

(2) Importing plant machinery

(3) Sidelining environmental issues

(4) Lifting our people to a life of dignity

15. Envisioning a developed India requires :

(1) Aspiration to become a major economic player

(2) Dependence upon projects designed abroad

(3) Focus on short-term projects

(4) Development of core technological strengths

16. Differentiation between acceptance and non-acceptance of certain stimuli in classroom communication is the basis of :

(1) selective expectation of performance

(2) selective affiliation to peer groups

(3) selective attention

(4) selective morality

17. Assertion (A) : The initial messages to students in the classroom by a teacher need not be critical to establish interactions later.

Reason (R) : More control over the communication process means more control over what the students are learning.

Code :

(1) Both (A) and (R) are true, and (R) is the correct explanation of (A).

(2) Both (A) and (R) are true, but (R) is not the correct explanation of (A).

(3) (A) is true, but (R) is false.

(4) (A) is false, but (R) is true.

18. Assertion (A) : To communicate well in the classroom is a natural ability.

Reason (R) : Effective teaching in the classroom demands knowledge of the communication process.

Code :

(1) Both **(A)** and **(R)** are true, and **(R)** is the correct explanation of **(A)**.

(2) Both **(A)** and **(R)** are true, but **(R)** is not the correct explanation of **(A)**.

(3) **(A)** is true, but **(R)** is false.

(4) **(A)** is false, but **(R)** is true.

19. Assertion (A) : Classroom communication is a transactional process.

Reason (R) : A teacher does not operate under the assumption that students' responses are purposive.

Select the **correct** code for your answer :

(1) Both **(A)** and **(R)** are true, and **(R)** is the correct explanation of **(A)**.

(2) Both **(A)** and **(R)** are true, but **(R)** is not the correct explanation of **(A)**.

(3) **(A)** is true, but **(R)** is false.

(4) **(A)** is false, but **(R)** is true.

20. Which of the following set of statements is correct for describing the human communication process ?

(a) Non-verbal communication can stimulate ideas.

(b) Communication is a learnt ability.

(c) Communication is not a universal panacea.

(d) Communication cannot break-down.

(e) More communication means more effective learning by students.

(f) Value of what is learnt through classroom communication is not an issue for students.

Code :

(1) (a), (c), (e) and (f)

(2) (b), (d), (e) and (f)

(3) (a), (b), (c) and (d)

(4) (a), (d), (e) and (f)

21. The next term in the series

–1, 5, 15, 29, ____?____, ... is :

(1) 36 (2) 47

(3) 59 (4) 63

22. The next term in the series
ABD, DGK, HMS, MTB, SBL, __?__, ... is :

(1) ZKU (2) ZCA
(3) ZKW (4) KZU

23. If VARANASI is coded as WCUESGZQ, then the code of KOLKATA will be :

(1) LOQOZEH (2) HLZEOOQ
(3) ZELHOQO (4) LQOOFZH

24. Introducing Rakesh to her husband a woman said, "His brother's father is the only son of my grandfather". The woman is related to Rakesh as :

(1) Aunt (2) Mother
(3) Sister (4) Daughter

25. Two numbers are in the ratio 2:5. If 16 is added to both the numbers, their ratio becomes 1 : 2. The numbers are :

(1) 16, 40 (2) 20, 50
(3) 28, 70 (4) 32, 80

26. Superiority of intellect depends upon its power of concentration on one theme in the same way as a concave mirror collects all the rays that strike upon it into one point.

What type of reasoning is entailed in the above statement ?

(1) Mathematical
(2) Psychological
(3) Analogical
(4) Deductive

27. Given below are two premises (A and B). Four conclusions are drawn from them. Select the code that states validly drawn conclusion(s) (taking the premises individually or jointly).

Premises :

(A) Most of the dancers are physically fit.
(B) Most of the singers are dancers.

Conclusions :

(a) Most of the singers are physically fit.
(b) Most of the dancers are singers.
(c) Most of the physically fit persons are dancers.
(d) Most of the physically fit persons are singers.

Code :

(1) (a) and (b) (2) (b) and (c)
(3) (c) and (d) (4) (d) and (a)

28. Which one among the following is a presupposition in inductive reasoning ?

(1) Law of identity
(2) Unchangeability in nature
(3) Harmony in nature
(4) Uniformity of nature

29. If the proposition 'domestic animals are hardly ferocious' is taken to be false, which of the following proposition/ propositions can be claimed to be certainly true ? Select the correct code :

Propositions :

(a) All domestic animals are ferocious.
(b) Most of the domestic animals are ferocious.
(c) No domestic animal is ferocious.
(d) Some domestic animals are non-ferocious.

Code :

(1) (a) and (b)
(2) (a) only
(3) (c) and (d)
(4) (b) only

30. Which one of the following statements is **not** correct in the context of Venn diagram method ?

(1) It is a method of testing the validity of arguments.
(2) It represents both the premises of a syllogism in one diagram.
(3) It requires two overlapping circles for the two premises of a standard-form categorical syllogism.
(4) It can be used to represent classes as well as propositions.

The table below embodies data on the production, exports and per capita consumption of rice in country P for the five years from 2012 to 2016. Answer questions 31-35 based on the data contained in the table.

Year-wise Production, Exports and Per Capita Consumption of Rice			
Year	Production (in million kg)	Exports (in million kg)	Per Capita Consumption (in kg)
2012	186.5	114	36.25
2013	202	114	35.2
2014	238	130	38.7
2015	221	116	40.5
2016	215	88	42

Where, Per Capita Consumption = (Consumption in million kg) ÷ (Population in million) and consumption (in million kg) = Production – Exports.

31. The percentage increase in the consumption of rice over the previous year was the highest in which year ?

(1) 2013 (2) 2014

(3) 2015 (4) 2016

32. What is the population of the country in the year 2014 (in million) ?

(1) 2.64 (2) 2.72

(3) 2.79 (4) 2.85

33. The ratio of exports to consumption in the given period was the highest in the year

(1) 2012 (2) 2013

(3) 2014 (4) 2015

34. In which year, the population of country was the highest ?

(1) 2013 (2) 2014

(3) 2015 (4) 2016

35. What is the average consumption of rice (in million kg) over the years 2012-2016 ?

(1) 104 (2) 102.1

(3) 108 (4) 100.1

36. Which of the following statements, regarding the term ICT is/are TRUE ?

P : ICT is an acronym that stands for Indian Classical Technology.

Q : Converging technologies that exemplify ICT include the merging of audio-visual, telephone and computer networks through a common cabling system.

(1) P only

(2) Q only

(3) P and Q

(4) Neither P nor Q

37. A new Laptop has been produced that weighs less, is smaller and uses less power than previous Laptop models. Which of the following technologies has been used to accomplish this ?

(1) Universal Serial Bus Mouse

(2) Faster Random Access Memory

(3) Blu Ray Drive

(4) Solid State Hard Drive

38. Given the following email fields, which of the email addresses will 'swami' be able to see when he rceives the message ?

To...	ram@test.com
Cc...	raj@test.com; ravi@test.com
Bcc...	swami@test.com; rama@test.com

(1) ram@test.com

(2) ram@test.com; raj@test.com; ravi@test.com

(3) ram@test.com; rama@test.com

(4) ram@test.com; rama@test.com; raj@test.com; ravi@test.com

39. Put the following units of storage into the correct order, starting with the smallest unit first and going down to the largest unit:

(a) Kilobyte (b) Byte

(c) Megabyte (d) Terabyte

(e) Gigabyte (f) Bit

Give your answer from the following code :

(1) (f), (b), (a), (c), (d), (e)

(2) (f), (b), (a), (d), (e), (c)

(3) (f), (b), (a), (c), (e), (d)

(4) (f), (b), (a), (d), (c), (e)

40. With regard to computer memory, which of the following statement(s) is/are TRUE ?

P : Read Only Memory (ROM) is 'volatile' memory.

Q : Random Access Memory (RAM) is 'volatile' memory.

R : Secondary Memory is 'volatiie' memory.

(1) P only (2) Q only

(3) P and Q only (4) P and R only

41. 'Fly ash' produced in thermal power plants is an ecofriendly resource for use in :

(a) agriculture as micro-nutrient

(b) wasteland development

(c) dam and water holding structures

(d) brick industry

Choose the **correct** answer from the code given below :

(1) (a), (b) and (d) only

(2) (b), (c) and (d) only

(3) (a), (c) and (d) only

(4) (a), (b), (c) and (d)

42. Which of the following types of natural disasters has no definite beginning and end?

(1) Earthquakes (2) Landslides

(3) Hurricanes (4) Droughts

43. **Assertion (A) :** Indoor air pollution is a serious health hazard.

Reason (R) : The dispersal of air pollutants is rather limited in indoor environment. Choose the **correct** answer from the code given below :

(1) Both **(A)** and **(R)** are true and **(R)** is the correct explanation of **(A)**.

(2) Both **(A)** and **(R)** are true but **(R)** is not the correct explanation of **(A)**.

(3) **(A)** is true and **(R)** is false.

(4) Both **(A)** and **(R)** are false.

44. In terms of their contribution to the total power generation in India, identify the correct sequence of energy sources - Thermal Power Plants (TPP), Large Hydropower Projects (LHP), Nuclear Energy (NE) and Renewable Energy (RE) which includes solar energy, wind energy, biomass and small hydropower projects.

(1) TPP > RE > LHP > NE

(2) TPP > LHP > RE > NE

(3) LHP > TPP > RE > NE

(4) LHP > TPP > NE > RE

45. Which of the following is considered as major source of pollution in rivers of India ?

(1) Unregulated small scale industry

(2) Untreated sewage

(3) Agricultural run-off

(4) Thermal power plants

46. India has the largest Higher Education System in the World after :

(a) The United States of America

(b) Australia

(c) China

(d) United Kingdom (U.K.)

Select the **correct** answer from the code given below :

(1) (a), (b), (c) and (d)

(2) (a), (b) and (c) only

(3) (a), (c) and (d) only

(4) (a) and (c) only

47. Prime Minister Research Fellowship is for students pursuing Ph.D programme in :

(1) State and Central Universities

(2) Central Universities, IISc, IITs, NITs, IISERs and IIITs

(3) IISc, IITs, NITs, IISERs, IIITs, State and Central Universities

(4) IITs and IISc

48. Leader of the Opposition is a member of committees which select:

(a) the Central Information Commissioner

(b) the Central Vigilance Commissioner

(c) the Chairperson of National Human Rights Commission

(d) the Chairperson of National Commission for Women

Select the **correct** answer from the code given below :

(1) (a), (b), (c) and (d)

(2) (a), (b) and (c) only

(3) (a), (c) and (d) only

(4) (a), (b) and (d) only

49. Which of the following statements are **correct** about gender budgeting ?

(a) It is a separate budget addressing the specific needs of women.

(b) It assesses the impact of government budget on women.

(c) It is an accounting exercise.

(d) It is another budgeting innovation.

Select the **correct** answer from the code given below :

(1) (b) and (d) only

(2) (a) and (d) only

(3) (a), (c) and (d) only

(4) (b), (c) and (d) only

50. Which of the following are the barriers to citizen-centric administration in India ?

(a) Wooden and inflexible attitude of the civil servants

(b) Ineffective implementation of laws and rules

(c) Awareness of rights and duties of citizens

(d) Lack of job opportunities for the youth

Select the **correct** answer from the code given below :

(1) (a), (b), (c) and (d)

(2) (a), (b) and (c) only

(3) (a), (b) and (d) only

(4) (a) and (b) only

ANSWERS

1. (3)	**2.** (1)	**3.** (3)	**4.** (4)	**5.** (3)	**6.** (1)	**7.** (4)	**8.** (2)	**9.** (4)	**10.** (3)
11. (3)	**12.** (1)	**13.** (2)	**14.** (4)	**15.** (4)	**16.** (3)	**17.** (4)	**18.** (4)	**19.** (3)	**20.** (3)
21. (2)	**22.** (3)	**23.** (4)	**24.** (3)	**25.** (4)	**26.** (3)	**27.** (2)	**28.** (4)	**29.** (1)	**30.** (3)
31. (2)	**32.** (3)	**33.** (1)	**34.** (4)	**35.** (4)	**36.** (2)	**37.** (4)	**38.** (2)	**39.** (3)	**40.** (2)
41. (4)	**42.** (4)	**43.** (1)	**44.** (1)	**45.** (2)	**46.** (4)	**47.** (4)	**48.** (2)	**49.** (1)	**50.** (4)

Solved Paper 2017 (NOVEMBER)

UGC NET

PAPER-I

Note : This paper consists of **Fifty (50)** objective type questions of **Two (2)** marks each. All questions are **compulsory**.

1. Which of the following set of statements best represents the nature and objective of teaching and learning ?

(a) Teaching is like selling and learning is like buying.

(b) Teaching is a social act while learning is a personal act.

(c) Teaching implies learning whereas learning does not imply teaching.

(d) Teaching is a kind of delivery of knowledge while learning is like receiving it.

(e) Teaching is an interaction and is triadic in nature whereas learning is an active engagement in a subject domain.

Code :

(1) (a), (d) and (e) (2) (b), (c) and (e)

(3) (a), (b) and (c) (4) (a), (b) and (d)

2. From the list given below identify the learner characteristics which would facilitate teaching-learning system to become effective. Choose the correct code to indicate your answer.

(a) Prior experience of learner

(b) Learner's family lineage

(c) Aptitude of the learner

(d) Learner's stage of development

(e) Learner's food habits and hobbies

(f) Learner's religious affiliation

Code :

(1) (a), (c) and (d) (2) (d), (e) and (f)

(3) (a), (d) and (e) (4) (b), (c) and (f)

3. Assertion (A) : All teaching implies learning.

Reason (R) : Learning to be useful must be derived from teaching.

Choose the correct answer from the following :

(1) Both (A) and (R) are true and (R) is the correct explanation of (A).

(2) Both (A) and (R) are true but (R) is not the correct explanation of (A).

(3) (A) is true, but (R)is false.

(4) (A) is false, but (R)is true.

4. On the basis of summative tests, a teacher is interpreting his/her students, performance in terms of their wellness life style evident in behaviour. This will be called :

(1) Formative testing

(2) Continuous and comprehensive evaluation

(3) Norm - referenced testing

(4) Criterion - referenced testing

5. Which one of the following is a key behaviour in effective teaching ?

(1) Using student ideas and contribution

(2) Structuring

(3) Instructional variety

(4) Questioning

6. Which of the following research types focuses on ameliorating the prevailing situations ?

(1) Fundamental Research

(2) Applied Research

(3) Action Research

(4) Experimental Research

7. A researcher attempts to evaluate the effect of method of feeding on anxiety - proneness of children. Which method of research would be appropriate for this ?

(1) Case study method

(2) Experimental method

(3) Ex-post-facto method

(4) Survey method

8. In which of the following arrangements a wider spectrum of ideas and issues may be made possible?

(1) Research Article

(2) Workshop mode

(3) Conference

(4) Symposium

9. In finalizing a thesis writing format which of the following would form part of supplementary pages?

(1) List of tables and figures

(2) Table of contents

(3) Conclusions of the study

(4) Bibliography and Appendices

10. Which of the following is susceptible to the issue of research ethics ?

(1) Inaccurate application of statistical techniques

(2) Faulty research design

(3) Choice of sampling techniques

(4) Reporting of research findings

Read the passage carefully and answer question numbers from 11 to 15.

Climate change is considered to be one of the most serious threats to sustainable development, with adverse impacts on the environment, human health, food security, economic activity, natural resources and physical infrastructure. Global climate varies naturally. According to theIntergovernmental Panel on Climate Change (IPCC), the effects of climate change have already been observed, and scientific findings indicate that precautionary and prompt action is necessary. Vulnerability to climate change is not just a function of geography or dependence on natural resources; it also has social, economic and political dimensions which influence how climate change affects different groups. Poor people rarely have insurance to cover loss of property due to natural calamities i.e. drought, floods, super cyclones etc. The poor communities are already struggling to cope with the existing challenges of poverty and climate variability and climate change could push many beyond their ability to cope or even survive. It is vital that these communities are helped to adapt to the changing dynamics of nature. Adaptation is a process through which societies make themselves better able to cope with an uncertain future. Adapting to climate change entails taking the right measures to reduce the negative effects of climate change (or exploit the positive ones) by making the appropriate adjustments and changes. These range from technological options such as increased sea defences or flood - proof houses on stilts to behavioural change at the individual level, such as reducing water use in times of drought. Other strategies include early warning systems for extreme events, better water management, improved risk management, various insurance options and biodiversity conservation. Because of the speed at which climate change is happening due to global temperature rise, it is urgent that the vulnerability of developing countries to climate change is reduced and their capacity to adapt is increased and national adaptation plans are implemented. Adapting to climate change will entail adjustments and changes at every level from community to national and international. Communities must build their resilience, including adopting appropriate technologies while making the most of traditional knowledge, and diversifying their livelihoods to cope with current and future climate stress. Local coping strategies and knowledge need to be used in synergy with government and local interventions. The need of adaptation interventions depends on national circumstances. There is a large body of knowledge and experience within local communities on coping with climatic variability and extreme weather events. Local communities have always aimed to adapt to variations in their climate. To do so, they have made preparations based on their resources and their knowledge accumulated through experience of past weather patterns. This includes times when they have also been forced to react to and recover from extreme events, such as floods, drought and hurricanes. Local coping strategies are an important element of planning for adaptation. Climate change is leading communities to experience climatic extremes more frequently, as well as new climate conditions and extremes. Traditional knowledge can help to provide efficient, appropriate and time - tested ways of advising and enabling adaptation to climate change in communities who are feeling the effects of climate changes due to global warming.

11. Given below are the factors of vulnerability of poor people to climate change. Select the code that contains the correct answer.

(a) Their dependence on natural resources

(b) Geographical attributes

(c) Lack of financial resources

(d) Lack of traditional knowledge

Code :

(1) (a), (b) and (c)

(2) (b), (c) and (d)

(3) (a), (b), (c) and (d)

(4) (c) only

12. Adaptation as a process enables societies to cope with :

(a) An uncertain future

(b) Adjustments and changes

(c) Negative impact of climate change

(d) Positive impact of climate change

Select the most appropriate answer from the following code :

(1) (a), (b), (c) and (d)

(2) (a) and (c)

(3) (b), (c) and (d)

(4) (c) only

13. To address the challenge of climate change, developing countries urgently require :

(1) Imposition of climate change tax

(2) Implementation of national adaptation policy at their level

(3) Adoption of short-term plans

(4) Adoption of technological solutions

14. The traditional knowledge should be used through:

(1) Its dissemination

(2) Improvement in national circumstances

(3) Synergy between government and local interventions

(4) Modern technology

15. The main focus of the passage is on :

(1) Combining traditional knowledge with appropriate technology

(2) Co-ordination between regional and national efforts

(3) Adaptation to climate change

(4) Social dimensions of climate change

16. The interaction between a teacher and students creates a zone of proximal :

(1) Difference

(2) Confusion

(3) Development

(4) Distortion

17. The spatial audio reproduction in a classroom can reduce the students':

(1) Cognitive load in understanding

(2) Respect for the teacher

(3) Motivation for excellence

(4) Interest in technology - orientation

18. The classroom communication should essentially be :

(1) Contrived (2) Empathetic

(3) Abstract (4) Non-descriptive

19. A good communicator begins his/her presentation with a :

(1) Complex question

(2) Non-sequitur

(3) Repetitive phrase

(4) Ice-breaker

20. In a classroom, the probability of message reception can be enhanced by :

(1) Establishing a viewpoint

(2) Exposing the ignorance of students

(3) Increasing the information load

(4) Using high decibel audio tools

21. In the series 1, 6, 15, 28, 45, ... the next term will be :

(1) 66 (2) 76

(3) 56 (4) 84

22. The next term in the series ABD, DGK, HMS, MTB, ... is :

(1) NSA

(2) SBL

(3) PSK

(4) RUH

23. In certain code, 'COVALENT' is coded as BWPDUOFM. The code of "ELEPHANT" will be:

(1) MFUIQRTW

(2) QMUBIADH

(3) QFMFUOBI

(4) EPHNTEAS

24. Ajay is a friend of Rakesh. Pointing to an old man Ajay asked Rakesh who is he ? Rakesh said "His son is my son's uncle". The old man is related to Rakesh as :

(1) Grandfather (2) Father-in-law

(3) Father (4) Uncle

25. A postman walked 20 m straight from his office, turned right and walked 10 m. After turning left he walked 10 m and after turning right walked 20 m. He again turned right and walked 70 m. How far he is from his office ?

(1) 50 m.

(2) 40 m.

(3) 60 m.

(4) 20 m.

26. It is Truism to say that no one was there when life first appeared on earth. Any assertion about life's origin, thus, should be treated as a theory.

The above two statements constitute :

(1) A historical explanation

(2) A narrative

(3) An argument

(4) A conjecture

27. Given below are four statements. Among them two are related in such a way that they can bothbe true but they cannot both be false. Select the code that indicates those two statements :

Statements :

(a) Honest people never suffer.

(b) Almost all honest people do suffer.

(c) Honest people hardly suffer.

(d) Each and every honest person suffers.

Code :

(1) (a) and (b)

(2) (a) and (c)

(3) (a) and (d)

(4) (b) and (c)

28. A deductive argument is invalid if :

(1) Its premises and conclusion are all true.

(2) Its premises and conclusion are all false.

(3) Its premises are all false but its conclusion is true.

(4) Its premises are all true but its conclusion is false.

29. Given below are two premises (a and b). From those two premises four conclusions (i), (ii),(iii) and (iv)are drawn. Select the code that states the conclusion/conclusions drawn validly (taking the premises singularly or jointly).

Premises :

(a) All bats are mammals.

(b) No birds are bats.

Conclusions :

(i) No birds are mammals.

(ii) Some birds are not mammals.

(iii) No bats are birds.

(iv) All mammals are bats.

Code :

(1) (i) only (2) (i) and (ii) only

(3) (iii) only (4) (iii) and (iv) only

30. Just as melting ice - cubes do not cause a glass of water to overflow, melting sea - ice does not increase oceanic volume.

What type of argument is it ?

(1) Analogical (2) Hypothetical

(3) Psychological (4) Statistical

Answer the questions 31 to 35 based on the data given in the table below.

Table : Number of registered vehicles in India and India's population.

Year	Total vehicles (Lakhs)	Two wheelers (Lakhs)	Cars, Jeeps, Taxis (Lakhs)	Buses (Lakhs)	Goods vehicles (Lakhs)	Others (Lakhs)	Population (India) (Millions)
1961	6.65	0.88	3.1	0.57	1.68	0.42	439.23
1971	18.65	5.76	6.82	0.94	3.43	1.70	548.15
1981	53.91	26.18	11.60	1.62	5.54	8.97	683.32
1991	213.74	142.00	29.54	3.31	13.56	25.33	846.42
2001	549.91	385.56	70.58	6.34	29.48	57.95	1028.73
2011	1417.58	1018.65	191.23	16.04	70.64	121.02	1210.19

31. The maximum decadal growth in population of India is registered in the period :

(1) 1961 - 1971 (2) 1991 - 2001

(3) 2001 - 2011 (4) 1981 - 1991

32. In which year the decadal growth (%) in number of cars surpassed that of the two wheelers ?

(1) 1991 (2) 2001

(3) 1981 (4) 2011

33. What was the average decadal growth in the number of cars during 1961 - 2011 ?

(1) ~ 131% (2) ~ 68%

(3) ~ 217% (4) ~ 157%

34. In the year 2001, out of total number of vehicles, the number of passenger vehicles (4 wheelers) accounted for :

(1) ~ 14% (2) ~ 24%

(3) ~ 31% (4) ~ 43%

35. What was the per capita ownership of two wheelers in India in the year 2011 ?

(1) ~ 0.084%

(2) ~ 0.0084%

(3) ~ 0.84%

(4) ~ 0.068%

36. What is the name for a webpage address ?

(1) Domain

(2) Directory

(3) Protocol

(4) URL

37. The data storage hierarchy consists of :

(1) Bytes, bits, fields, records, files and databases

(2) Bits, bytes, fields, records, files and databases

(3) Bits, bytes, records, fields, files and databases

(4) Bits, bytes, fields, files, records and databases

38. Which of the following domains is used for - profit businesses ?

(1) .org

(2) .net

(3) .edu

(4) .com

39. What is the full form of USB as used in computer related activities ?

(1) Ultra Security Block

(2) Universal Security Block

(3) Universal Serial Bus

(4) United Serial Bus

40. Which of the following represents billion characters ?

(1) Terabytes

(2) Megabytes

(3) Kilobytes

(4) Gigabytes

41. Which of the following pollutants is the major cause of respiratory diseases ?

(1) Suspended fine particles

(2) Nitrogen oxides

(3) Carbon monoxide

(4) Volatile organic compounds

42. **Assertion (A) :** In urban areas, smog episodes occur frequently in winters.

Reason (R) : In winters, a lot of biomass is burnt by people for heating purposes or to keep themselves warm.

Choose the correct answer from the code given below :

(1) Both (A) and (R)are true and (R) is the correct explanation of (A)

(2) Both (A) and (R)are true but (R) is not the correct explanation of (A)

(3) (A) is true and (R)is false

(4) Both (A) and (R)are false

43. Occurrence of natural hazards is affected by :

(a) Land use changes

(b) Drainage and construction

(c) Ozone depletion

(d) Climate change

Choose the correct answer from the code given below :

(1) (a), (c) and (d)

(2) (a), (b) and (c)

(3) (a), (b) and (d)

(4) (b), (c) and (d)

44. Which of the following pollutant gases is not produced both naturally and as a result of industrial activity ?

(1) Chlorofluoro carbons

(2) Nitrous oxide

(3) Methane

(4) Carbon dioxide

45. Among the following fuels of energy, which is the most environment friendly ?

(1) Ethanol

(2) Biogas

(3) CNG

(4) Hydrogen

46. Which of the following are the goals of higher education in India ?

(a) Access

(b) Equity

(c) Quality and Excellence

(d) Relevance

(e) Value based education

(f) Compulsory and free education

Select the correct answer from the code given below :

(1) (a), (b) and (e) only

(2) (a), (b), (e) and (f)

(3) (a), (b), (c), (d) and (e)

(4) (a), (b), (c), (d), (e) and (f)

47. Which of the following has been ranked the best college in the country (2017) as per the National Institutional Ranking Framework (NIRF) ?

(1) Miranda House, Delhi

(2) St. Stephen's College, Delhi

(3) Fergusson College, Pune

(4) Maharaja's College, Mysore

48. Which of the following universities has received the Visitor's Award for the best Central University in India in Feb. 2017 ?

(1) Jawaharlal Nehru University

(2) Banaras Hindu University

(3) Tezpur University

(4) University of Hyderabad

49. Who among the following can be removed by the President without Parliament's resolution ?

(1) Judge of a High Court

(2) Governor of a State

(3) Chief Election Commissioner

(4) Comptroller and Auditor - General

50. Which of the following come(s) within the ambit of the term 'corruption'?

(a) Misuse of official position

(b) Deviation from rules, laws and norms

(c) Non-action when action is required

(d) Harm to public good

Select the correct answer from the code given below :

(1) (a) only

(2) (a) and (b) only

(3) (a), (b) and (d)

(4) (a), (b), (c) and (d)

ANSWERS

1. (2)	**2.** (1)	**3.** (1)	**4.** (3)	**5.** (1)	**6.** (2)	**7.** (2)	**8.** (3)	**9.** (4)	**10.** (1)
11. (1)	**12.** (2)	**13.** (2)	**14.** (3)	**15.** (4)	**16.** (3)	**17.** (4)	**18.** (3)	**19.** (4)	**20.** (1)
21. (1)	**22.** (2)	**23.** (3)	**24.** (3)	**25.** (1)	**26.** (3)	**27.** (2)	**28.** (4)	**29.** (3)	**30.** (1)
31. (1)	**32.** (4)	**33.** (1)	**34.** (2)	**35.** (3)	**36.** (4)	**37.** (2)	**38.** (4)	**39.** (3)	**40.** (4)
41. (3)	**42.** (2)	**43.** (1)	**44.** (2)	**45.** (2)	**46.** (4)	**47.** (1)	**48.** (1)	**49.** (2)	**50.** (4)

Solved Paper 2017 (JANUARY)

UGC NET

PAPER-I

Note : • This paper contains **Sixty (60)** multiple-choice questions, each question carrying **two (2)** marks.

• Candidate is expected to answer any **Fifty (50)** questions.

• In case more than **Fifty (50)** questions are attempted, only the first **Fifty (50)** questions will be evaluated.

1. The principal of a school conducts an interview session of teachers and students with a view to explore the possibility of their enhanced participation in school programmes. This endeavour may be related to which type of research ?

(1) Evaluation Research

(2) Fundamental Research

(3) Action Research

(4) Applied Research

2. In doing action research what is the usual sequence of steps ?

(1) Reflect, observe, plan, act

(2) Plan, act, observe, reflect

(3) Plan, reflect, observe, act

(4) Act, observe, plan, reflect

3. Which sequence of research steps is logical in the list given below ?

(1) Problem formulation, Analysis, Development of Research design, Hypothesis making, Collection of data, Arriving at generalizations and conclusions.

(2) Development of Research design, Hypothesis making, Problem formulation, Data analysis, Arriving at conclusions and data collection.

(3) Problem formulation, Hypothesis making, Development of a Research design, Collection of data, Data analysis and formulation of generalizations and conclusions.

(4) Problem formulation, Deciding about the sample and data collection tools, Formulation of hypothesis, Collection and interpretation of research evidence.

4. Below are given two sets – research methods (Set-I) and data collection tools (Set-II). Match the two sets and indicate your answer by selecting the correct code:

Set-I (Research Methods)	**Set-II (Data Collection Tools)**
a. Experimental method	i. Using primary and secondary sources
b. Ex post-facto method	ii. Questionnaire
c. Descriptive survey method	iii. Standardized tests
d. Historical method	iv. Typical characteristic tests

Codes :

	a	b	c	d
(1)	ii	i	iii	iv
(2)	iii	iv	ii	i
(3)	ii	iii	i	iv
(4)	ii	iv	iii	i

5. The issue of 'research ethics' may be considered pertinent at which stage of research ?

(1) At the stage of problem formulation and its definition

(2) At the stage of defining the population of research

(3) At the stage of data collection and interpretation

(4) At the stage of reporting the findings.

6. In which of the following, reporting format is formally prescribed ?

(1) Doctoral level thesis

(2) Conference of researchers

(3) Workshops and seminars

(4) Symposia

Read the following passage carefully and answer questions from 7 to 12 :

The last great war, which nearly shook the foundations of the modern world, had little impact on Indian literature beyond aggravating the popular revulsion against violence and adding to the growing disillusionment with the 'humane pretensions' of the Western World. This was eloquently voiced in Tagore's later poems and his last testament, *Crisis in Civilisation*. The Indian intelligentsia was in a state of moral dilemma. On the one hand, it could not help sympathising with England's dogged courage in the hour of peril, with the Russians fighting with their backs to the wall against the ruthless Nazi hordes, and with China groaning under the heel of Japanese militarism; on the other hand, their own country was practically under military occupation of their own soil, and an Indian army under Subhas Bose was trying from the opposite camp to liberate their country. No creative impulse could issue from such confusion of loyalties. One would imagine that the achievement of Indian independence in 1947, which came in the wake of the Allies' victory and was followed by the collapse of colonialism in the neighbouring countries of South-East Asia, would have released an upsurge of creative energy. No doubt it did, but unfortunately it was soon submerged in the great agony of partition, with its inhuman slaughter of the innocents and the uprooting of millions of people from their homeland, followed by the martyrdom of Mahatma Gandhi. These tragedies, along with Pakistan's invasion of Kashmir and its later atrocities in Bangladesh, did indeed provoke a poignant writing, particularly in the languages of the regions most affected, Bengali, Hindi, Kashmiri, Punjabi, Sindhi and Urdu. But poignant or passionate writing does not by itself make great literature. What reserves of enthusiasm and confidence survived these disasters have been mainly absorbed in the task of national reconstruction and economic development. Great literature has always emerged out of chains of convulsions. Indian literature is richer today in volume, range and variety than it ever was in the past.

Based on the passage answer the following questions from 7 to 12 :

7. What was the impact of the last great war on Indian literature ?

(1) It had no impact.

(2) It aggravated popular revulsion against violence.

(3) It shook the foundations of literature.

(4) It offered eloquent support to the Western World.

8. What did Tagore articulate in his last testament?

(1) Offered support to Subhas Bose.

(2) Exposed the humane pretensions of the Western World.

(3) Expressed loyalty to England.

(4) Encouraged the liberation of countries.

9. What was the stance of Indian intelligentsia during the period of great war ?

(1) Indifference to Russia's plight.

(2) They favoured Japanese militarism.

(3) They prompted creativity out of confused loyalties.

(4) They expressed sympathy for England's dogged courage.

10. Identify the factor responsible for the submergence of creative energy in Indian literature.

(1) Military occupation of one's own soil.

(2) Resistance to colonial occupation.

(3) Great agony of partition.

(4) Victory of Allies.

11. What was the aftermath that survived tragedies in Kashmir and Bangladesh ?

(1) Suspicion of other countries

(2) Continuance of rivalry

(3) Menace of war

(4) National reconstruction

12. The passage has the message that

(1) Disasters are inevitable.

(2) Great literature emerges out of chains of convulsions.

(3) Indian literature does not have a marked landscape.

(4) Literature has no relation with war and independence.

13. Effective communication pre-supposes

(1) Non-alignment (2) Domination

(3) Passivity (4) Understanding

14. When verbal and non-verbal messages are contradictory, it is said that most people believe in

(1) indeterminate messages

(2) verbal messages

(3) non-verbal messages

(4) aggressive messages

15. The typical feature of an information-rich classroom lecture is in the nature of being

(1) Sedentary (2) Staggered

(3) Factual (4) Sectoral

16. Expressive communication is driven by

(1) Passive aggression

(2) Encoder's personality characteristics

(3) External clues

(4) Encoder-decoder contract

17. Positive classroom communication leads to

(1) Coercion (2) Submission

(3) Confrontation (4) Persuasion

18. Classroom communication is the basis of

(1) Social identity

(2) External inanities

(3) Biased passivity

(4) Group aggression

19. The missing term in the series 1, 4, 27, 16, ?, 36, 343, ... is

(1) 30 (2) 49

(3) 125 (4) 81

20. The next term in the following series YEB, WFD, UHG, SKI, ? will be

(1) TLO (2) QOL

(3) QLO (4) GQP

21. If A is coded as C, M as I, N as P, S as O, I as A, P as N, E as M, O as E and C as S, then the code of COMPANIES will be

(1) SPEINMOAC (2) NCPSEIOMA

(3) SMOPIEACN (4) SEINCPAMO

22. Among the following, identify the continuous type of data :

(1) Number of languages a person speaks

(2) Number of children in a household

(3) Population of cities

(4) Weight of students in a class

23. Ali buys a glass, a pencil box and a cup and pays ₹ 21 to the shopkeeper. Rakesh buys a cup, two pencil boxes and a glass and pays ₹ 28 to the shopkeeper. Preeti buys two glasses, a cup and two pencil boxes and pays ₹ 35 to the shopkeeper. The cost of 10 cups will be

(1) ₹ 40 (2) ₹ 60

(3) ₹ 80 (4) ₹ 70

24. Out of four cities given below three are alike in some manner while the fourth one is different. Identify the odd one

(1) Lucknow (2) Rishikesh

(3) Allahabad (4) Patna

25. Given below are some characteristics of reasoning. Select the code that states a characteristic which is not of deductive reasoning:

(1) The conclusion must be based on observation and experiment.

(2) The conclusion should be supported by the premise/premises.

(3) The conclusion must follow from the premise/premises necessarily.

(4) The argument may be valid or invalid.

26. If two standard form categorical propositions with the same subject and predicate are related in such a manner that if one is undetermined the other must be undetermined, what is their relation?

(1) Contrary (2) Subcontrary
(3) Contradictory (4) Sub-altern

27. Men and woman may have different reproductive strategies but neither can be considered inferior or superior to the other, any more than a bird's wings can be considered superior or inferior to a fish's fins. What type of argument it is ?

(1) Biological (2) Physiological
(3) Analogical (4) Hypothetical

28. Among the following propositions two are related in such a way that they cannot both be true but can both be false. Select the code that states those two propositions.

Propositions :

(a) Every student is attentive.
(b) Some students are attentive.
(c) Students are never attentive.
(d) Some students are not attentive.

Codes :

(1) (a) and (b) (2) (a) and (c)
(3) (b) and (c) (4) (c) and (d)

29. Given below are two premises ((a) and (b)). From those two premises four conclusions (i), (ii), (iii) & (iv)are drawn. Select the code that states the conclusions validly drawn from the premises (taking singly or jointly.)

Premises :

(a) Untouchability is a curse.
(b) All hot pans are untouchable.

Conclusions :

(i) All hot pans are curse.
(ii) Some untouchable things are hot pans.
(iii) All curses are untouchability.
(iv) Some curses are untoucha-bility.

Codes :

(1) (i) and (ii) (2) (ii) and (iii)
(3) (iii) and (iv) (4) (ii) and (iv)

30. If the statement 'None but the brave wins the race' is false which of the following statements can be claimed to be true ? Select the correct code :

(1) All brave persons win the race.
(2) Some persons who win the race are not brave.
(3) Some persons who win the race are brave.
(4) No person who wins the race is brave.

The table below embodies data on the sales revenue (₹ in lakh) generated by a publishing house during the years 2012-15 while selling books, magazines and journals as three categories of items. Answer questions 31 – 33 based on the data contained in the table.

	Sales Revenue (₹ in lakh)			
Year / Items	**2012**	**2013**	**2014**	**2015**
Journals	46	47	45	44
Magazines	31	39	46	51
Books	73	77	78	78
Total				

31. In 2015, approximately what percent of total revenue came from books ?

(1) 45% (2) 55%
(3) 35% (4) 25%

32. The number of years in which there was an increase in revenue from at least two categories of items, is

(1) 0
(2) 1
(3) 2
(4) 3

33. If the year 2016 were to show the same growth in terms of total sales revenue as the year 2015 over the year 2014, then the revenue in the year 2016 must be approximately :

(1) ₹ 194 lakh
(2) ₹ 187 lakh
(3) ₹ 172 lakh
(4) ₹ 177 lakh

A University professor maintains data on MCA students tabulated by performance and gender of the students. The data is kept on a computer hard disk, but accidently some of it is lost because of a computer virus. Only the following could be recovered :

	Number of MCA Students			
Performance/ Gender	**Average**	**Good**	**Excellent**	**Total**
Male			10	
Female				32
Total		30		

Panic buttons were pressed but to no avail. An expert committee was formed, which decided that the following facts were self evident :

(a) Half the students were either excellent or good.

(b) 40% of the students were females.

(c) One-third of the male students were average.

Answer questions **34 – 36** based on the data given above :

34. How many female students are excellent ?

(1) 0 (2) 8

(3) 16 (4) 32

35. What proportion of female students are good ?

(1) 0 (2) 0.25

(3) 0.50 (4) 0.75

36. Approximately, what proportion of good students are male ?

(1) 0 (2) 0.73

(3) 0.43 (4) 0.27

37. Which of the following statement (s) is/are TRUE?

S1 : The decimal number 11 is larger than the hexadecimal number 11.

S2 : In the binary number 1110.101, the fractional part has the decimal value as 0.625.

(1) S1 only

(2) S2 only

(3) Both S1 and S2

(4) Neither S1 nor S2

38. Read the following two statements :

I : Information and Communication Technology (ICT) is considered a subset of Information Technology (IT).

II : The 'right to use' a piece of software is termed as copyright.

Which of the above statement(s) is/are CORRECT?

(1) Both I and II

(2) Neither I nor II

(3) II only

(4) I only

39. Which of the following correctly lists computer memory types from highest to lowest speed ?

(1) Secondary Storage; Main Memory (RAM); Cache Memory; CPU Registers

(2) CPU Registers; Cache Memory; Secondary Storage; Main Memory (RAM)

(3) CPU Registers; Cache Memory; Main Memory (RAM); Secondary Storage

(4) Cache Memory; CPU Registers; Main Memory (RAM); Secondary Storage

40. Which of the following is a characteristic of Web2.0 applications ?

(1) Multiple users schedule their time to use Web 2.0 applications one by one.

(2) Web 2.0 applications are focused on the ability for people to collaborate and share information online.

(3) Web 2.0 applications provide users with content rather than facilitating users to create it.

(4) Web 2.0 applications use only static pages.

41. With regard to a word processing software, the process of combining static information in a publication together with variable information in a data source to create one merged publication is called

(1) Electronic mail

(2) Data sourcing

(3) Mail merge

(4) Spam mail

42. DVD technology uses an optical media to store the digital data. DVD is an acronym for

(1) Digital Vector Disc

(2) Digital Volume Disc

(3) Digital Versatile Disc

(4) Digital Visualization Disc

43. **Assertion (A):** Sustainable development is critical to well being of human society.

Reason (R): Environmentally sound policies do not harm the environment or deplete the natural resources.

Choose the correct code :

(1) Both (A) and (R) are correct and (R) is the correct explanation of (A).

(2) Both (A) and (R) are correct, but (R) is not the correct explanation of (A).

(3) (A) is true and (R) is false.

(4) (A) is false and (R) is true.

44. The dominant source of pollution due to oxides of nitrogen (NO_X) in urban areas is

(1) road transport

(2) commercial sector

(3) energy use in industry

(4) power plants

45. Which of the following is not a water-brone disease?

(1) Typhoid

(2) Hepatitis

(3) Cholera

(4) Dengue

46. Indian government's target for power production from small hydro projects by the year 2022 is

(1) 1 Giga-Watt (2) 5 Giga-Watt

(3) 10 Giga-Watt (4) 15 Giga-Watt

47. In which country, the recent international agreement on phasing out Hydro Fluoro Carbons(HFCs) was signed ?

(1) Rwanda (2) Morocco

(3) South Africa (4) Algeria

48. Which of the following natural hazards is not hydro-meteorological ?

(1) Snow avalanche

(2) Sea erosion

(3) Tropical cyclone

(4) Tsunami

49. Which of the following are the demerits of globalisation of higher education ?

(a) Exposure to global curriculum

(b) Promotion of elitism in education

(c) Commodification of higher education

(d) Increase in the cost of education

Select the correct answer from the codes given below :

Codes :

(1) (a) and (d)

(2) (a), (c) and (d)

(3) (b), (c) and (d)

(4) (a), (b), (c) and (d)

50. Which of the following statements are correct about deemed universities ?

(a) The Governor of the State is the chancellor of deemed universities.

(b) They can design their own syllabus and course work.

(c) They can frame their own guidelines regarding admission and fees.

(d) They can grant degrees.

Select the correct answer from the codes given below :

Codes :

(1) (a), (b) and (c) (2) (b), (c) and (d)

(3) (a), (c) and (d) (4) (a), (b), (c) and (d)

51. The purpose of value education is best served by focussing on

(1) Cultural practices prevailing in the society.

(2) Norms of conduct laid down by a social group.

(3) Concern for human values.

(4) Religious and moral practices and instructions.

52. Which of the following statements are correct ?

(a) Rajya Sabha is a Permanent House which can be dissolved only during national emergency.

(b) Rajya Sabha does not represent the local interests of the States.

(c) Members of the Rajya Sabha are not bound to vote at the dictates of the states they represent.

(d) No Union territory has a representative in the Rajya Sabha.

Select the correct answer from the codes given below :

Codes :

(1) (a) and (d)

(2) (b) and (c)

(3) (b), (c) and (d)

(4) (a), (b), (c) and (d)

53. Which of the following are not necessarily the immediate consequences of the proclamation of the President's Rule in a State ?

(a) Dissolution of the State Assembly.

(b) Removal of the Council of Ministers in the State.

(c) Takeover of the State administration by the Union Government.

(d) Appointment of a new Chief Secretary.

Select the correct answer from the codes given below :

Codes :

(1) (a) & (d) (2) (a), (b) & (c)

(3) (a), (b), (c) & (d) (4) (b) & (c)

54. Instead of holding the office during the pleasure of the President who among the following hold(s) office during good behaviour?

(a) Governor of a State

(b) Attorney General of India

(c) Judges of the High Court

(d) Administrator of a Union Territory

Select the correct answer from the codes given below :

Codes :

(1) (a) only (2) (c) only

(3) (a) and (c) (4) (a), (b), (c) and (d)

55. Which of the following set of statements represents acceptable propositions in respect of teaching-learning relationships? Choose the correct code to indicate your answer.

(i) When students fail in a test, it is the teacher who fails.

(ii) Every teaching must aim at ensuring learning.

(iii) There can be teaching without learning taking place.

(iv) There can be no learning without teaching.

(v) A teacher teaches but learns also.

(vi) Real learning implies rote learning.

Codes :

(1) (ii), (iii), (iv) and (v)

(2) (i), (ii), (iii) and (v)

(3) (iii), (iv), (v) and (vi)

(4) (i), (ii), (v) and (vi)

56. Assertion (A): Learning is a life long process.

Reason (R): Learning to be useful must be linked with life processes.

Choose the correct answer from the following code:

(1) Both (A) and (R) are true and (R) is the correct explanation of (A).

(2) Both (A) and (R) are true, but (R) is not the correct explanation of (A).

(3) (A) is true, but (R) is false.

(4) (A) is false, but (R) is true.

57. Effectiveness of teaching has to be judged in terms of

(1) Course coverage

(2) Students' interest

(3) Learning outcomes of students

(4) Use of teaching aids in the classroom

58. In which teaching method learner's participation is made optimal and proactive?

(1) Discussion method

(2) Buzz session method

(3) Brainstorming session method

(4) Project method

59. One of the most powerful factors affecting teaching effectiveness is related to the

(1) Social system of the country

(2) Economic status of the society

(3) Prevailing political system

(4) Educational system

60. Assertion (A): Formative evaluation tends to accelerate the pace of learning.

Reason (R): As against summative evaluation, formative evaluation is highly reliable.

Choose the correct answer from the following code:

(1) Both (A) and (R)are true and (R) is the correct explanation of (A).

(2) Both (A) and (R) are true, but (R) is not the correct explanation of (A).

(3) (A) is true, but (R) is false.

(4) (A) is false, but (R) is true.

ANSWERS

1. (3)	**2.** (2)	**3.** (3)	**4.** (2)	**5.** (3)	**6.** (1)	**7.** (2)	**8.** (2)	**9.** (4)	**10.** (3)
11. (4)	**12.** (2)	**13.** (4)	**14.** (3)	**15.** (3)	**16.** (2)	**17.** (4)	**18.** (1)	**19.** (3)	**20.** (2)
21. (4)	**22.** (4)	**23.** (4)	**24.** (1)	**25.** (1)	**26.** (3)	**27.** (3)	**28.** (2)	**29.** (4)	**30.** (2)
31. (1)	**32.** (3)	**33.** (4)	**34.** (1)	**35.** (2)	**36.** (2)	**37.** (2)	**38.** (2)	**39.** (3)	**40.** (2)
41. (3)	**42.** (3)	**43.** (2)	**44.** (1)	**45.** (4)	**46.** (2)	**47.** (1)	**48.** (4)	**49.** (3)	**50.** (2)
51. (3)	**52.** (2)	**53.** (1)	**54.** (2)	**55.** (2)	**56.** (1)	**57.** (3)	**58.** (4)	**59.** (4)	**60.** (3)

Solved Paper 2016 (AUGUST)

UGC NET

PAPER-I

Note :

- This paper consists of **Sixty (60)** multiple choice questions, each question carrying **two (2)** marks.
- Candidate is expected to answer any **Fifty (50)** questions.
- In case more than **Fifty (50)** questions are attempted, only the first **Fifty (50)** questions will be evaluated.

1. In a Ph.D. thesis which one is the correct sequence for showing scheme of Chapterisation ?

(1) Survey of related studies, Introduction, Design of the study, Data-Analysis and interpretation, Conclusions and generalisations, suggested further study, References, Appendix

(2) Introduction, Design of study, Data Analysis and Interpretation, Generalizations, Conclusions and Survey of related studies and suggestions for further research, References and Appendix

(3) Introduction, Survey of related studies, Design of study, Data-presentation; analysis & Interpretation, Formulation of generalization & Conclusions, Suggestions for further research, References & Appendix

(4) Survey of related studies, References, Introduction, Design of study, Data analysis and interpretation, Conclusions and generalizations, Suggestions for further research, Appendix

2. Which of the following is not the critical feature of qualitative research ?

(1) Actual settings are the direct source of data.

(2) Data take the forms of words or pictures.

(3) Seeking to establish relationships among measured social facts.

(4) Researcher becomes immersed in the situation, present or past related to the phenomena.

3. A detailed description of methodology of research is required in

(1) Thesis/Dissertation

(2) Symposium/Workshop

(3) Seminar paper/Articles

(4) Conference and Seminar Papers

4. Research ethics has a direct connection more often with which stages of research?

(1) Defining and delimiting the scope of research.

(2) Problem formulation and reporting of research findings.

(3) Defining the population and deciding the sampling technique for research.

(4) Deciding about statistical techniques and data analysis.

Read the following passage carefully and answer questions from 5 to 10 :

Many aspects of the motion-picture industry and its constituent companies are dissimilar to those observable in advanced-technology industries and firms. For instance, company longevity does not represent a consistent concern across the two organisational contexts. In the advanced-technology company for example, one new-product innovation – which is expected to generate financial returns to the firm – is insufficient for the company to be successful.

Rather, a stream of new product innovations is required. By contrast with the independent production company of this case, each new film – which is expected to generate financial returns to the principals – is sufficient for the company to be successful. Any subsequent new films involving the firm's participants will be produced by a different independent company.

As another instance, people's learning is expected to have different contributors and beneficiaries across the two organizational contexts. In the advanced-technology company, for example, each new product innovation provides an opportunity for participants on the project team to learn and acquire experience, and this same company intends to retain such participants, hence, benefit from their increased experience on the next project. By contrast with the independent production company, each new film provides an opportunity for participants on the project team to learn and acquire this experience also, but this same company has little or no expectation of retaining such participants, and hence, benefitting from their increased experience in the next project.

Experience is paramount in the motion-picture industry. Generally, on film projects, budgets are very tight, and schedules are very demanding. People are hired largely based on their experience and are expected to perform well immediately when called to do so. There is negligible slack time or margin for learning through trial and error, but experienced people learn exactly through trial and error. Because experience is valued so highly and film-production houses have such short time horizons, entry into the industry is very difficult for most people. Further, the role played by schools and colleges is minimal in this industry. Some skills and techniques can be learned and refined through formal education (e.g., acting schools, theatre, film degrees), but the majority come through direct experience. Mentoring plays an important role. True, the film business focuses heavily on exploitation over exploration. Yet success of the industry as a whole is critically dependent upon learning and exploration overtime.

Answer the following questions :

5. What is not a consistent concern across the two organisational contexts ?

(1) Dissimilarity

(2) Product package

(3) Financial return

(4) Company longevity

6. What will be sufficient for an independent production company to be successful ?

(1) New product innovations

(2) Financial returns from each new film

(3) Active role by firm's participants

(4) Organisational context

7. What does an advanced-technology company expect from the learning experience of its participants ?

(1) Benefit for the next project

(2) Opportunity for more learning

(3) Little expectation of retaining them

(4) Help in marketing the previous product

8. What is not the expectation of an independent production company in the case of its participants ?

(1) Absence from the next project.

(2) Retention for the next project.

(3) Participation in the current project.

(4) Use of opportunity to acquire experience.

9. Why do film production houses value experience highly ?

(1) Because of the importance of trial and error methods.

(2) Because of the margin for learning.

(3) Because of short time horizons.

(4) Because it allows easy entry to everyone into the film world.

10. According to the author, what has been the focus of film business ?

(1) Formal education

(2) Mentoring

(3) Exploitation

(4) Indirect experience

11. Internal and external factors that affect message reception by the students in the classroom are referred to as

(1) feedback (2) fragmentation

(3) channelisation (4) noise

12. A teacher in a classroom has immediate control over

(1) the self, selected methods of communication and the message.

(2) the audience, the noise and the reception.

(3) the feedback, the technology and the audience experience.

(4) the communication channel, other communicators, and external factors.

13. What do communicated words carry in a classroom situation ?

(1) Inspiration, controversy and introspection

(2) Diversion, criticism and irrationality

(3) Insipidity, irrationality, and non-acceptance

(4) Power, structure and tradition

14. As a good classroom communicator, you are supposed to know your

(1) audience emotions

(2) silent cues

(3) artful pauses

(4) counter arguments

15. Figure out the components of non-verbal communication in a classroom from the following :

(1) Facial expression, cultural space and seating arrangement

(2) Speed of utterance, feel good factor and acoustics

(3) High sound, physical ambience and teacher-learner distance

(4) Facial expression, kinesics and personal space

16. Which of the following are the basic factors of effective listening ?

(1) Opinionation, stare and glare and interruptions

(2) Aggressive questioning, continuous cues and frequent movement

(3) Me-too-ism, glancing sideways, and offering advice

(4) Acknowledgement of thoughts, reflection, and asking open-ended questions

17. In a particular code, HOSPITALS is coded as HSOLSAPTI. The code of BIOLOGICALS will be

(1) BLICOALIOSG

(2) BOLGICAILOS

(3) SBLAOILOBCG

(4) BSILOALCOIG

18. In the series

1, 5, 13, 25, 41, ...

the next term is

(1) 59 (2) 63

(3) 61 (4) 68

19. At present, a mother is 3 times older than her son. After 5 years, the sum of their ages will be 70 years. The age of the mother after 10 years will be

(1) 40 (2) 55

(3) 45 (4) 60

20. In the series

AYD, BVF, DRH, GMJ, ? the next term is

(1) GLK (2) HLM

(3) LHM (4) KGL

21. C and D are sisters. A and B are brothers. E is son of A and brother of D. B is related to C as

(1) Brother (2) Son

(3) Uncle (4) Father-in-law

22. Anil played 8 cricket matches. The mean (average) of the runs was found to be 80. After playing four more matches, the mean of the runs of all the matches was found to be 70.

The total runs made in the last four matches is

(1) 400 (2) 300

(3) 200 (4) 100

23. If two propositions are connected in such a way that they cannot both be false although they may both be true, then their relationship is called

(1) Contrary (2) Subcontrary

(3) Contradictory (4) Subalternation

24. Which one among the following is not a characteristic of a deductive type of argument ?

(1) The conclusion follows from the premise/premises necessarily.

(2) The argument admits degree of complexity.

(3) The argument provides us knowledge about matters of fact.

(4) The argument must be either valid or invalid.

25. Select the code which states the condition of an invalid deductive argument :

(1) All the premises are true but the conclusion is false.

(2) Some of the premises are true but the conclusion is false.

(3) All the premises are false and the conclusion is also false.

(4) All the premises are true and the conclusion is also true.

26. Given below are two premises, with four conclusions drawn from them (taking singly or together); which conclusions are validly drawn ? Select the correct answer from the codes given below :

Premises :

(*i*) All bats are mammals.

(*ii*) Birds are not bats.

Conclusions :

(*a*) Birds are not mammals.

(*b*) Bats are not birds.

(*c*) All mammals are bats.

(*d*) Some mammals are bats.

Codes :

(1) (*a*), (*b*) and (*d*) (2) (*b*) and (*d*)

(3) (*a*) and (*c*) (4) (*b*), (*c*) and (*d*)

27. When a definition implies a proposal to use the definiendum to mean what is meant by the definiens it is called

(1) Lexical definition

(2) Stipulative definition

(3) Precising definition

(4) Persuasive definition

28. Select the code which is not correct :

An analogical argument is strengthened by

(1) increasing the number of entities.

(2) increasing the number of similar respects.

(3) reducing the claim made earlier stronger.

(4) making the conclusion stronger when premises remain unchanged.

Consider the following two tables (I and II) that show the percentage of students in each faculty at University and the number of foreign students in the Science faculty. These percentages have been rounded to the nearest whole number. There are a total of 1049 students in the science faculty. Study these tables I and II and answer the questions that follow **(Questions 29 – 31) :**

I : Students Facultywise

Name of Faculty	% of Students
Computing	22
Business	14
Science	23
Engineering	9
Arts	21
Medicine	5
Law	6

II : Foreign Students in Science Faculty

Foreign Students	Number of Science Students
American	79
Australian	4
African	2
Chinese	6
European	21

29. Approximately, what percentage of students in the Science faculty is that of foreign students ?

(1) 14% (2) 9%

(3) 30% (4) 11%

30. Approximately, how many students belong to the Engineering faculty ?

(1) 420 (2) 410

(3) 390 (4) 400

31. In case, there are 34 European medical students, then approximately, what is their percentage in the medicine faculty?

(1) 13% (2) 18%

(3) 12% (4) 15%

A college has a total of 800 MCA students, 80% of whom are in class MCA-III and remaining are equally divided between class MCA-I and class MCA-II. The proportion of female students and the proportion of vegetarian students in the college are indicated as under through the table.

Answer questions 32 to 34 based on this information.

Proportion of females and proportion of vegetarians in each class

Class	Female (F)	Vegetarian (V)
MCA-I	0.40	
MCA-II	0.45	0.50
MCA-III		0.55
Total	0.525	0.53

For example, in the table above, 0.525 is the total proportion of female students and 0.53 is the total proportion of vegetarian students in the college.

32. What is the percentage of female students in class MCA-III ?

(1) 40 (2) 45

(3) 50 (4) 55

33. What is the percentage of vegetarian students in class MCA-I ?

(1) 40 (2) 45

(3) 50 (4) 55

34. How many total non-vegetarian students are there in class MCA-I and class MCA-II ?

(1) 72 (2) 88

(3) 78 (4) 92

35. Which of the following statements regarding the features of Information and Communication Technology (ICT) is/are true ?

I. ICT are the main instruments for the creation of computer networks and the applications based on them.

II. ICT support the spread of information and knowledge, separating the content from the place where it belongs physically.

III. The digital and virtual nature of most of ICT products allow the expenditure for them to be maximized.

Codes :

(1) I and II only (2) I and III only

(3) II and III only (4) I, II and III

36. If one GigaByte is equal to 2^{30} Bytes of data storage, then 1024 TeraBytes is equal to _____ bits of data storage.

(1) 2^{50} (2) 2^{53}

(3) 2^{40} (4) 2^{56}

37. The software used to navigate through the web is known as

(1) Website

(2) Web Browser

(3) Internet

(4) World Wide Web

38. With regard to e-mail, what does Bcc : mean ?

(1) Blind Computer Communication : The users specified in the Bcc : field will get the e-mail and see the addresses in the to : and cc : fields.

(2) Blind Carbon Copy : The users specified in the Bcc : field will get the e-mail and see the addresses in the to : and cc : fields.

(3) Blind Computer Communication : The users specified in the Bcc : field will get the e-mail but it will be an audio file because this is how blind people get e-mail.

(4) Blind Carbon Copy : The users specified in the Bcc : field will get the e-mail but will not see the addresses in the to : and cc : fields.

39. Random Access Memory (RAM), a form of computer storage, is a ______ memory.

(1) Non-volatile (2) Volatile

(3) Permanent (4) Secondary

40. In Computer Networking, HTTP is referred to as a stateless protocol as servers do not maintain any information about past client requests. HTTP is an acronym for

(1) Hyper Text Translation Protocol

(2) Hyper Text Transfer Protocol

(3) High TeraByte Transfer Protocol

(4) Hypervisor Test Translation Protocol

41. The arsenic pollution in ground water in Bangladesh and parts of India is due to

(1) industrial waste

(2) thermal power plants

(3) natural sources

(4) agricultural practices

42. Among the following air pollutants which directly impacts human health as well as climate ?

(1) Soot

(2) Sulphur dioxide

(3) Oxides of nitrogen

(4) Chlorofluoro carbons

43. Assertion (A) : The problems of environmental sustainability are difficult to resolve.

Reason (R) : Our understanding how environment works and how different human choices affect environment is inadequate.

Choose the correct code :

(1) Both (A) and (R) are correct and (R) is the correct explanation of (A).

(2) Both (A) and (R) are correct, but (R) is not the correct explanation of (A).

(3) (A) is true and (R) is false.

(4) (A) is false and (R) is true.

44. The percentage share of electrical power from solar energy in the total electric power generation from all renewable energy sources sought to be achieved by Indian government by the year 2022, is

(1) ~ 57.1% (2) ~ 65.5%

(3) ~ 47.5% (4) ~ 75%

45. As part of Intended Nationally Determined contributions, Indian government through additional forest and tree cover has resolved to create an additional carbon sink (in terms of carbon dioxide equivalent) by year 2030 to the extent of

(1) 3.5 to 4 billion tons

(2) 2.5 to 3 billion tons

(3) 1.5 to 2 billion tons

(4) 1 to 1.5 billion tons

46. Which of the following is a meteorological hazard ?

(1) Avalanche (2) Coastal erosion

(3) Landslide (4) Blizzard

47. Which of the following universities/ institutes is ranked first in the India Rankings 2016 ?

(1) Jawaharlal Nehru University, New Delhi

(2) Central University, Hyderabad

(3) Indian Institute of Science, Bangalore

(4) Institute of Chemical Technology, Mumbai

48. Which of the following statements are correct about distance education in India?

(*a*) It supplements formal education.

(*b*) It reduces the cost of education.

(*c*) It replaces the formal education.

(*d*) It enhances access to education.

Select the correct answer from the codes given below :

Codes :

(1) (*a*), (*b*), (*c*) and (*d*)

(2) (*a*), (*c*) and (*d*)

(3) (*a*), (*b*) and (*d*)

(4) (*b*), (*c*) and (*d*)

49. Which of the following are statutory bodies ?

(*a*) Election Commission of India

(*b*) University Grants Commission (UGC)

(*c*) All India Council for Technical Education (AICTE)

(*d*) National Assessment and Accreditation Council (NAAC)

Select the correct answer from the codes given below :

Codes :

(1) (*a*), (*b*) and (*c*) (2) (*b*), (*c*) and (*d*)

(3) (*b*) and (*c*) (4) (*b*) and (*d*)

50. Which of the following statements are not correct in respect of Rajya Sabha ?

(*a*) It has same powers as those of Lok Sabha.

(*b*) It can pass a vote of no-confidence against the Council of Ministers.

(*c*) It can amend a money bill.

(*d*) It can be dissolved during emergency.

Select the correct answer from the codes given below :

Codes :

(1) (*b*) and (*c*)

(2) (*b*), (*c*) and (*d*)

(3) (*a*), (*b*) and (*c*)

(4) (*a*), (*b*), (*c*) and (*d*)

51. Which of the following statement(s) is/are correct about the powers of the Governor of a State ?

(*a*) He has the power to dissolve the Legislative Assembly.

(*b*) He has the power to appoint judges of the State High Court.

(*c*) He has the power to grant pardon in case of death sentence.

(*d*) He has diplomatic powers.

Select the correct answer from the codes given below :

Codes :

(1) (*a*) only (2) (*a*) and (*b*)

(3) (*a*), (*b*) and (*d*) (4) (*a*), (*b*) and (*c*)

52. In which of the following cases, the principle of natural justice (Hear the other party) must be followed ?

(*a*) Dismissal of an employee

(*b*) Supersession of a municipality

(*c*) Threat to national security

(*d*) Disciplinary action against a student or an employee

Select the correct answer from the codes given below :

Codes :

(1) (*a*) and (*b*)

(2) (*a*) and (*d*)

(3) (*a*), (*b*) and (*d*)

(4) (*a*), (*b*), (*c*) and (*d*)

53. Which of the following set of statements reflects the basic characteristics of teaching ?

Select the correct alternative from the codes :

(*i*) Teaching is the same as training.

(*ii*) There is no difference between instruction and conditioning when we teach.

(*iii*) Teaching is related to learning.

(*iv*) Teaching is a 'task' word while learning is an 'achievement' word.

(*v*) Teaching means giving information.

(*vi*) One may teach without learning taking place.

Codes :

(1) (*i*), (*ii*) and (*iii*)

(2) (*iii*), (*iv*) and (*vi*)

(3) (*ii*), (*iii*) and (*v*)

(4) (*i*), (*iv*) and (*vi*)

54. Which of the following factors affect teaching ?

Choose the correct code to indicate your answer.

(*i*) Teacher's internal locus of control.

(*ii*) Learner-motivation.

(*iii*) Teacher's biographical data.

(*iv*) Teacher's self efficacy.

(*v*) Learner's interest in co-curricular activities.

(*vi*) Teacher's skill in managing and monitoring.

(*vii*) Teacher's knowledge of the subject including general knowledge.

Codes :

(1) (*i*), (*ii*), (*iv*), (*vi*) and (*vii*)

(2) (*i*), (*ii*), (*iii*), (*iv*) and (*v*)

(3) (*iii*), (*iv*), (*v*), (*vi*) and (*vii*)

(4) (*ii*), (*iii*), (*iv*), (*v*) and (*vi*)

55. Which combination of methods of teaching is likely to optimise learning ?

(1) Lecturing, discussions and seminar method

(2) Interactive discussions, planned lectures and PowerPoint based presentations

(3) Interactive lecture sessions followed by buzz sessions, brainstorming and projects

(4) Lecturing, demonstrations and PowerPoint based presentations

56. Assertion (A) : Teaching aids have to be considered as effective supplements to instruction.

Reason (R) : They keep the students in good humour.

Choose the correct answer from the codes given below :

Codes :

(1) Both (A) and (R) are true and (R) is the correct explanation of (A).

(2) Both (A) and (R) are true, but (R) is not the correct explanation of (A).

(3) (A) is true, but (R) is false.

(4) (A) is false, but (R) is true.

57. The purpose of formative evaluation is to

(1) grade students' learning outcomes.

(2) accelerate students' learning performance.

(3) check students' performance graph.

(4) provide feedback to teacher effectiveness.

58. Which of the following learner characteristics are likely to influence the effectiveness of teaching aids and evaluation systems to ensure positive results ?

(1) Learner's family background, age and habitation.

(2) Learner's parentage, socio-economic background and performance in learning of the concerned subject.

(3) Learner's stage of development, social background and personal interests.

(4) Learner's maturity level, academic performance level and motivational dispositions.

59. For advancing knowledge, the latest strategy used by mankind is

(1) consulting an authority

(2) deductive reasoning

(3) scientific thinking

(4) inductive reasoning

60. There are two sets given below, Set-I consists of methods of research and Set-II indicates their procedural characteristics. Match the two sets and choose your answer from the codes given below :

Set – I (Research method)

a. Experimental method

b. Expost facto method

c. Descriptive method

d. Symbolic interactionism

e. Action research

Set – II (Procedural Characteristics)

i. Interventions to ameliorate a given situation

ii. Explaining patterns of behaviour in terms of meanings and their representations which people share.

iii. Manipulating an independent variable in controlled conditions and measuring its effect on dependent variable.

iv. Depending on primary and secondary sources of data.

v. Obtaining information concerning the current status of phenomena.

vi. Observing the effect on dependent variable and making probes into factors/variables which explain it.

vii. Exegetic analysis.

Codes :

	a	*b*	*c*	*d*	*e*
(1)	*i*	*iii*	*iv*	*v*	*vii*
(2)	*iii*	*iv*	*v*	*vi*	*vii*
(3)	*i*	*ii*	*iii*	*iv*	*v*
(4)	*iii*	*vi*	*v*	*ii*	*i*

ANSWERS

1. (3)	**2.** (3)	**3.** (1)	**4.** (2)	**5.** (4)	**6.** (2)	**7.** (1)	**8.** (2)	**9.** (3)	**10.** (3)
11. (4)	**12.** (1)	**13.** (4)	**14.** (3)	**15.** (4)	**16.** (4)	**17.** (4)	**18.** (3)	**19.** (2)	**20.** (4)
21. (3)	**22.** (3)	**23.** (2)	**24.** (3)	**25.** (1)	**26.** (2)	**27.** (2)	**28.** (4)	**29.** (4)	**30.** (2)
31. (4)	**32.** (4)	**33.** (1)	**34.** (2)	**35.** (1)	**36.** (2)	**37.** (2)	**38.** (2)	**39.** (2)	**40.** (2)
41. (3)	**42.** (1)	**43.** (1)	**44.** (1)	**45.** (2)	**46.** (4)	**47.** (3)	**48.** (3)	**49.** (3)	**50.** (4)
51. (1)	**52.** (3)	**53.** (2)	**54.** (1)	**55.** (3)	**56.** (2)	**57.** (2)	**58.** (4)	**59.** (3)	**60.** (4)

Solved Paper 2016 (July)

UGC NET

PAPER-I

Note : • This paper contains **Sixty (60)** multiple choice questions, each question carrying **two (2)** marks.

• Candidate is expected to answer any **Fifty (50)** questions.

• In case more than **Fifty (50)** questions are attempted, only the first **Fifty (50)** questions will be evaluated.

1. Which of the following is the largest source of water pollution in major rivers of India ?

(1) Untreated sewage

(2) Agriculture run-off

(3) Unregulated small scale industries

(4) Religious practices

2. Sustainable development goals have specific targets to be achieved by

(1) 2022 (2) 2030

(3) 2040 (4) 2050

3. Indian government's target of producing power from biomass by the year 2022, is

(1) 50 MW (2) 25 MW

(3) 15 MW (4) 10 MW

4. Assertion (A) : Conserving our soil resources is critical to human survival.

Reason (R) : Soil is home to many microorganisms and contains minerals.

Choose the correct code :

(1) Both (A) and (R) are correct and (R) is the correct explanation of (A).

(2) Both (A) and (R) are correct but (R) is not the correct explanation of (A).

(3) (A) is true and (R) is false.

(4) (A) is false and (R) is true.

5. World Meteorological Organisation's (WMO) objective has been to reduce the number of deaths due to hydrometeorological disasters over the decade 2010-2019 by (with reference to the decade 1994-2003)

(1) 25% (2) 50%

(3) 75% (4) 80%

6. is a type of memory circuitry that holds the computer's start-up routine.

(1) RIM (Read Initial Memory)

(2) RAM (Random Access Memory)

(3) ROM (Read Only Memory)

(4) Cache Memory

7. An ASCII is a character-encoding scheme that is employed by personal computers in order to represent various characters, numbers and control keys that the computer user selects on the keyboard. ASCII is an acronym for

(1) American Standard Code for Information Interchange

(2) Americn Standard Code for Intelligent Information

(3) American Standard Code for Information Integrity

(4) American Standard Code for Isolated Information

8. Identify the air pollutant in urban areas which irritates eyes and also respiratory tract of human beings.

(1) Particulate matter

(2) Oxides of nitrogen

(3) Surface ozone

(4) Carbon monoxide

9. Which of the following statements about the Indian political system is/are correct ?

(a) The President is both Head of the State and Head of the Government.

(b) Parliament is Supreme.

(c) The Supreme Court is the guardian of the Constitution.

(d) The Directive Principles of State Policy are justiciable.

Select the correct answer from the codes given below :

(1) (a), (b), (c) and (d)

(2) (b), (c) and (d)

(3) (b) and (c)

(4) (c) only

10. Which of the following are the fundamental duties ?

(a) To respect the National Flag.

(b) To protect and improve the natural environment.

(c) For a parent to provide opportunities for education to his/her child.

(d) To protect monuments and places of national importance.

Select the correct answer from the codes given :

Codes :

(1) (a), (b) and (c)

(2) (a), (b) and (d)

(3) (a), (c) and (d)

(4) (a), (b), (c) and (d)

11. Which of the following statements are correct in respect of Niti Aayog ?

(a) It is a constitutional body.

(b) It is a statutory body.

(c) It is neither a constitutional body nor a statutory body.

(d) It is a think-tank.

Select the correct answer from the codes given below :

(1) (a) and (d)

(2) (b) and(d)

(3) and (d)

(4) (b), (c) and (d)

12. Which of the following core values among the institutions of higher education are promoted by the NAAC (National Assessment and Accreditation Council) ?

(a) Contributing to national development.

(b) Fostering global competencies among the students:

(c) Inculcating a value system among students and teachers.

(d) Promoting the optimum utilization of the in frastructure.

Select the correct answer from the codes given below :

Codes :

(1) (b), (c) and (d)

(2) (a), (b) and (c)

(3) (a), (c) and (d)

(a), (b), (c) and (d)

13. The best way for providing value education is through

(1) discussions on scriptural texts

(2) lectures / discourses on values

(3) seminars / symposia on values

(4) mentoring/ reflective sessions on values

14. The National Judicial Appointments Commission (NJAC) has been declared unconstitutional by

(1) The Supreme Court of India

(2) The High Court

(3) The High Court and the Supreme Court both

(4) The President of India

15. Which set of learner characteristics may be considered helpful in designing effective. teaching-learning systems ? Select the correct alternative from the codes given below :

(i) Prior experience of learners in respect of the subject.

(ii) Interpersonal relationships of learner's family friends.

(iii) Ability of the learners in respect of the subject,

(iv) Student's language background.

(v) Interest of students in following the prescribed dress code.

(vi) Motivational-orientation of the students.

Codes :

(1) (i), (ii), (iii) and (iv)

(2) (i), (iii), (iv) and (vi)

(3) (ii), (iii), (iv) and (v)

(4) (iii), (iv), (v) and (vi)

16. A college level assistant professor has planned his/her lectures with an intent to develop cognitive dimensions of students centered on skills of analysis and synthesis. Below, given are two sets of items Set-I consisting of levels of cognitive interchange and Set-II comprising basic requirements for promoting them. Match the two sets and indicate your answer by choosing the correct alternative from the code :

Set-I (*Levels of Cognitive Interchange*)

a. Memory level

b. Understanding level

c. Reflective level

Set-II (*Basic requirements for promoting cognitive Interchange*)

i. Giving opportunity for discriminating examples and non-examples of a point.

ii. Recording the important points made during the presentations.

iii. Asking the students to discuss various items of information.

iv. Critically analyzing the points to be made and discussed.

Codes:

	a	b	c
(1)	ii	iv	i
(2)	iii	iv	ii
(3)	ii	i	iv
(4)	i	ii	iii

17. Match the items of the first set with that of the second set in respect of evaluation system. Choose the correct code :

Set-I

a. Formative evaluation

b. Summative evaluation

c. Continuous and comprehensive evaluation

d. Norm and criterion referenced test

Set-II

i. Evaluating cognitive and co-cognitive aspects with regularity

ii. Tests and their interpretations based on a group and certain yardsticks

iii. Grading the final learning outcomes comprehensive evaluation

iv. Quizzes and discussions tests

Codes:

	a	b	c	d
(1)	iv	iii	i	ii
(2)	i	ii	iii	iv
(3)	iii	iv	ii	i
(4)	i	iii	iv	ii

18. Select the alternative which consists of positive factors contributing to effectiveness of teaching:

List of factors :

(a) Teacher's knowledge of the subject.

(b) Teacher's socio-economic background.

(c) Communication skill of the teacher.

(d) Teacher's ability to please the students.

(e) Teacher's personal contact with students.

(f) Teacher's competence in managing and monitoring the classroom transactions.

Codes:

(1) (b), (c) and (d)

(2) (c), (d) and (f)

(3) (b), (d) and (e)

(4) (a), (c) and (f)

19. The use of teaching aids is justified on the grounds of

(1) attracting students' attention in the class room.

(2) minimising indiscipline problems in the classroom.

(3) optimising learning outcomes of students.

(4) effective engagement of students in learning tasks.

20. Assertion (A): The purpose of higher education is to promote critical and creative thinking abilities among students.

Reason (R) : These abilities ensure job placements.

Choose the correct answer from the following code :

(1) Both (A) and (R) are true and (R) is the correct explanation of (A).

(2) Both (A) and (R) are true but (R) is notthe correct explanation of (A).

(3) (A) is true but (R) is false.

(4) (A) is false but (R) is true.

21. In qualitative research paradigm, which of the following features may be considered critical ?

(1) Data collection with standardised research tools.

(2) Sampling design with probability sample techniques.

(3) Data collection with bottom-up empirical evidences.

(4) Data gathering to take place with top-down systematic evidences.

22. From the following list of statements identify the set which has negative implications for 'research ethics' :

(i) A researcher critically looks at the findings of another research.

(ii) Related studies are cited without proper references,

(iii) Research findings are made the basis for policy making.

(iv) Conduct of practitioner is screened in terms of reported research evidences.

(v) A research study is replicated with a view to verify the evidences from other researches.

(vi) Both policy making and policy implementing processes are regulated in terms of preliminary studies.

Codes:

(1) (i), (ii) and (iii)

(2) (ii), (iii) and (iv)

(3) (ii), (iv) and (vi)

(4) (i), (iii) and (v)

23. In a research on the effect of child-rearing practices on stress-proneness of children in completing school projects, the hypothesis formulated is that 'child rearing practices do influence stress-proneness'. At the data-analysis stage a null hypothesis is advanced to find out the tenability of research hypothesis. On the basis of the evidence available, the null hypothesis is rejected at 0.01 level of significance. What decision may be warranted in respect of the research hypothesis ?

(1) The research hypothesis will also be rejected.

(2) The research hypothesis will be accepted.

(3) Both the research hypothesis and the null hypothesis will be rejected.

(4) No decision can be taken in respect of the research hypothesis.

24. A researcher intends to explore the effect of possible factors for the organization of effective mid-day meal interventions. Which research method will be most appropriate for this study?

(1) Historical method

(2) Descriptive survey method

(3) Experimental method

(4) Ex-post-facto method

25. Which of the following is an initial mandatory requirement for pursuing research ?

(1) Developing a research design

(2) Formulating a research question

(3) Deciding about the data analysis procedure

(4) Formulating a research hypothesis

26. The format of thesis writing is the same as in

(1) preparation of a research paperl/ article

(2) writing of seminar presentation

(3) a research dissertation

(4) presenting a workshop/conference paper

Read the following passage carefully and answer question numbers from 27 to 32 :

In terms of labour, for decades the relatively low cost and high quality of Japanese workers conferred considerable competitive advantage across numerous durable goods and consumer electronics industries (eg. Machinery, automobiles, televisions, radios). Then labour-based advantages shifted to South Korea, then to Malaysia, Mexico and other nations. Today, China appears to be capitalizing best on the basis of labour. Japanese firms still remain competitive in markets for such durable goods, electronics and other products, but the labour force is no longer sufficient for competitive advantage over manufacturers in other industrializing nations. Such shifting of labour-based advantage is clearly not limited to manufacturing industries. Today, a huge number of IT and service jobs are moving from Europe and North America to India, Singapore, and like countries with relatively well-educated, low-cost workforces possessing technical skills. However, as educational levels and technical skills continue to rise in other countries, India, Singapore, and like nations enjoying labour-based competitive advantage today are likely to find such advantage cannot be sustained through emergence of new competitors.

In terms of capital, for centuries the days of gold coins and later even paper money restricted financial flows. Subsequently regional concentrations were formed where large banks, industries and markets coalesced. But today capital flows internationally at rapid speed. Global commerce no longer requires regional interactions among business players. Regional capital concentrations in places such as New York, London and Tokyo still persist, of course, but the capital concentrated there is no longer sufficient for competitive advantage over other capitalists distributed worldwide. Only if an organization is able to combine, integrate and apply its resources (eg. Land, labour, capital, IT) in an effective manner that is not readily imitable by competitors can such an organization enjoy competitive advantage sustainable overtime.

In a knowledge-based theory of the firm, this idea is extended to view organizational knowledge as a resource with atleast the same level of power and importance as the traditional economic inputs. An organization with superior knowledge can achieve competitive advantage in markets that appreciate the application of such knowledge. Semiconductors, genetic engineering, pharmaceuticals, software, military warfare, and like knowledge-intensive competitive arenas provide both time-proven and current examples. Consider semiconductors (e.g. computer chips), which are made principally of sand and common metals. These ubiquitous and powerful electronic devices are designed within common office buildings, using commercially available tools, and fabricated within factories in many industrialized nations. Hence, land is not the key competitive resource in the semiconductor industry.

"Based on the passage answer the following questions :

27. What is required to ensure competitive advantages in specific markets ?

(1) Access to capital

(2) Common office buildings

(3) Superior knowledge

(4) Common metals

28. The passage also mentions about the trend of

(1) Global financial flow

(2) Absence of competition in manufacturing industry

(3) Regionalisation of capitalists

(4) Organizational incompatibility

29. What does the author lay stress on in the passage ?

(1) International commerce

(2) Labour-Intensive industries

(3) Capital resource management

(4) Knowledge-driven competitive advantage

30. Which country enjoyed competitive advantages in automobile industry for decades ?

(1) South Korea (2) Japan

(3) Mexico (4) Malaysia

31. Why labour-based competitive advantages of India and Singapore cannot be sustained in IT and service sectors?

(1) Due to diminishing levels of skill.

(2) Due to capital-intensive technology making inroads.

(3) Because of new competitors.

(4) Because of shifting of labour-based advantage in manufacturing industries.

32. How can an organisation enjoy competitive advantage sustainable overtime ?

(1) Through regional capital flows.

(2) Through regional interactions among business players.

(3) By making large banks, industries and markets coalesced.

(4) By effective use of various instrumentalities.

33. The choice of communication partners is influenced by factors of

(1) Proximity, utility, loneliness

(2) Utility, secrecy, dissonance

(3) Secrecy, dissonance, deception

(4) Dissimilarity, dissonance, deviance

34. As a teacher, select the best option to ensure your effective presence in the classroom.

(1) Use of peer command

(2) Making aggressive statements

(3) Adoption of well-established posture

(4) Being authoritarian

35. Every communicator has to experience

(1) Manipulated emotions

(2) Anticipatory excitement

(3) The issue of homophiles

(4) Status dislocation

36. Imagine you are working in an educational institution where people are of equal status? Which method of communication is best suited and normally employed in such a context ?

(1) Horizontal communication

(2) Vertical communication

(3) Corporate communication

(4) Cross communication

37. Identify the important element a teacher has to take cognizance of while addressing students in a classroom.

(1) Avoidance of proximity

(2) Voice modulation

(3) Repetitive pause

(4) Fixed posture

38. What are the barriers to effective communication ?

(1) Moralising, being judgemental and comments of consolation.

(2) Dialogue, summary and self-review.

(3) Use of simple words, cool reaction and defensive attitude.

(4) Personal statements, eye contact and simple narration.

39. A person walks 10 m infront and 10 m to the right. Then every time turning to his left, he walks 5,15 and 15 m respectively. How far is he now from his starting point ?

(1) 20 m

(2) 15 m

(3) 10 m

(4) 5 m

40. A is sister of B. F is daughter of G. C is mother of B. D is father of C. E is mother of D. A is related to D as

(1) Grand daughter

(2) Daughter

(3) Daughter-in-law

(4) Sister

41. In the series

AB, EDC, FGHI, ...?...., OPQRST, the missing term is

(1) JKLMN

(2) JMKNL

(3) NMLKJ

(4) NMKLJ

42. Among the following propositions two are related in such a way that one is the denial of the other. Which are those propositions ? Select the correct code :

Propositions :

(a) All women are equal to men

(b) Some women are equal to men

(c) Some women are not equal to men

(d) No women are equal to men

Codes :

(1) (a) and (b)

(2) (a) and (d)

(3) (c) and (d)

(4) (a) and (c)

43. In certain code, SELECTION is coded as QCJCARGML. The code of AMERICANS will be

(1) YKCPGAYLQ

(2) BNFSJDBMR

(3) QLYAGPCKY

(4) YQKLCYPAG

44. In the series 3, 11, 23, 39, 59 .....

The next term will be

(1) 63

(2) 73

(3) 83

(4) 93

45. Two railway tickets from city A to B and three tickets from city A to C cost ₹ 177. Three tickets from city A to B and two tickets from city A to C cost ₹ 173. The fare for city B from city A will be ?

(1) 25
(2) 27
(3) 30
(4) 33

46. Select the code which is not correct in the context of deductive argument with two premises:

(1) An argument with one true premise, one false premise and a false conclusion may be valid.
(2) An argument with two true premises and a false conclusion may be valid.
(3) An argument with one true premise, one false premise and a true conclusion may be valid.
(4) An argument with two false premises and a false conclusion may be valid.

47. Given below are two premises and four conclusions are drawn from them (taking singly or together). Select the code that states the conclusions validly drawn.

Premises:

(i) All religious persons are emotional.
(ii) Ram is a religious person.

Conclusions:

(*a*) Ram is emotional,
(b) All emotional persons are religious.
(c) Ram is not a non-religious person.
(d) Some religious persons are not emotional.

Codes:

(1) (a), (b), (c) and (d)
(2) (a) only
(3) (a) and (c) only
(4) (b) and (c) only

48. If the proposition 'All thieves are poor' is false, which of the following propositions can be claimed certainly to be true ?

Propositions :

(1) Some thieves are poor.
(2) Some thieves are not poor.
(3) No thief is poor.
(4) No poor person is a thief.

49. Consider the following statement and select the correct code stating the nature of the argument involved in it:

To suppose that the earth is the only populated world in the infinite space is as absurd as to assert that in an entire field of millet only one grain will grow.

(1) Astronomical (2) Anthropological
(3) Deductive (4) Analogical

50. Select the code which is not correct about Venn diagram:

(1) Venn diagram represents propositions as well as classes.
(2) It can provide clear method of notation.
(3) It can be either valid or invalid.
(4) It can provide the direct method of testing the validity.

Directions : The following table shows the percentage profit (%) earned by two companies A and B during the years 2011-15. Answer questions 51-53 based on the data contained in the table :

Profit carned by two companies

Year	Percentage Profit (%)	
	A	B
2011	20	30
2012	35	40
2013	45	35
2014	40	50
2015	25	35

Where, percent (%) Profit

$$= \frac{\text{Income} - \text{Expenditure}}{\text{Expenditure}} \times 100$$

51. If the total expenditure of the two companies was ₹ 9 lakh in the year 2012 and the expenditure of A and B were in the ratio 2 : 1, then what was the income of the company A in that year ?

(1) ₹ 9.2 lakh (2) ₹ 8.1 lakh

(3) ₹ 7.2 lakh (4) ₹ 6.0 lakh

52. What is the average percentage profit earned by the company B ?

(1) 35% (2) 42%

(3) 38% (4) 40%

53. In which year, the percentage profit earned by the company B is less than that of company A?

(1) 2012

(2) 2013

(3) 2014

(4) 2015

54. The following table shows the number of people in different age groups who responded to a survey about their favourite style of music. Use this information to answer the questions

Style of Music ↓ / Age →	Number of people (Years) 15-20	(Years) 21-30	(Years) 31+
Classical	6	4	17
Pop	7	5	5
Rock	6	12	14
Jazz	1	4	11
Blues	2	3	15
Hip-Hop	9	3	4

54. Approximately what percentage of the total sample were aged 21-30 ?

(1) 31%

(2) 23%

(3) 25%

(4) 14%

55. Approximately what percentage of the total sample indicates that Hip-Hop is their favourite style of music?

(1) 6% (2) 8%

(3) 14% (4) 12%

56. What percentage of respondents aged 31+ indicated a favourite style other that classical music ?

(1) 64% (2) 60%

(3) 75% (4) 50%

57. An unsolicited e-mail message sent to many recipients at once is a

(1) Worm (2) Virus

(3) Threat (4) Spam

58. The statement "the study, design, development, implementation, support or management of computer-based information systems, particularly software applications and computer Hardware" refers to

(1) Information Technology (IT)

(2) Information and Collaborative Technology (ICT)

(3) Information and Data Technology (IDT)

(4) Artificial Intelligence (AI)

59. If the binary equivalent of the decimal number 48 is 110000, then the binary equivalent of the decimal number 51 is given by

(1) 110011 (c) 110010

(3) 110001 (4) 110100

60. The process of copying files to a CD-ROM is known as

(1) Burning

(2) Zipping

(3) Digitizing

(4) Ripping

ANSWERS

1. (1)	**2.** (2)	**3.** (4)	**4.** (2)	**5.** (2)	**6.** (3)	**7.** (1)	**8.** (3)	**9.** (4)	**10.** (1)
11. (3)	**12.** (2)	**13.** (4)	**14.** (1)	**15.** (2)	**16.** (3)	**17.** (1)	**18.** (4)	**19.** (3)	**20.** (2)
21. (3)	**22.** (3)	**23.** (2)	**24.** (4)	**25.** (2)	**26.** (3)	**27.** (3)	**28.** (1)	**29.** (4)	**30.** (2)
31. (3)	**32.** (4)	**33.** (1)	**34.** (3)	**35.** (2)	**36.** (1)	**37.** (2)	**38.** (1)	**39.** (4)	**40.** (1)
41. (3)	**42.** (4)	**43.** (1)	**44.** (3)	**45.** (4)	**46.** (2)	**47.** (3)	**48.** (2)	**49.** (4)	**50.** (3)
51. (2)	**52.** (3)	**53.** (2)	**54.** (3)	**55.** (4)	**56.** (3)	**57.** (4)	**58.** (1)	**59.** (1)	**60.** (1)

■■

Solved Paper 2015 (December)

UGC NET

PAPER-I

Note : This paper consists of **Sixty (60)** multiple-choice type of questions, out of which the candidate would be required to answer **any Fifty (50)** questions. In the event of candidate attempting more than **Fifty (50)** questions, the **first Fifty (50)** questions attempted by the Candidate would be evaluated.

1. Greater the handicap of the students coming to the educational institutions, greater the demand on the :

(1) Family (2) Society

(3) Teacher (4) State

2. What are the characteristics of Continuous and Comprehensive Evaluation ?

(a) It increases the workload on students by taking multiple tests.

(b) It replaces marks with grades.

(c) It evaluates every aspect of the student.

(d) It helps in reducing examination phobia.

Select the correct answer from the codes given below :

(1) (a), (b), (c) and (d)

(2) (b) and (d)

(3) (a), (b) and (c)

(4) (b), (c) and (d)

3. Which of the following attributes denote great strengths of a teacher ?

(a) Full-time active involvement in the institutional management

(b) Setting examples

(c) Willingness to put assumptions to the test

(d) Acknowledging mistakes

Select the correct answer from the codes given below :

(1) (a), (b) and (d)

(2) (b), (c) and (d)

(3) (a), (c) and (d)

(4) (a), (b), (c) and (d)

4. Which one of the following statements is correct in the context of multiple - choice type questions ?

(1) They are more objective than true-false type questions.

(2) They are less objective than essay type questions.

(3) They are more subjective than short-answer type questions.

(4) They are more subjective than true-false type questions.

5. As Chairman of an independent commission on education, Jacques Delors report to UNESCO was titled :

(1) International Commission on Education Report

(2) Millennium Development Report

(3) Learning : The Treasure Within

(4) World Declaration on Education for All

6. What are required for good teaching ?

(a) Diagnosis

(b) Remedy

(c) Direction

(d) Feedback

Select the correct answer from the codes given below :

(1) (a), (b), (c) and (d)

(2) (a) and (b)

(3) (b), (c) and (d)

(4) (c) and (d)

7. Which of the following statements is not true in the context of participatory research ?

(1) It recognizes knowledge as power.

(2) It emphasises on people as experts.

(3) It is a collective process of enquiry.

(4) Its sole purpose is production of knowledge.

8. Which of the following statements is true in the context of the testing of a hypothesis ?

(1) It is only the alternative hypothesis, that can be tested.

(2) It is only the null hypothesis, that can be tested.

(3) Both, the alternative and the null hypotheses can be tested.

(4) Both, the alternative and the null hypotheses cannot be tested.

9. Which of the following are the basic rules of APA style of referencing format ?

(a) Italicize titles of shorter works such as journal articles or essays

(b) Invert authors' names (last name first)

(c) Italicize titles of longer works such as books and journals

(d) Alphabetically index reference list

Select the correct answer from the codes given below :

(1) (a) and (b)

(2) (b), (c) and (d)

(3) (c) and (d)

(4) (a), (b), (c) and (d)

10. Which of the following are the characteristics of a seminar ?

(a) It is a form of academic instruction.

(b) It involves questioning, discussion and debates.

(c) It involves large groups of individuals.

(d) It needs involvement of skilled persons.

Select the correct answer from the codes given below :

(1) (b) and (c) (2) (b) and (d)

(3) (b), (c) and (d) (4) (a), (b) and (d)

11. A researcher is interested in studying the prospects of a particular political party in an urban area. What tool should he prefer for the study ?

(1) Rating scale (2) Interview

(3) Questionnaire (4) Schedule

12. Ethical norms in research do not involve guidelines for :

(1) Thesis format

(2) Copyright

(3) Patenting policy

(4) Data sharing policies

Read the following passage carefully and answer question numbers 13 to 17.

I did that thing recently where you have to sign a big card - which is a horror unto itself, especially as the keeper of the Big Card was leaning over me at the time. Suddenly I was on the spot, a rabbit in the headlights, torn between doing a fun message or some sort of in-joke or a drawing. Instead overwhelmed by the myriad options available to me, I decided to just write : "Good luck, best, Joel".

It was then that I realised, to my horror, that I had forgotten how to write. My entire existence is "tap letters into computer". My shopping lists are hidden in the notes function of my phone. If I need to remember something I send an e-mail to myself. A pen is something I chew when I'm struggling to think. Paper is something I pile beneath my laptop to make it a more comfortable height for me to type on.

A poll of 1,000 teens by the stationers, Bic found that one in 10 don't own a pen, a third have never written a letter, and half of 13 to 19 years - old have never been forced to sit down and write a thank you letter. More than 80% have never written a love letter, 56% don't have letter paper at home. And a quarter have never known the unique torture of writing a birthday card. The most a teen ever has to use a pen is on an exam paper.

Bic, have you heard of mobile phones ? Have you heard of e-mail, facebook and snap chatting ? This is the future. Pens are dead. Paper is dead. Handwriting is a relic.

"Handwriting is one of the most creative outlets we have and should be given the same importance as other art forms such as sketching, painting or photography."

Answer the following questions :

13. When confronted with signing a big card, the author felt like "a rabbit in the headlight". What does this phrase mean?

(1) A state of confusion

(2) A state of pleasure

(3) A state of anxiety

(4) A state of pain

14. According to the author, which one is not the most creative outlet of pursuit ?

(1) Handwriting (2) Photography

(3) Sketching (4) Reading

15. The entire existence of the author revolves round :

(a) Computer

(b) Mobile phone

(c) Typewriter

Identify the correct answer from the codes given below :

(1) (b) only

(2) (a) and (b) only

(3) (a), (b) and (c)

(4) (b) and (c) only

16. How many teens, as per the Bic survey, do not own a pen ?

(1) 800 (2) 560

(3) 500 (4) 100

17. What is the main concern of the author ?

(1) That the teens use social networks for communication.

(2) That the teens use mobile phones.

(3) That the teens use computer.

(4) That the teens have forgotten the art of handwriting.

18. The main objectives of student evaluation of teachers are :

(a) To gather information about student weaknesses.

(b) To make teachers take teaching seriously.

(c) To help teachers adopt innovative methods of teaching.

(d) To identify the areas of further improvement in teacher traits.

Identify the correct answer from the codes given below :

(1) (a) and (b) only

(2) (b), (c) and (d) only

(3) (a), (b) and (c) only

(4) (a) only

19. Using the central point of the classroom communication as the beginning of a dynamic pattern of ideas is referred to as:

(1) Systemisation

(2) Problem - orientation

(3) Idea protocol

(4) Mind mapping

20. Aspects of the voice, other than the speech are known as :

(1) Physical language

(2) Personal language

(3) Para language

(4) Delivery language

21. Every type of communication is affected by its :

(1) Reception (2) Transmission

(3) Non-regulation (4) Context

22. Attitudes, actions and appearances in the context of classroom communication are considered as :

(1) Verbal (2) Non-verbal

(3) Impersonal (4) Irrational

23. Most often, the teacher - student communication is :

(1) Spurious (2) Critical

(3) Utilitarian (4) Confrontational

24. In a classroom, a communicator's trust level is determined by :

(1) the use of hyperbole

(2) the change of voice level

(3) the use of abstract concepts

(4) eye contact

25. The next term in the series 2, 5, 10, 17, 26, 37, ? is :

(1) 50 (2) 57

(3) 62 (4) 72

26. A group of 210 students appeared in some test. The mean of $\frac{1}{3}$rd of students is found to be 60. The mean of the remaining students is found to be 78. The mean of the whole group will be :

(1) 80 (2) 76

(3) 74 (4) 72

27. Anil after travelling 6 km towards East from his house realized that he has travelled in a wrong direction. He turned and travelled 12 km towards West, turned right and travelled 8 km to reach his office. The straight distance of the office from his house is :

(1) 20 km (2) 14 km

(3) 12 km (4) 10 km

28. The next term in the series : B2E, D5H, F12K, H27N, ? is :

(1) J 5 6 I (2) I 6 2 Q

(3) Q 6 2 J (4) J 5 8 Q

29. A party was held in which a grandmother, father, mother, four sons, their wives and one son and two daughters to each of the sons were present. The number of females present in the party is :

(1) 12 (2) 14

(3) 18 (4) 24

30. P and Q are brothers. R and S are sisters. The son of P is brother of S. Q is related to R as :

(1) Son (2) Brother

(3) Uncle (4) Father

31. Consider the argument given below :

'Pre - employment testing of teachers is quite fair because doctors, architects and engineers who are now employed had to face such a testing.'

What type of argument it is ?

(1) Deductive (2) Analogical

(3) Psychological (4) Biological

32. Among the following propositions two are related in such a way that they can both be true although they cannot both be false. Which are those propositions ? Select the correct code

Propositions :

(a) Some priests are cunning.

(b) No priest is cunning.

(c) All priests are cunning.

(d) Some priests are not cunning.

Codes :

(1) (a) and (b)

(2) (c) and (d)

(3) (a) and (c)

(4) (a) and (d)

33. A Cluster of propositions with a structure that exhibits some inference is called :

(1) An inference (2) An argument

(3) An explanation (4) A valid argument

34. Consider the following **assertion (A)** and **Reason (R)** and select the correct code given below :

(A) : No man is perfect.

(R) : Some men are not perfect.

(1) Both **(A)** and **(R)** are true but **(R)** does not provide sufficient reason for **(A)**.

(2) Both **(A)** and **(R)** are true and **(R)** provides sufficient reason for **(A)**.

(3) **(A)** is true but **(R)** is false.

(4) **(A)** is false but **(R)** is true.

35. A definition that has a meaning that is deliberately assigned to some symbol is called :

(1) Lexical (2) Precising

(3) Stipulative (4) Persuasive

36. If the proposition 'No men are honest' is taken to be false which of the following proposition/ propositions can be claimed certainly to be true ?

Propositions :

(1) All men are honest

(2) Some men are honest

(3) Some men are not honest

(4) No honest person is man

Given below in the table is the decadal data of Population and Electrical Power Production of a country.

Year	Population (million)	Electrical Power Production(GW)*
1951	20	10
1961	21	20
1971	24	25
1981	27	40
1991	30	50
2001	32	80
2011	35	100
		*1 GW = 100 million watt

Based on the above table, answer the questions from Sl. No. 37 to 42.

37. Which decade registered the maximum growth rate (%) of population ?

(1) 1961-71 (2) 1971-81

(3) 1991-2001 (4) 2001-2011

38. Average decadal growth rate (%) of population is :

(1) ~ 12.21% (2) ~ 9.82%

(3) ~ 6.73% (4) ~ 5%

39. Based on the average decadal growth rate, what will be the population in the year 2021 ?

(1) 40.34 million (2) 38.49 million

(3) 37.28 million (4) 36.62 million

40. In the year 1951, what was the power availability per person ?

(1) 100 W (2) 200 W

(3) 400 W (4) 500 W

41. In which decade, the average power availability per person was maximum ?

(1) 1981-1991 (2) 1991-2001

(3) 2001-2011 (4) 1971-1981

42. By what percentage (%) the power production increased from 1951 to 2011 ?

(1) 100% (2) 300%

(3) 600% (4) 900%

43. NMEICT stands for :

(1) National Mission on Education through ICT

(2) National Mission on E-governance through ICT

(3) National Mission on E-commerce through ICT

(4) National Mission on E-learning through ICT

44. Which of the following is an instant messaging application ?

(a) WhatsApp

(b) Google Talk

(c) Viber

Select the correct answer from the codes given below :

(1) (a) and (b) only

(2) (b) and (c) only

(3) (a) only

(4) (a), (b) and (c)

45. In a Computer a byte generally consists of :

(1) 4 bits (2) 8 bits

(3) 16 bits (4) 10 bits

46. Which of the following is not an input device ?

(1) Microphone (2) Keyboard

(3) Joystick (4) Monitor

47. Which of the following is an open source software ?

(1) MS Word

(2) Windows

(3) Mozilla Firefox

(4) Acrobat Reader

48. Which of the following enables us to send the same letter to different persons in MS Word ?

(1) Mail join (2) Mail copy

(3) Mail insert (4) Mail merge

49. Inside rural homes, the source/sources of Nitrogen Oxide Pollution may be :

(a) Unvented gas stoves

(b) Wood stoves

(c) Kerosene heaters

Choose the correct code :

(1) (a) and (b) only

(2) (b) and (c) only

(3) (b) only

(4) (a), (b) and (c)

50. Which of the following pollutants can cause cancer in humans ?

(1) Pesticides (2) Mercury

(3) Lead (4) Ozone

51. **Assertion (A) :** People population control measures do not necessarily help in checking environmental degradation.

Reason (R) : The relationship between population growth and environmental degradation is rather complex.

Choose the correct answer from the following :

(1) Both **(A)** and **(R)** are true and **(R)** is the correct explanation of **(A)**.

(2) Both **(A)** and **(R)** are true but **(R)** is not the correct explanation of **(A)**.

(3) **(A)** is true but **(R)** is false.

(4) **(A)** is false but **(R)** is true.

52. Which of the following phenomena is not a natural hazard ?

(1) Wildfire

(2) Lightning

(3) Landslide

(4) Chemical contamination

53. As part of National Climate Change Policy, Indian government is planning to raise the installed capacity of renewable energy by the year 2030 to :

(1) 175 GW (2) 200 GW

(3) 250 GW (4) 350 GW

54. At present, in terms of per capita energy consumption (kWh/year), identify the correct sequence.

(1) Brazil > Russia > China > India

(2) Russia > China > India > Brazil

(3) Russia > China > Brazil > India

(4) China > Russia > Brazil > India

55. Which of the following are the objectives of Rashtriya Uchchatar Shiksha Abhiyan (RUSA)?

(a) To improve the overall quality of state institutions.

(b) To ensure adequate availability of quality faculty.

(c) To create new institutions through upgradation of existing autonomous colleges.

(d) To downgrade universities with poor infrastructure into autonomous colleges.

Select the correct answer from the codes given below :

(1) (a), (b), (c) and (d)

(2) (a), (b) and (c)

(3) (a), (c) and (d)

(4) (a), (b) and (d)

56. The grounds on which discrimination in admission to educational institutions is constitutionally prohibited are :

(a) Religion

(b) Sex

(c) Place of birth

(d) Nationality

Select the correct answer from the codes given below :

(1) (b), (c) and (d)

(2) (a), (b) and (c)

(3) (a), (b) and (d)

(4) (a), (b), (c) and (d)

57. Which of the following statements are correct about Lok Sabha ?

(a) The Constitution puts a limit on the size of the Lok Sabha.

(b) The size and shape of the Parliamentary Constituencies is determined by the Election Commission.

(c) First - past - the Post electoral system is followed.

(d) The Speaker of Lok Sabha does not have a casting vote in case of an equality of votes.

Select the correct answer from the codes given below :

(1) (a) and (c)

(2) (a), (b) and (c)

(3) (a), (c) and (d)

(4) (a), (b), (c) and (d)

58. Public Order as an item in the Constitution figures in :

(1) the Union List

(2) the State List

(3) the Concurrent List

(4) the Residuary Powers

59. The term of office of the Advocate General of a State is :

(1) 4 years

(2) 5 years

(3) 6 years or 65 years of age whichever is earlier

(4) not fixed

60. Which among the following States has the highest number of seats in the Lok Sabha?

(1) Maharashtra (2) Rajasthan

(3) Tamil Nadu (4) West Bengal

ANSWERS

1. (3)	**2.** (4)	**3.** (2)	**4.** (1)	**5.** (3)	**6.** (1)	**7.** (4)	**8.** (2)	**9.** (2)	**10.** (4)
11. (3)	**12.** (1)	**13.** (1)	**14.** (4)	**15.** (2)	**16.** (4)	**17.** (4)	**18.** (2)	**19.** (4)	**20.** (3)
21. (4)	**22.** (2)	**23.** (3)	**24.** (4)	**25.** (1)	**26.** (4)	**27.** (4)	**28.** (4)	**29.** (2)	**30.** (3)
31. (2)	**32.** (4)	**33.** (2)	**34.** (1)	**35.** (3)	**36.** (2)	**37.** (1)	**38.** (2)	**39.** (2)	**40.** (4)
41. (3)	**42.** (4)	**43.** (1)	**44.** (4)	**45.** (2)	**46.** (4)	**47.** (3)	**48.** (4)	**49.** (4)	**50.** (1)
51. (1)	**52.** (4)	**53.** (4)	**54.** (3)	**55.** (2)	**56.** (2)	**57.** (1)	**58.** (2)	**59.** (4)	**60.** (1)

■■

JUNE – 2015

UGC-NET

PAPER – I

Note : This paper contains **Sixty (60)** multiple choice questions, each question carrying **two (2) marks**.

- Candidate is expected to answer any **Fifty (50)** questions.
- In case more than **Fifty (50)** questions are attempted, only the **first Fifty (50)** questions will be evaluated.

1. Which of the following is the highest level of cognitive ability ?

(1) Knowing

(2) Understanding

(3) Analysing

(4) Evaluating

2. Which of the following factors does **not** impact teaching ?

(1) Teacher's knowledge

(2) Class room activities that encourage learning

(3) Socio-economic background of teachers and students

(4) Learning through experience

3. Which of the following statements about teaching aids are correct ?

(a) They help in retaining concepts for longer duration.

(b) They help students learn better.

(c) They make teaching learning process interesting.

(d) They enhance rote learning.

Select the correct answer from the codes given below :

(1) (a), (b), (c) and (d)

(2) (a), (b) and (c)

(3) (b), (c) and (d)

(4) (a), (b) and (d)

4. Techniques used by a teacher to teach include :

(a) Lecture

(b) Interactive lecture

(c) Group work

(d) Self study

Select the correct answer from the codes given below :

(1) (a), (b) and (c)

(2) (a), (b), (c) and (d)

(3) (b), (c) and (d)

(4) (a), (b) and (d)

5. Achievement tests are commonly used for the purpose of :

(1) Making selections for a specific job

(2) Selecting candidates for a course

(3) Identifying strengths and weaknesses of learners

(4) Assessing the amount of learning after teaching

6. A good teacher is one who :

(1) gives useful information

(2) explains concepts and principles

(3) gives printed notes to students

(4) inspires students to learn

7. Which of the following statements regarding the meaning of research are correct ?
   (a) Research refers to a series of systematic activity or activities undertaken to find out the solution of a problem.
   (b) It is a systematic, logical and an unbiased process wherein verification of hypothesis, data analysis, interpretation and formation of principles can be done.
   (c) It is an intellectual enquiry or quest towards truth.
   (d) It leads to enhancement of knowledge.

   Select the correct answer from the codes given below :
   (1) (a), (b) and (c)
   (2) (b), (c) and (d)
   (3) (a), (c) and (d)
   (4) (a), (b), (c) and (d)

8. A good thesis writing should involve :
   (a) reduction of punctuation and grammatical errors to a minimum.
   (b) careful checking of references.
   (c) consistency in the way the thesis is written.
   (d) a clear and well written abstract.

   Select the correct answer from the codes given below :
   (1) (a), (b), (c) and (d)
   (2) (a), (b) and (c)
   (3) (a), (b) and (d)
   (4) (b), (c) and (d)

9. Jean Piaget gave a theory of cognitive development of humans on the basis of his :
   (1) Fundamental Research
   (2) Applied Research
   (3) Action Research
   (4) Evaluation Research

10. "Male and female students perform equally well in a numerical aptitude test." This statement indicates a :
   (1) research hypothesis
   (2) null hypothesis
   (3) directional hypothesis
   (4) statistical hypothesis

11. The conclusions/findings of which type of research cannot be generalized to other situations ?
   (1) Historical Research
   (2) Descriptive Research
   (3) Experimental Research
   (4) Causal Comparative Research

12. Which of the following steps are required to design a questionnaire ?
   (a) Writing primary and secondary aims of the study.
   (b) Review of the current literature.
   (c) Prepare a draft of questionnaire.
   (d) Revision of the draft.

   Select the correct answer from the codes given below :
   (1) (a), (b) and (c)
   (2) (a), (c) and (d)
   (3) (b), (c) and (d)
   (4) (a), (b), (c) and (d)

Read the following passage carefully and answer questions 13 to 18.

Story telling is not in our genes. Neither it is an evolutionary history. It is the essence of what makes us Human.

Human beings progress by telling stories. One event can result in a great variety of stories being told about it. Sometimes those stories differ greatly. Which stories are picked up and repeated and which ones are dropped and forgotten often determines how we progress. Our history, knowledge and understanding are all the collections of the few stories that survive. This includes the stories that we tell each other about the future. And how the future will turn out depends partly, possibly largely, on which stories we collectively choose to believe.

Some stories are designed to spread fear and concern. This is because some story-tellers feel that there is a need to raise some tensions. Some stories are frightening, they are like totemic warnings : "Fail to act now and we are all doomed." Then there are stories that indicate that all will be fine so long as we leave everything upto a few especially able adults. Currently, this trend is being led by those who call themselves "rational optimists". They tend to claim that it is human nature to compete and to succeed and also to profit at the expense of others. The rational optimists however, do not realize how humanity has progressed overtime through amiable social networks and how large groups work in less selfishness and in the process accommodate rich and poor, high and low alike. This aspect in story-telling is considered by the 'Practical Possibles', who sit between those who say all is fine and cheerful and be individualistic in your approach to a successful future, and those who ordain pessimism and fear that we are doomed.

What the future holds for us is which stories we hold on to and how we act on them.

Answer the following questions :

13. Our knowledge is a collection of :

(1) all stories that we have heard during our life-time

(2) some stories that we remember

(3) a few stories that survive

(4) some important stories

14. Story telling is :

(1) an art

(2) a science

(3) in our genes

(4) the essence of what makes us human

15. How the future will turn out to be, depends upon the stories ?

(1) We collectively choose to believe in

(2) Which are repeatedly narrated

(3) Designed to spread fear and tension

(4) Designed to make prophecy

16. Rational optimists :

(a) Look for opportunities.

(b) Are sensible and cheerful.

(c) Are selfishly driven.

Identify the correct answer from the codes given below :

(1) (a), (b) and (c)

(2) (a) only

(3) (a) and (b) only

(4) (b) and (c) only

17. Humans become less selfish when :

(1) they work in large groups

(2) they listen to frightening stories

(3) they listen to cheerful stories

(4) they work in solitude

18. 'Practical Possibles' are the ones who :

(1) follow Midway Path

(2) are doom-mongers

(3) are self-centred

(4) are cheerful and carefree

19. Effectiveness of communication can be traced from which of the following ?

(a) Attitude surveys

(b) Performance records

(c) Students attendance

(d) Selection of communication channel

Select the correct answer from the codes given below :

(1) (a), (b), (c) and (d)

(2) (a), (b) and (c)

(3) (b), (c) and (d)

(4) (a), (b) and (d)

20. **Assertion (A)** : Formal communication tends to be fast and flexible.

Reason (R) : Formal communication is a systematic and orderly flow of information.

(1) Both (A) and (R) are correct and (R) is correct explanation of (A)

(2) Both (A) and (R) are correct, but (R) is not correct explanation of (A)

(3) (A) is correct but, (R) is false

(4) (A) is false but, (R) is correct

21. Which of the following are the characteristic features of communication ?

(a) Communication involves exchange of ideas, facts and opinions.

(b) Communication involves both information and understanding.

(c) Communication is a continuous process.

(d) Communication is a circular process.

Select the correct answer from the codes given below :

(1) (a), (b) and (c)

(2) (a), (b) and (d)

(3) (b), (c) and (d)

(4) (a), (b), (c) and (d)

22. The term 'grapevine' is also known as :

(1) Downward communication

(2) Informal communication

(3) Upward communication

(4) Horizontal communication

23. Which of the following is **not** a principle of effective communication ?

(1) Persuasive and convincing dialogue

(2) Participation of the audience

(3) One-way transfer of information

(4) Strategic use of grapevine

24. In communication, the language is :

(1) The verbal code

(2) Intrapersonal

(3) The symbolic code

(4) The non-verbal code

25. The next term in the series is :

2, 5, 9, 19, 37, ?

(1) 73

(2) 75

(3) 78

(4) 80

26. In certain code MATHURA is coded as JXQEROX. The code of HOTELS will be :

(1) LEQIBP

(2) ELQBIP

(3) LEBIQP

(4) ELIPQB

27. One day Prakash left home and walked 10 km towards south, turned right and walked 5 km, turned right and walked 10 km and turned left and walked 10 km. How many km will he have to walk to reach his home straight ?

(1) 10

(2) 20

(3) 15

(4) 30

28. A girl introduced a boy as the son of the daughter of the father of her uncle. The boy is related to the girl as :

(1) Brother

(2) Uncle

(3) Nephew

(4) Son

29. In an examination 10,000 students appeared. The result revealed the number of students who have :

passed in all five subjects = 5583

passed in three subjects only = 1400

passed in two subjects only = 1200
passed in one subject only = 735
failed in English only = 75
failed in Physics only = 145
failed in Chemistry only = 140
failed in Mathematics only = 200
failed in Bio-science only = 157

The number of students passed in at least four subjects is :

(1) 6300
(2) 6900
(3) 7300
(4) 7900

30. At present a person is 4 times older than his son and is 3 years older than his wife. After 3 years the age of the son will be 15 years. The age of the person's wife after 5 years will be;

(1) 42
(2) 48
(3) 45
(4) 50

31. If we want to seek new knowledge of facts about the world, we must rely on reason of the type:

(1) Inductive
(2) Deductive
(3) Demonstrative
(4) Physiological

32. A deductive argument is invalid if :

(1) Its premises and conclusions are all false
(2) Its premises are true but its conclusion is false
(3) Its premises are false but its conclusion is true
(4) Its premises and conclusions are all true

33. Inductive reasoning is grounded on :

(1) Integrity of nature
(2) Unity of nature
(3) Uniformity of nature
(4) Harmony of nature

34. Among the following statements **two** are contradictory to each other. Select the correct code that represents them :

Statements :

(a) All poets are philosophers.
(b) Some poets are philosophers.
(c) Some poets are not philosophers.
(d) No philosopher is a poet.

Codes :

(1) (a) and (b) (2) (a) and (d)
(3) (a) and (c) (4) (b) and (c)

35. Which of the codes given below contains only the **correct** statements ? Select the code :

Statements :

(a) Venn diagram represents the arguments graphically.
(b) Venn diagram can enhance our understanding.
(c) Venn diagram may be called valid or invalid.
(d) Venn diagram is clear method of notation.

Codes :

(1) (a), (b) and (c)
(2) (a), (b) and (d)
(3) (b), (c) and (d)
(4) (a), (c) and (d)

36. When the purpose of a definition is to explain the use or to eliminate ambiguity the definition is called :

(1) Stipulative
(2) Theoretical
(3) Lexical
(4) Persuasive

Question numbers 37 to 42 are based on the tabulated data given below :

A company has 20 employees with their age (in years) and salary (in thousand rupees per month) mentioned against each of them :

S.No.	Age (in years)	Salary (in thousand rupees per month)
1.	44	35
2.	32	20
3.	54	45
4.	42	35
5.	31	20
6.	53	60
7.	42	50
8.	51	55
9.	34	25
10.	41	30
11.	33	30
12.	31	35
13.	30	35
14.	37	40
15.	44	45
16.	36	35
17.	34	35
18.	49	50
19.	43	45
20.	45	50

37. Classify the data of age of each employee in class interval of 5 years. Which class interval of 5 years has the maximum average salary ?

(1) 35 - 40 years (2) 40 - 45 years

(3) 45 - 50 years (4) 50 - 55 years

38. What is the frequency (%) in the class interval of 30 - 35 years ?

(1) 20 % (2) 25 %

(3) 30 % (4) 35 %

39. What is the average age of the employees?

(1) 40.3 years (2) 38.6 years

(3) 47.2 years (4) 45.3 years

40. What is the fraction (%) of employees getting salary ₹ 40,000 per month ?

(1) 45% (2) 50%

(3) 35% (4) 32%

41. What is the average salary (in thousand per month) in the age group 40 - 50 years?

(1) 35 (2) 42.5

(3) 40.5 (4) 36.5

42. What is the fraction of employees getting salary less than the average salary of all the employees ?

(1) 45% (2) 50%

(3) 55% (4) 47%

43. Encoding or scrambling data for transmission across a network is known as :

(1) Protection (2) Detection

(3) Encryption (4) Decryption

44. Which of the following is **not** an output device ?

(1) Printer (2) Speaker

(3) Monitor (4) Keyboard

45. Which of the following represents one billion characters ?

(1) Kilobyte (2) Megabyte

(3) Gigabyte (4) Terabyte

46. Which of the following is **not** open source software ?

(1) Internet explorer

(2) Fedora Linux

(3) Open office

(4) Apache HTTP server

47. Which one of the following represents the binary equivalent of the decimal number 25 ?

(1) 10101 (2) 01101

(3) 11001 (4) 11011

48. Which is an instant messenger that is used for chatting ?
(1) Altavista
(2) MAC
(3) Microsoft Office
(4) Google Talk

49. In which of the countries per capita use of water is maximum ?
(1) USA
(2) European Union
(3) China
(4) India

50. India's contribution to total global carbon dioxide emissions is about :
(1) ~ 3%
(2) ~ 6%
(3) ~ 10%
(4) ~ 15%

51. Two earthquakes A and B happen to be of magnitude 5 and 6 respectively on Richter Scale. The ratio of the energies released E_B/E_A will be approximately :
(1) ~ 8
(2) ~ 16
(3) ~ 32
(4) ~ 64

52. Which of the following combinations represent renewable natural resources ?
(1) Fertile soil, fresh water and natural gas
(2) Clean air, phosphates and biological diversity
(3) Fishes, fertile soil and fresh water
(4) Oil, forests and tides

53. In the recently launched Air Quality Index in India, which of the following pollutants is **not** included ?
(1) Carbon monoxide
(2) Fine particulate matter
(3) Ozone
(4) Chlorofluorocarbons

54. The factors which are most important in determining the impact of anthropogenic activities on environment are :
(1) Population, affluence per person, land available per person
(2) Population, affluence per person and the technology used for exploiting resources
(3) Atmospheric conditions, population and forest cover
(4) Population, forest cover and land available per person

55. The session of the parliament is summoned by :
(1) The President
(2) The Prime Minister
(3) The Speaker of the Lok Sabha
(4) The Speaker of the Lok Sabha and the Chairman of the Rajya Sabha

56. Civil Service Day is celebrated in India on :
(1) 21st April
(2) 24th April
(3) 21st June
(4) 7th July

57. The South Asia University is situated in the city of :
(1) Colombo
(2) Dhaka
(3) New Delhi
(4) Kathmandu

58. The University Grants Commission was established with which of the following aims ?
(a) Promotion of research and development in higher education
(b) Identifying and sustaining institutions of potential learning
(c) Capacity building of teachers
(d) Providing autonomy to each and every higher educational institution in India

Select the correct answer from the codes given below :

(1) (a), (b), (c) and (d)

(2) (a), (b) and (c)

(3) (b), (c) and (d)

(4) (a), (b) and (d)

59. The Gross Enrolment Ratio (GER) in institutions of higher education in India at present (2015) is about:

(1) 8 percent (2) 12 percent

(3) 19 percent (4) 23 percent

60. The total number of central universities in India in April 2015 was :

(1) 08

(2) 14

(3) 27

(4) 43

ANSWERS

1. (4)	**2.** (3)	**3.** (2)	**4.** (1)	**5.** (4)	**6.** (4)	**7.** (4)	**8.** (1)	**9.** (1)	**10.** (2)
11. (1)	**12.** (4)	**13.** (3)	**14.** (4)	**15.** (1)	**16.** (1)	**17.** (1)	**18.** (1)	**19.** (2)	**20.** (4)
21. (4)	**22.** (2)	**23.** (3)	**24.** (1)	**25.** (2)	**26.** (2)	**27.** (3)	**28.** (1)	**29.** (1)	**30.** (4)
31. (1)	**32.** (2)	**33.** (3)	**34.** (3)	**35.** (2)	**36.** (3)	**37.** (4)	**38.** (4)	**39.** (1)	**40.** (1)
41. (2)	**42.** (3)	**43.** (3)	**44.** (4)	**45.** (3)	**46.** (1)	**47.** (3)	**48.** (4)	**49.** (2)	**50.** (2)
51. (3)	**52.** (3)	**53.** (4)	**54.** (2)	**55.** (1)	**56.** (1)	**57.** (3)	**58.** (2)	**59.** (3)	**60.** (4)

Solved Paper 2014 (December)
UGC NET
PAPER-I

Note : • This paper contains **Sixty (60)** multiple choice questions, each question carrying **two (2)** marks.
• Candidate is expected to answer any **Fifty (50)** questions.
• In case more than **Fifty (50)** questions are attempted, only the first **Fifty (50)** questions will be evaluated.

1. The term "Yellow Journalism" refers to
   (*a*) Sensational news about terrorism and violence
   (*b*) Sensationalism and exaggeration to attract readers / viewers.
   (*c*) Sensational news about arts and culture.
   (*d*) Sensational news prints in yellow paper.

2. In the classroom, the teacher sends the message either as words or images. The students are really
   (*a*) Encoders (*b*) Decoders
   (*c*) Agitators (*d*) Propagators

3. Media is known as
   (*a*) First Estate (*b*) Second Estate
   (*c*) Third Estate (*d*) Fourth Estate

4. The mode of communication that involves a single source transmitting information to a large number of receivers simultaneously, is called
   (*a*) Group Communication
   (*b*) Mass Communication
   (*c*) Intrapersonal Communication
   (*d*) Interpersonal Communication

5. A smart classroom is a teaching space which has
   (*i*) Smart portion with a touch panel control system.
   (*ii*) PC/Laptop connection and DVD/VCR player.
   (*iii*) Document camera and specialized software
   (*iv*) Projector and screen

   Select the correct answer from the codes given below :
   (*a*) (*i*) and (*ii*) only
   (*b*) (*ii*) and (*iv*) only
   (*c*) (*i*), (*ii*) and (*iii*) only
   (*d*) (*i*), (*ii*), (*iii*) and (*iv*)

6. Digital Empowerment means
   (*i*) Universal digit literacy
   (*ii*) Universal access to all digital resources
   (*iii*) Collaborative digital platform for participative governance.
   (*iv*) Probability of all entitlements for individuals through cloud.

   Choose the correct answer from the codes given below :
   (*a*) (*i*) and (*ii*) only
   (*b*) (*ii*) and (*iii*) only
   (*c*) (*i*), (*ii*) and (*iii*) only
   (*d*) (*i*), (*ii*), (*iii*) and (*iv*)

7. The next term in the series: 2, 7, 28, 63, 126, ____ is
   (*a*) 215 (*b*) 245
   (*c*) 276 (*d*) 296

8. The next term in the series: AB, ED, IH, NM, ____ is
   (*a*) TS (*b*) ST
   (*c*) TU (*d*) SU

9. If STREAMERS is coded as UVTGALDQR, then KNOWLEDGE will be coded as
   (*a*) MQPYLCDFD (*b*) MPQYLDCFD
   (*c*) MYQLDFCD (*d*) YMQPLDDFC

10. A is brother of B. B is the brother of C. C is the husband of D. E is the father of A. D is related to E as
    (*a*) Daughter (*b*) Daughter-in-law
    (*c*) Sister-in-law (*d*) Sister

11. Two numbers are in the ration 3:5. If 9 is subtracted from the numbers, the ratio becomes 12:23. The numbers are

(*a*) 30, 50 (*b*) 36, 60
(*c*) 33, 55 (*d*) 42, 70

12. The mean of the ages of father and his son is 27 years. After 18 years, father will be twice as old as his son. Their present ages are

(*a*) 42, 12 (*b*) 40, 14
(*c*) 30, 24 (*d*) 36, 18

Read the following passage carefully and answer questions 13 to 17:

The literary distaste for politics, however, seems to be focused not so much on the largely murky practice of politics in itself as a subject of literary representation but rather more on how it is often depicted in literature, i.e., on the very politics of such representation. A political novel often turns out to be not merely a novel about politics but a novel with a politics of its own, for it seeks not merely to show us how things are but has fairly definite ideas about how things should be, and precisely what one should think and do in order to make things move in that desired direction. In short, it seeks to convert and enlist the reader to a particular cause or ideology; it often is (in an only too familiar phrase) not literature but propaganda. This is said to violate the very spirit of literature which is to broaden our understanding of the world and the range of our sympathies rather than to narrow them down through partisan commitment. As John Keats said, 'We hate poetry that has a palpable design upon us'.

Another reason why politics does not seem amenable to the highest kind of literary representation seems to arise from the fact that politics by its very nature is constituted of ideas and ideologies. If political situations do not lend themselves to happy literary treatment, political ideas present perhaps an even greater problem in this regard. Literature, it is argued, is about human experiences rather than about intellectual abstractions; it deals in what is called the 'felt reality' of human flesh and blood, and in sap and savour. (rasa) rather than in and and lifeless ideas. In an extensive discussion of the matter in her book Ideas and the Novel, the American novelist Mary McCarthy observed that 'ideas are still today felt to be unsightly in the novel' though that was not so in 'former days', i.e., in the 18th and 19th centuries. Her formulation of the precise nature of the incompatibility between ideas on the one hand and the novel on the other betrays perhaps a divided conscience in the matter and a sense of dilemma shared by many writers and readers : 'An idea cannot have loose ends, but a novel, I almost think, needs them. Nevertheless, there is enough in common for the novelists to feel... the attraction of ideas while taking up arms against them — most often with weapons of mockery.'

13. According to the passage, a political novel often turns out to be a

(*a*) Literary distaste for politics
(*b*) Literary representation of politics
(*c*) Novels with its own politics
(*d*) Depiction of murky practice of politics

14. A political novel reveals

(*a*) Reality of the tings
(*b*) Writer's perception
(*c*) Particular ideology of the readers
(*d*) The spirit of literature

15. The constructs of politics by its nature is

(*a*) Prevalent political situation
(*b*) Ideas and Ideologies
(*c*) Political propaganda
(*d*) Understanding of human nature

16. Literature deals with

(*a*) Human experiences in politics
(*b*) Intellectual abstractions
(*c*) Dry and empty ideas
(*d*) Felt reality of human life

17. The observation of the novelist, May McCarthy reveals

(*a*) Unseen felt ideas of today in the novel
(*b*) Dichotomy of conscience on political ideas and novels
(*c*) Compatibility between idea and novel
(*d*) Endless idea and novels

18. When in a group of propositions, one proposition is claimed to follow from the others, that group of propositions is called

(*a*) An argument
(*b*) A valid argument
(*c*) An explanation
(*d*) An invalid argument

19. Namita and Samita are brilliant and studious. Anita and karabi are obedient and irregular. Babita and Namita are irregular but brilliant. Samita and Kabita are regular and obedient. Who among them is/are brilliant, obedient, regular and studious?

(*a*) Samita alone (*b*) Namita and Samita

(*c*) Kabita alone (*d*) Anita alone

20. Warrior is related to sword, carpenter is related to saw, farmer is related to plough. In the same way, the author is related to

(*a*) Book (*b*) Fame

(*c*) Reader (*d*) Pen

21. Given below is a diagram of three circles A, B and C over-lapping each other? The circle A represents the class of honest people, the circle B represent the class of sincere people and circle C represents the class of politicians. p, q, r, s, U, X, Y represent different regions. Select the code that represents the region indicating the class of honest politicians who are not sincere.

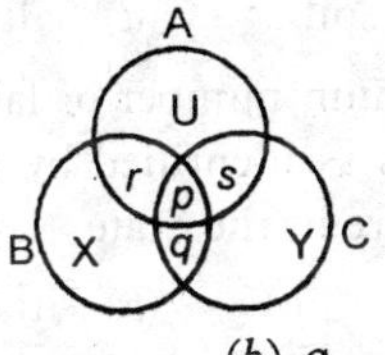

(*a*) X (*b*) q

(*c*) p (*d*) s

22. "A man ought no more to value himself for being wiser than a woman if he owes his advantage to a better education, than he ought to boast of his courage for beating a man when his hands were tied." The above passage is an instance of

(*a*) Deductive argument

(*b*) Hypothetical argument

(*c*) Analogical argument

(*d*) Factual argument

23. By which of the following proposition, the proposition "wise men are hardly afraid of death" is contradicted?

(*a*) Some wise men are afraid of death.

(*b*) All wise men are afraid of death.

(*c*) No wise men is afraid of death.

(*d*) Some wise men are not afraid of death.

For a county CO_2 emissions (million metric tons) from various sectors are given in the following table. Answer the questions (24 to 29) base on the data given

CO_2 emissions (million metric tones)					
Sector / Year	Power	Industry	Commercial	Agriculture	Domestic
2005	500	200	150	80	100
2006	600	300	200	90	110
2007	650	320	250	100	120
2008	700	400	300	150	150
2009	800	450	320	200	180

24. What is the percentage (%) growth of CO_2 emission from power sector during 2005 to 2009?

(*a*) 60 (*b*) 50

(*c*) 40 (*d*) 80

25. Which sector has recorded maximum growth in CO_2 emission during 2005 to 2009 ?

(*a*) Power (*b*) Industry

(*c*) Commercial (*d*) Agriculture

26. By what percentage (%), the total emissions of CO_2 have increased from 2005 to 2009 ?

(*a*) ~ 89.32% (*b*) ~ 57.62%

(*c*) ~ 40.32% (*d*) ~ 113.12%

27. What is the average annual growth rate of CO_2 emission in power sector ?

(*a*) ~ 12.57% (*b*) ~ 16.87%

(*c*) ~ 30.81% (*d*) ~ 50.25%

28. What is the percentage contribution of power sector to total CO_2 emission in the year 2008?

(*a*) ~ 30.82% (*b*) ~ 41.18%

(*c*) ~ 51.38% (*d*) ~ 60.25%

29. In which year, the contribution (%) of industry to total sectoral CO_2 emission was minimum?

(*a*) 2005 (*b*) 2006

(*c*) 2007 (*d*) 2008

30. Symbols A-F are used in which one of the following ?

(*a*) Binary number system

(*b*) Decimal number system

(*c*) Hexadecimal number system

(*d*) Octal number system

31. Which one of the following is not a search engine ?

(a) Google (b) Chrome

(c) Yahoo (d) Bing

32. CSS stands for

(a) Cascading Style Sheets

(b) Collecting Style Sheets

(c) Comparative Style Sheets

(d) Comprehensive Style Sheets

33. MOOC stands for

(a) Media Online Open Course

(b) Massachusetts Open Online Course

(c) Massive Open Online Course

(d) Myrind Open Online Course

34. Binary equivalent of decimal number 35 is

(a) 100011 (b) 110001

(c) 110101 (d) 101011

35. gif, jpg, bmp, png are used as extensions for files which store

(a) Audio data (b) Image data

(c) Video data (d) Text data

36. Which of the anthropogenic activity accounts for more than 2/3rd of global water consumption?

(a) Agriculture

(b) Hydropower generation

(c) Industry

(d) Domestic and Municipal usage

37. One of the anthropogenic sources of gaseous pollutants chlorofluorocarbons (CFCs) in air is

(a) Cement Industry

(b) Fertiliser industry

(c) Foam industry

(d) Pesticide industry

38. In terms of total CO_2 emissions from a country, identity the correct sequence :

(a) U.S.A. > China > India > Russia

(b) China > U.S.A. > India > Russia

(c) China > U.S.A. > Russia > India

(d) U.S.A. > China > Russia > India

39. Match List – I and List – II and identify the correct code :

A. World Health Day — *i.* 16th September

B. World Population Day — *ii.* 1st December

C. World Ozone Day — *iii.* 11th July

D. World AIDS Day — *iv.* 7th April

Codes :

	A	B	C	D
(a)	i	ii	iii	iv
(b)	iv	iii	i	ii
(c)	ii	iii	iv	i
(d)	iii	iv	ii	i

40. The cyclone "Hudhud" hit the coast of which State ?

(a) Andhra Pradesh (b) Karnataka

(c) Kerala (d) Gujarat

41. Which of the following is not a renewable natural resource?

(a) Clean air (b) Fresh water

(c) Fertile soil (d) Salt

42. The maximum number of fake institutions / universities as identified by the UGC in the year 2014 are in the State / Union territory of

(a) Bihar (b) Uttar Pradesh

(c) Tamil Nadu (d) Delhi

43. Which of the following institutions are empowered to confer or grant degrees under the UGC Act, 1956 ?

(a) A university established by an Act of Parliament.

(b) A university established by an Act of Legislature.

(c) A university / institution established by a linguistic minority.

(d) An institution which is a deemed to be university.

Select the correct answers from the codes given below :

(a) 1 and 2

(b) 1, 2 and 3

(c) 1, 2 and 4

(d) 1, 2, 3 and 4

44. Which of the following are the tools of good governance ?

1. Social Audit
2. Separation of Powers
3. Citizen's Charter
4. Right to Information

Select the correct answer from the codes given below :

(*a*) 1, 3 and 4 (*b*) 2, 3 and 4
(*c*) 1 and 4 (*d*) 1, 2, 3, and 4

45. Which of the following powers, the President has in relation to Lok Sabha ?

1. Summoning
2. Adjournment- sine die
3. Prorogation
4. Dissolution

Select the correct answer from the codes given below :

(*a*) 1 and 4 (*b*) 1, 2 and 3
(*c*) 1, 3 and 4 (*d*) 1, 2, 3 and 4

46. The interval between two sessions of parliament must not exceed

(*a*) 3 months (*b*) 6 months
(*c*) 4 months (*d*) 100 days

47. Right to privacy as a Fundamental Right is implied in

(*a*) Right to Freedom
(*b*) Right to Life and Personal Liberty
(*c*) Right to Equality
(*d*) Right against Exploitation

48. Which of the following organizations deals with "capacity building programe" on Educational Planning ?

(*a*) NCERT (*b*) UGC
(*c*) NAAC (*d*) NUEPA

49. "Education is the manifestation of perfection already in man" was stated by

(*a*) M. K. Gandhi
(*b*) R. N. Tagore
(*c*) Swami Vivekanand
(*d*) Sri Aurobindo

50. Which of the following is not a prescribed level of teaching ?

(*a*) Memory (*b*) Understanding
(*c*) Reflective (*d*) Differentiation

51. Maximum participation of students during teaching is possible through

(*a*) Lecture method
(*b*) Demonstration method
(*c*) Inductive method
(*d*) Textbook method

52. Diagnostic evaluation ascertains

(*a*) Students performance at the beginning of instructions.
(*b*) Learning progress and failures during instructions.
(*c*) Degree of achievements of instructions at the end.
(*d*) Causes and remedies of persistent learning problems during instructions.

53. Instructional aides are used by the teacher to

(*a*) Glorify the class
(*b*) Attract the students
(*c*) Clarify the concepts
(*d*) Ensure discipline

54. Attitude of the teacher that affects teaching pertains to

(*a*) Affective domain
(*b*) Cognitive domain
(*c*) Connative domain
(*d*) Psychomotor domain

55. When planning to do a social research, it is better to

(*a*) Approach the topic with an open mind
(*b*) Do a pilot study before getting stuck into it
(*c*) Be familiar with literature on the topic
(*d*) Forget about theory because this is a very practical

56. When academicians are called to deliver lecture or presentations to an audience on certain topics or a set of topics of educational nature, it is called

(*a*) Training Program
(*b*) Seminar
(*c*) Workshop
(*d*) Symposium

57. The core elements of dissertation are

(*a*) Introduction; Data Collection; Data Analysis; Conclusions and Recommendations

(*b*) Executive Summary; Literature review; Data gathered; Conclusions; Bibliography

(*c*) Research Plan; Research Data; Analysis; References

(*d*) Introduction; Literature Review; Research Methodology; Results; Discussion and Conclusion

58. What is a Research Design ?

(*a*) A way of conducting research that is not grounded in theory.

(*b*) The choice between using qualitative or quantitative methods.

(*c*) The style in which you present your research findings e.g. a graph.

(*d*) A framework for every stage of the collection and analysis of data.

59. "Sampling Cases" means

(*a*) Sampling using a sampling frame

(*b*) Identifying people who are suitable for research

(*c*) Literally the researcher's brief case

(*d*) Sampling of people, newspapers, television programmes etc.

60. The frequency distribution of a research data which is symmetrical in shape similar to a normal distribution but center peak is much higher, is

(*a*) Skewed

(*b*) Mesokurtic

(*c*) Leptokurtic

(*d*) Platykurtic

ANSWERS

1. (*b*)	**2.** (*b*)	**3.** (*d*)	**4.** (*b*)	**5.** (*b, d*)	**6.** (*d*)	**7.** (*a*)	**8.** (*a*)	**9.** (*b*)	**10.** (*b*)
11. (*c*)	**12.** (*a*)	**13.** (*c*)	**14.** (*b*)	**15.** (*c*)	**16.** (*d*)	**17.** (*b*)	**18.** (*a*)	**19.** (*a*)	**20.** (*d*)
21. (*d*)	**22.** (*c*)	**23.** (*b*)	**24.** (*a*)	**25.** (*d*)	**26.** (*a*)	**27.** (*a*)	**28.** (*b*)	**29.** (*a*)	**30.** (*c*)
31. (*b*)	**32.** (*a*)	**33.** (*c*)	**34.** (*a*)	**35.** (*b*)	**36.** (*a*)	**37.** (*c*)	**38.** (*b*)	**39.** (*b*)	**40.** (*a*)
41. (*d*)	**42.** (*b*)	**43.** (*c*)	**44.** (*d*)	**45.** (*c*)	**46.** (*b*)	**47.** (*b*)	**48.** (*d*)	**49.** (*c*)	**50.** (*d*)
51. (*c*)	**52.** (*d*)	**53.** (*c*)	**54.** (*a*)	**55.** (*a*)	**56.** (*b*)	**57.** (*d*)	**58.** (*d*)	**59.** (*d*)	**60.** (*c*)

Solved Paper 2014 (June)

UGC NET

PAPER-I

Note : • This paper contains **Sixty (60)** multiple choice questions, each question carrying **two (2)** marks.

• Candidate is expected to answer any **Fifty (50)** questions.

• In case more than **Fifty (50)** questions are attempted, only the first **Fifty (50)** questions will be evaluated.

1. Break-down in verbal communication is described as

(*a*) Short circuit (*b*) Contradiction

(*c*) Unevenness (*d*) Entropy

2. The Telephone Model of Communication was first developed in the area of

(*a*) Technological theory

(*b*) Dispersion theory

(*c*) Minimal effects theory

(*d*) Information theory

3. The Dada Saheb Phalke Award for 2013 has been conferred on

(*a*) Karan Johar (*b*) Amir Khan

(*c*) Asha Bhonsle (*d*) Gulzar

4. Photographs are not easy to

(*a*) publish (*b*) secure

(*c*) decode (*d*) change

5. The grains that appear on a television set when operated are also referred to as

(*a*) sparks (*b*) green dots

(*c*) snow (*d*) rain drops

6. In circular communication, the encoder becomes a decoder when there is

(*a*) noise (*b*) audience

(*c*) criticality (*d*) feedback

7. In a post-office, stamps of three different denominations of ₹ 7, ₹ 8, ₹ 10 are available. The exact amount for which one cannot buy stamps is

(*a*) 19 (*b*) 20

(*c*) 23 (*d*) 29

8. In certain coding method, the word QUESTION is encoded as DOMESTIC. In this coding, what is the code word for the word RESPONSE?

(*a*) OMESUCEM (*b*) OMESICSM

(*c*) OMESICEM (*d*) OMESISCM

9. If the series 4, 5, 8, 13, 14, 17, 22, ... is continued in the same pattern, which one of the following is not a term of this series ?

(*a*) 31 (*b*) 32

(*c*) 33 (*d*) 35

10. Complete the series BB, FE, II, ML, PP, ... by choosing one of the following option given:

(*a*) TS (*b*) ST

(*c*) RS (*d*) SR

11. A man started walking from his house towards south. After walking 6 km, he turned to his left and walked 5 km. Then he walked further 3 km after turning left. He then turned to his left and continued his walk for 9 km. How far is he away from his house ?

(*a*) 3 km (*b*) 4 km

(*c*) 5 km (*d*) 6 km

12. One writes all numbers from 50 to 99 without the digits 2 and 7. How many numbers have been written ?

(*a*) 32 (*b*) 36

(*c*) 40 (*d*) 38

13. "If a large diamond is cut up into little bits, it will lose its value just as an army is divided up into small units of soldiers, it loses its strength."

The argument put above may be called as

(*a*) Analogical (*b*) Deductive

(*c*) Statistical (*d*) Causal

14. Given below are some characteristics of logical argument. Select the code which expresses a characteristic which is not of inductive in character.

(*a*) The conclusion is claimed to follow from its premises.

(*b*) The conclusion is based on causal relation.

(*c*) The conclusion conclusively follows from its premises.

(*d*) The conclusion is based on observation and experiment.

15. If two propositions having the same subject and predicate terms can both be true but can not both be false, the relation between those two propositions is called

(*a*) contradictory (*b*) contrary

(*c*) subcontrary (*d*) subaltern

16. Given below are two premises and four conclusions drawn from those premises. Select the code that expresses conclusion drawn validly from the premises (separately or jointly).

Premises :

A. All dogs are mammals.

B. No cats are dogs.

Conclusions :

(*i*) No cats are mammals.

(*ii*) Some cats are mammals.

(*iii*) No dogs are cats.

(*iv*) No dogs are non-mammals.

Codes :

(*a*) (*i*) only

(*b*) (*i*) and (*ii*)

(*c*) (*iii*) and (*iv*)

(*d*) (*ii*) and (*iii*)

17. Given below is a diagram of three circles A, B & C inter-related with each other. The circle A represents the class of Indians, the circle B represents the class of scientists and circle C represents the class of politicians. p, q, r, s ... represent different regions. Select the code containing the region that indicates the class of Indian scientists who are not politicians.

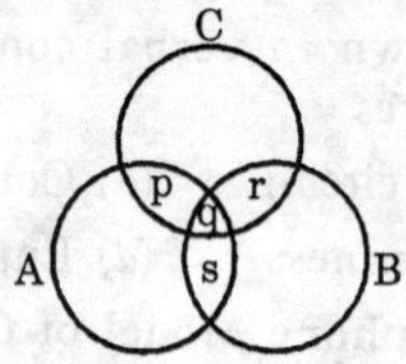

Codes :

(*a*) q and s only

(*b*) s only

(*c*) s and r only

(*d*) p, q and s only

Read the following table carefully. Based upon this table answer questions from 18 to 22 :

Net Area under Irrigation by sources in a country (Thousand Hectares)

Year	Government canals	Private canals	Tanks	Tube wells & Other wells	Other sources	Total
1997-98	17117	211	2593	32090	3102	55173
1998-99	17093	212	2792	33988	3326	57411
1999-00	16842	194	2535	34623	2915	57109
2000-01	15748	203	2449	33796	2880	55076
2001-02	15031	209	2179	34906	4347	56672
2002-03	13863	206	1802	34250	3657	53778
2003-04	14444	206	1908	35779	4281	56618
2004-05	14696	206	1727	34785	7453	58867
2005-06	15268	207	2034	35372	7314	60196

18. Which of the following sources of Irrigation has registered the largest percentage of decline in Net area under irrigation during 1997-98 and 2005-06 ?

(*a*) Government canals

(*b*) Private canals

(*c*) Tanks

(*d*) Other sources

19. Find out the source of Irrigation that has registered the maximum improvement in terms of percentage of Net irrigated area during 2002-03 and 2003-04.

(*a*) Government canals

(*b*) Tanks

(*c*) Tube wells and other wells

(*d*) Other sources

20. In which of the following years, Net irrigation by tanks increased at the highest rate ?
(a) 1998-99 (b) 2000-01
(c) 2003-04 (d) 2005-06

21. Identify the source of Irrigation that has recorded the maximum incidence of negative growth in terms of Net irrigated area during the years given in the table.
(a) Government canals
(b) Private canals
(c) Tube wells and other wells
(d) Other sources

22. In which of the following years, share of the tube wells and other wells in the total net irrigated area was the highest ?
(a) 1998-99 (b) 2000-01
(c) 2002-03 (d) 2004-05

23. The acronym FTP stands for
(a) File Transfer Protocol
(b) Fast Transfer Protocol
(c) File Tracking Protocol
(d) File Transfer Procedure

24. Which one of the following is not a/an image/graphic file format ?
(a) PNG (b) GIF
(c) BMP (d) GUI

25. The first web browser is
(a) Internet Explorer
(b) Netscape
(c) World Wide Web
(d) Firefox

26. When a computer is booting, BIOS is loaded to the memory by
(a) RAM (b) ROM
(c) CD-ROM (d) TCP

27. Which one of the following is not the same as the other three ?
(a) MAC address (b) Hardware address
(c) Physical address (d) IP address

28. Identify the IP address from the following :
(a) 300 · 215 · 317 · 3
(b) 302 · 215@ 417 · 5
(c) 202 · 50 · 20 · 148
(d) 202 – 50 – 20 – 148

29. The population of India is about 1.2 billion. Take the average consumption of energy per person per year in India as 30 Mega Joules. If this consumption is met by carbon based fuels and the rate of carbon emissions per kilojoule is 15 × 106 kgs, the total carbon emissions per year from India will be
(a) 54 million metric tons
(b) 540 million metric tons
(c) 5400 million metric tons
(d) 2400 million metric tons

30. Which of the following cities has been worst affected by urban smog in recent times ?
(a) Paris (b) London
(c) Los Angeles (d) Beijing

31. The primary source of organic pollution in fresh water bodies is
(a) run-off urban areas
(b) run-off from agricultural forms
(c) sewage effluents
(d) industrial effluents

32. 'Lahar' is a natural disaster involving
(a) eruption of large amount of material
(b) strong winds
(c) strong water waves
(d) strong winds and water waves

33. In order to avoid catastrophic consequences of climate change, there is general agreement among the countries of the world to limit the rise in average surface temperature of earth compared to that of pre-industrial times by
(a) 1.5 °C to 2 °C (b) 2.0 °C to 3.5 °C
(c) 0.5 °C to 1.0 °C (d) 0.25 °C to 0.5 °C

34. The National Disaster Management Authority functions under the Union Ministry of
(a) Environment (b) Water Resources
(c) Home Affairs (d) Defence

35. Match List – I and List – II and select the correct answer from the codes given below :

List – I	List – II
A. Flood	1. Lack of rainfall of sufficient duration
B. Drought	2. Tremors produced by the passage of vibratory waves through the rocks of the earth

C. Earthquake	3. A vent through which molted substances come out
D. Volcano	4. Excess rain and uneven distribution of water

Codes :

	A	B	C	D
(*a*)	4	1	2	3
(*b*)	2	3	4	1
(*c*)	3	4	2	1
(*d*)	4	3	1	2

36. Which one of the following green house gases has the shortest residence time in the atmosphere?

(*a*) Chlorofluorocarbon

(*b*) Carbon dioxide

(*c*) Methane

(*d*) Nitrous oxide

37. Consider the following statements and select the correct answer from the code given below:

i. Rajasthan receives the highest solar radiation in the country.

ii. India has the fifth largest installed wind power in the world.

iii. The maximum amount of wind power is contributed by Tamil Nadu.

iv. The primary source of uranium in India is Jaduguda.

Codes :

(*a*) *i* and *ii* (*b*) *i*, *ii* and *iii*

(*c*) *ii* and *iii* (*d*) *i* and *iv*

38. Who among the following is the de facto executive head of the Planning Commission?

(*a*) Chairman

(*b*) Deputy Chairman

(*c*) Minister of State for Planning

(*d*) Member Secretary

39. Education as a subject of legislation figures in the

(*a*) Union List

(*b*) State List

(*c*) Concurrent List

(*d*) Residuary Powers

40. Which of the following are Central Universities ?

1. Pondicherry University
2. Vishwa Bharati
3. H.N.B. Garhwal University
4. Kurukshetra University

Select the correct answer from the code given below :

Codes :

(*a*) 1, 2 and 3 (*b*) 1, 3 and 4

(*c*) 2, 3 and 4 (*d*) 1, 2 and 4

41. Consider the statement which is followed by two arguments (*i*) and (*ii*).

Statement : India should have a very strong and powerful Lokpal.

Arguments :

(*i*) Yes, it will go a long in eliminating corruption in bureaucracy.

(*ii*) No, it will discourage honest officers from making quick decisions.

Codes :

(*a*) Only argument (*i*) is strong.

(*b*) Only argument (*ii*) is strong.

(*c*) Both the arguments are strong.

(*d*) Neither of the arguments is strong.

42. Which of the following universities has adopted the meta university concept ?

(*a*) Assam University

(*b*) Delhi University

(*c*) Hyderabad University

(*d*) Pondicherry University

43. Which of the following statements are correct about a Central University ?

1. Central University is established under an Act of Parliament.
2. The President of India acts as the visitor of the University.
3. The President has the power to nominate some members to the Executive Committee or the Board of Management of the University.

4. The President occasionally presides over the meetings of the Executive Committee or Court.

Select the correct answer from the code given below :

Codes :

(*a*) 1, 2 and 4 (*b*) 1, 3 and 4

(*c*) 1, 2 and 3 (*d*) 1, 2, 3 and 4

44. Which one of the following is considered a sign of motivated teaching ?

(*a*) Students asking questions

(*b*) Maximum attendance of the students

(*c*) Pin drop silence in the classroom

(*d*) Students taking notes

45. Which one of the following is the best method of teaching ?

(*a*) Lecture (*b*) Discussion

(*c*) Demonstration (*d*) Narration

46. Dyslexia is associated with

(*a*) mental disorder

(*b*) behavioural disorder

(*c*) reading disorder

(*d*) writing disorder

47. The e-content generation for undergraduate courses has been assigned by the Ministry of Human Resource Development to

(*a*) INFLIBNET

(*b*) Consortium for Educational Communication

(*c*) National Knowledge Commission

(*d*) Indira Gandhi National Open University

48. Classroom communication is normally considered as

(*a*) effective (*b*) cognitive

(*c*) affective (*d*) selective

49. Who among the following, propounded the concept of paradigm ?

(*a*) Peter Haggett (*b*) Von Thunen

(*c*) Thomas Kuhn (*d*) John K. Wright

50. In a thesis, figures and tables are included in

(*a*) the appendix

(*b*) a separate chapter

(*c*) the concluding chapter

(*d*) the text itself

51. A thesis statement is

(*a*) an observation (*b*) a fact

(*c*) an assertion (*d*) a discussion

52. The research approach of Max Weber to understand how people create meanings in natural settings is identified as

(*a*) positive paradigm

(*b*) critical paradigm

(*c*) natural paradigm

(*d*) interpretative paradigm

53. Which one of the following is a nonprobability sampling ?

(*a*) Simple random (*b*) Purposive

(*c*) Systematic (*d*) Stratified ü

54. Identify the category of evaluation that assesses the learning progress to provide continuous feedback to the students during instruction.

(*a*) Placement (*b*) Diagnostic

(*c*) Formative (*d*) Summative

55. The research stream of immediate application is

(*a*) Conceptual research

(*b*) Action research

(*c*) Fundamental research

(*d*) Empirical research

Read the following passage carefully and answer questions 56 to 60 :

Traditional Indian Values must be viewed both from the angle of the individual and from that of the geographically delimited agglomeration of peoples or groups enjoying a common system of leadership which we call the 'State'. The Indian 'State's' special feature is the peaceful, or perhaps mostly peaceful, co-existence of social groups of various historical provenances which mutually adhere in a geographical, economic, and political sense, without ever assimilating to each other in social terms, in ways of thinking, or even in language. Modern Indian law will determine certain rules, especially in relation to the regime of the family, upon the basis of how the loin-cloth is tied, or how the turban is worn, for this may identify the litigants as members of a regional group, and therefore as participants in its traditional law, though their ancestors left the region three or four centuries earlier. The use of the word 'State' above must not mislead us. There was no such thing as a conflict between the individual and the State, atleast before foreign governments became established, just as there was no concept of state 'sovereignty' or of any church-and-state dichotomy.

Modern Indian 'secularism' has an admittedly peculiar feature : It requires the state to make a fair distribution of attention and support amongst all religions. These blessed aspects of India's famed tolerance (Indian kings so rarely persecuted religious groups that the exceptions prove the rule) at once struck Portuguese and other European visitors to the West Coast of India in the sixteenth century, and the impression made upon them in this and other ways gave rise, at one remove, to the basic constitution of Thomas More's Utopia. There is little about modern India that strikes one at once as Utopian : but the insistence upon the inculcation of norms, and the absence of bigotry and institutionalized exploitation of human or natural resources, are two very different features which link the realities of India and her tradition with the essence of all Utopians.

56. Which of the following is a special feature of the Indian State ?
   (*a*) Peaceful co-existence of people under a common system of leadership
   (*b*) Peaceful co-existence of social groups of different historical provenances attached to each other in a geographical, economic and political sense
   (*c*) Social integration of all groups
   (*d*) Cultural assimilation of all social groups.

57. The author uses the word 'State' to highlight
   (*a*) Antagonistic relationship between the state and the individual throughout the period of history.
   (*b*) Absence of conflict between the state and the individuals upto a point in time.
   (*c*) The concept of state sovereignty.
   (*d*) Dependence on religion.

58. Which one is the peculiar feature of modern Indian 'Secularism' ?
   (*a*) No discrimination on religious considerations
   (*b*) Total indifference to religion
   (*c*) No space for social identity
   (*d*) Disregard for social law

59. The basic construction of Thomas More's Utopia was inspired by
   (*a*) Indian tradition of religious tolerance.
   (*b*) Persecution of religious groups by Indian rulers.
   (*c*) Social inequality in India.
   (*d*) European perception of Indian State.

60. What is the striking feature of modern India ?
   (*a*) A replica of Utopian State
   (*b*) Uniform laws
   (*c*) Adherence to traditional values
   (*d*) Absence of Bigotry

ANSWERS

1. (*d*)	2. (*d*)	3. (*d*)	4. (*c*)	5. (*c*)	6. (*d*)	7. (*a*)	8. (*c*)	9. (*c*)	10. (*a*)
11. (*c*)	12. (*a*)	13. (*a*)	14. (*c*)	15. (*c*)	16. (*c*)	17. (*b*)	18. (*c*)	19. (*d*)	20. (*d*)
21. (*a*)	22. (*c*)	23. (*a*)	24. (*d*)	25. (*c*)	26. (*b*)	27. (*d*)	28. (*c*)	29. (*)	30. (*d*)
31. (*c*)	32. (*a*)	33. (*a*)	34. (*c*)	35. (*a*)	36. (*c*)	37. (*d*)	38. (*b*)	39. (*c*)	40. (*a*)
41. (*a*)	42. (*b*)	43. (*c*)	44. (*a*)	45. (*c*)	46. (*c*)	47. (*b*)	48. (*c*)	49. (*c*)	50. (*d*)
51. (*c*)	52. (*d*)	53. (*b*)	54. (*c*)	55. (*b*)	56. (*b*)	57. (*b*)	58. (*a*)	59. (*a*)	60. (*d*)

[Note : "*" denotes marks given to all candidates.]

Solved Paper 2013 (December)

UGC NET

PAPER-I

Note : • This paper contains **Sixty (60)** multiple choice questions, each question carrying **two (2)** marks.

• Candidate is expected to answer any **Fifty (50)** questions.

• In case more than **Fifty (50)** questions are attempted, only the first **Fifty (50)** questions will be evaluated.

1. Which is the main objective of research ?

(*a*) To review the literature

(*b*) To summarize what is already known

(*c*) To get an academic degree

(*d*) To discover new facts or to make fresh interpretation of known facts

2. Sampling error decreases with the

(*a*) decrease in sample size

(*b*) increase in sample size

(*c*) process of randomization

(*d*) process of analysis

3. The principles of fundamental research are used in

(*a*) action research

(*b*) applied research

(*c*) philosophical research

(*d*) historical research

4. Users who use media for their own ends are identified as

(*a*) Passive audience (*b*) Active audience

(*c*) Positive audience (*d*) Negative audience

5. Classroom communication can be described as

(*a*) Exploration

(*b*) Institutionalisation

(*c*) Unsignified narration

(*d*) Discourse

6. Ideological codes shape our collective

(*a*) Productions (*b*) Perceptions

(*c*) Consumptions (*d*) Creations

7. In communication, myths have power, but are

(*a*) uncultural. (*b*) insignificant.

(*c*) imprecise. (*d*) unpreferred.

8. The first multi-lingual news agency of India was

(*a*) Samachar

(*b*) API

(*c*) Hindustan Samachar

(*d*) Samachar Bharati

9. Organisational communication can also be equated with

(*a*) intra-personal communication.

(*b*) inter-personal communication.

(*c*) group communication.

(*d*) mass communication.

10. If two propositions having the same subject and predicate terms are such that one is the denial of the other, the relationship between them is called

(*a*) Contradictory (*b*) Contrary

(*c*) Sub-contrary (*d*) Sub-alternation

11. Ananya and Krishna can speak and follow English. Bulbul can write and speak Hindi as Archana does. Archana talks with Ananya also in Bengali. Krishna can not follow Bengali. Bulbul talks with Ananya in Hindi. Who can speak and follow English, Hindi and Bengali ?

(*a*) Archana (*b*) Bulbul

(*c*) Ananya (*d*) Krishna

12. A stipulative definition may be said to be

(*a*) Always true

(*b*) Always false

(*c*) Sometimes true, sometimes false

(*d*) Neither true nor false

13. When the conclusion of an argument follows from its premise/premises conclusively, the argument is called

(*a*) Circular argument

(*b*) Inductive argument

(*c*) Deductive argument

(*d*) Analogical argument

14. Saturn and Mars are planets like the earth. They borrow light from the Sun and moves around the Sun as the Earth does. So those planets are inhabited by various orders of creatures as the earth is.

What type of argument is contained in the above passage ?

(*a*) Deductive (*b*) Astrological

(*c*) Analogical (*d*) Mathematical

15. Given below are two premises. Four conclusions are drawn from those two premises in four codes. Select the code that states the conclusion validly drawn.

Premises :

(*i*) All saints are religious. (major)

(*ii*) Some honest persons are saints. (minor)

Codes :

(*a*) All saints are honest.

(*b*) Some saints are honest.

(*c*) Some honest persons are religious.

(*d*) All religious persons are honest.

Following table provides details about the Foreign Tourist Arrivals (FTAs) in India from different regions of the world in different years. Study the table carefully and answer questions from **16 to 19** based on this table.

Region	Number of Foreign Tourist Arrivals		
	2007	2008	2009
Western Europe	1686083	1799525	1610086
North America	1007276	1027297	1024469
South Asia	982428	1051846	982633
South East Asia	303475	332925	348495
East Asia	352037	355230	318292
West Asia	171661	215542	201110
Total FTAs in India	5081504	5282603	5108579

16. Find out the region that contributed around 20 percent of the total foreign tourist arrivals in India in 2009.

(*a*) Western Europe (*b*) North America

(*c*) South Asia (*d*) South East Asia

17. Which of the following regions has recorded the highest negative growth rate of foreign tourist arrivals in India in 2009 ?

(*a*) Western Europe (*b*) North America

(*c*) South Asia (*d*) West Asia

18. Find out the region that has been showing declining trend in terms of share of foreign tourist arrivals in India in 2008 and 2009.

(*a*) Western Europe (*b*) South East Asia

(*c*) East Asia (*d*) West Asia

19. Identify the region that has shown hyper growth rate of foreign tourist arrivals than the growth rate of the total FTAs in India in 2008.

(*a*) Western Europe (*b*) North America

(*c*) South Asia (*d*) East Asia

20. The post-industrial society is designated as

(*a*) Information society

(*b*) Technology society

(*c*) Mediated society

(*d*) Non-agricultural society

21. The initial efforts for internet based communication was for

(*a*) Commercial communication

(*b*) Military purposes

(*c*) Personal interaction

(*d*) Political campaigns

22. Internal communication within institutions is done through

(*a*) LAN (*b*) WAN

(*c*) EBB (*d*) MMS

23. Virtual reality provides

(*a*) Sharp pictures

(*b*) Individual audio

(*c*) Participatory experience

(*d*) Preview of new films

24. The first virtual university of India came up in

(*a*) Andhra Pradesh (*b*) Maharashtra

(*c*) Uttar Pradesh (*d*) Tamil Nadu

25. Arrange the following books in chronological order in which they appeared. Use the code given below :

(*i*) Limits to Growth

(*ii*) Silent Spring

(*iii*)Our Common Future

(*iv*) Resourceful Earth

Codes :

(*a*) (*i*), (*iii*), (*iv*), (*ii*) (*b*) (*ii*), (*iii*), (*i*), (*iv*)

(*c*) (*ii*), (*i*), (*iii*), (*iv*) (*d*) (*i*), (*ii*), (*iii*), (*iv*)

26. Which one of the following continents is at a greater risk of desertification ?

(*a*) Africa (*b*) Asia

(*c*) South America (*d*) North America

27. "Women are closer to nature than men." What kind of perspective is this ?

(*a*) Realist (*b*) Essentialist

(*c*) Feminist (*d*) Deep ecology

28. Which one of the following is not a matter a global concern in the removal of tropical forests?

(*a*) Their ability to absorb the chemicals that contribute to depletion of ozone layer.

(*b*) Their role in maintaining the oxygen and carbon balance of the earth.

(*c*) Their ability to regulate surface and air temperatures, moisture content and reflectivity.

(*d*) Their contribution to the biological diversity of the planet.

29. The most comprehensive approach to address the problems of manenvironment interaction is one of the following :

(*a*) Natural Resource Conservation Approach

(*b*) Urban-industrial Growth Oriented Approach

(*c*) Rural-agricultural Growth Oriented Approach

(*d*) Watershed Development Approach

30. The major source of the pollutant gas, carbon mono-oxide (CO), in urban areas is

(*a*) Thermal power sector

(*b*) Transport sector

(*c*) Industrial sector

(*d*) Domestic sector

31. In a fuel cell driven vehicle, the energy is obtained from the combustion of

(*a*) Methane (*b*) Hydrogen

(*c*) LPG (*d*) CNG

32. Which one of the following Councils has been disbanded in 2013 ?

(*a*) Distance Education Council (DEC)

(*b*) National Council for Teacher Education (NCTE)

(*c*) National Council of Educational Research and Training (NCERT)

(*d*) National Assessment and Accreditation Council (NAAC)

33. Which of the following statements are correct about the National Assessment and Accreditation Council ?

1. It is an autonomous institution.
2. It is tasked with the responsibility of assessing and accrediting institutions of higher education.
3. It is located in Delhi.
4. It has regional offices.

Select the correct answer from the codes given below :

Codes :

(*a*) 1 and 3 (*b*) 1 and 2

(*c*) 1, 2 and 4 (*d*) 2, 3 and 4

34. The power of the Supreme Court of India to decide disputes between two or more States falls under its

(*a*) Advisory Jurisdiction

(*b*) Appellate Jurisdiction

(*c*) Original Jurisdiction

(*d*) Writ Jurisdiction

35. Which of the following statements are correct ?

1. There are seven Union Territories in India.
2. Two Union Territories have Legislative Assemblies
3. One Union Territory has a High Court.
4. One Union Territory is the capital of two States.

Select the correct answer from the codes given below :

(*a*) 1 and 3 only (*b*) 2 and 4 only

(*c*) 2, 3 and 4 only (*d*) 1, 2, 3 and 4

36. Which of the following statements are correct about the Central Information Commission ?

1. The Central Information Commission is a statutory body.
2. The Chief Information Commissioner and other Information Commissioners are appointed by the President of India.
3. The Commission can impose a penalty upto a maximum of ₹ 25,000/-
4. It can punish an errant officer.

Select the correct answer from the codes given below :

Codes :

(*a*) 1 and 2 only (*b*) 1, 2 and 4
(*c*) 1, 2 and 3 (*d*) 2, 3 and 4

37. Who among the following conducted the CNN-IBN – The Hindu 2013 Election Tracker Survey across 267 constituencies in 18 States ?

(*a*) The Centre for the Study of Developing Societies (CSDS)
(*b*) The Association for Democratic Reforms (ADR)
(*c*) CNN and IBN
(*d*) CNN, IBN and The Hindu

38. In certain code TEACHER is written as VGCEJGT. The code of CHILDREN will be

(*a*) EKNJFTGP (*b*) EJKNFTGP
(*c*) KNJFGTP (*d*) None of these

39. A person has to buy both apples and mangoes. The cost of one apple is ₹ 7/- whereas that of a mango is ₹ 5/-. If the person has ₹ 38, the number of apples he can buy is

(*a*) 1 (*b*) 2
(*c*) 3 (*d*) 4

40. A man pointing to a lady said, "The son of her only brother is the brother of my wife". The lady is related to the man as

(*a*) Mother's sister
(*b*) Grand mother
(*c*) Mother-in-law
(*d*) Sister of Father-in-law

41. In this series
6, 4, 1, 2, 2, 8, 7, 4, 2, 1, 5, 3, 8, 6, 2, 2, 7, 1, 4, 1, 3, 5, 8, 6, how many pairs of successive numbers have a difference of 2 each ?

(*a*) 4 (*b*) 5
(*c*) 6 (*d*) 8

42. The mean marks obtained by a class of 40 students is 65. The mean marks of half of the students is found to be 45. The mean marks of the remaining students is

(*a*) 85 (*b*) 60
(*c*) 70 (*d*) 65

43. Anil is twice as old as Sunita. Three years ago, he was three times as old as Sunita. The present age of Anil is

(*a*) 6 years (*b*) 8 years
(*c*) 12 years (*d*) 16 years

44. Which of the following is a social network ?

(*a*) amazon.com (*b*) eBay
(*c*) gmail.com (*d*) Twitter

45. The population information is called parameter while the corresponding sample information is known as

(*a*) Universe (*b*) Inference
(*c*) Sampling design (*d*) Statistics

Read the following passage carefully and answer questions 46 to 51 :

Heritage conservation practices improved worldwide after the International Centre for the Study of the Preservation and Restoration of Cultural Property (ICCROM) was established with UNESCO's assistance in 1959. The inter-governmental organisation with 126 member states has done a commendable job by training more than 4,000 professionals, providing practice standards, and sharing technical expertise. In this golden jubilee year, as we acknowledge its key role in global conservation, an assessment of international practices would be meaningful to the Indian conservation movement. Consistent investment, rigorous attention, and dedicated research and dissemination are some of the positive lessons to imbibe. Countries such as Italy have demonstrated that prioritising heritage with significant budget provision pays. On the other hand, India, which is no less endowed in terms of cultural capital, has a long way to go. Surveys indicate that in addition to the 6,600 protected monuments, there are over 60,000 equally valuable heritage structures that await attention. Besides the small group in the service of Archaeological Survey of India, there are only about 150 trained conservation professionals. In order to overcome this severe shortage the emphasis has been on setting up dedicated labs and training institutions. It would make much better sense for conservation to be made part of mainstream research and engineering institutes, as has been done in Europe.

Increasing funding and building institutions are the relatively easy part. The real challenge is to redefine international approaches to address local contexts. Conservation cannot limit itself to enhancing the art-historical value of the heritage structures, which international charters perhaps overemphasise. The effort has to be broad-based : It must also serve as a means to improving the quality of life in the area where the heritage structures are located. The first task therefore is to integrate conservation efforts with sound development plans that take care of people living in the heritage vicinity. Unlike in western countries, many traditional building crafts survive in India, and conservation practices offer an avenue to support them. This has been acknowledged by the Indian National Trust for Art and Cultural Heritage charter for conservation but is yet to receive substantial state support. More strength for heritage conservation can be mobilised by aligning it with the green building movement. Heritage structures are essentially eco-friendly and conservation could become a vital part of the sustainable building practices campaign in future.

46. The outlook for conservation heritage changed

(*a*) after the establishment of the International Centre for the Study of the Preservation and Restoration of Cultural Property.

(*b*) after training the specialists in the field.

(*c*) after extending UNESCO's assistance to the educational institutions.

(*d*) after ASI's measures to protect the monuments.

47. The inter-government organization was appreciated because of

(*a*) increasing number of members to 126.

(*b*) imparting training to professionals and sharing technical expertise.

(*c*) consistent investment in conservation.

(*d*) its proactive role in renovation and restoration.

48. Indian conservation movement will be successful if there would be

(*a*) Financial support from the Government of India.

(*b*) Non-governmental organisations role and participation in the conservation movement.

(*c*) consistent investment, rigorous attention, and dedicated research and dissemination of awareness for conservation.

(*d*) Archaeological Survey of India's meaningful assistance.

49. As per the surveys of historical monuments in India, there is very small number of protected monuments. As per given the total number of monuments and enlisted number of protected monuments, percentage comes to

(*a*) 10 percent (*b*) 11 percent

(*c*) 12 percent (*d*) 13 percent

50. What should India learn from Europe to conserve our cultural heritage ?

(*i*) There should be significant budget provision to conserve our cultural heritage.

(*ii*) Establish dedicated labs and training institutions.

(*iii*) Force the government to provide sufficient funds.

(*iv*) Conservation should be made part of mainstream research and engineering institutes.

Choose correct answer from the codes given below :

(*a*) (*i*), (*ii*), (*iii*), (*iv*) (*b*) (*i*), (*ii*), (*iv*)

(*c*) (*i*), (*ii*) (*d*) (*i*), (*iii*), (*iv*)

51. INTACH is known for its contribution for conservation of our cultural heritage. The full form of INTACH is

(*a*) International Trust for Art and Cultural Heritage.

(*b*) Intra-national Trust for Art and Cultural Heritage

(*c*) Integrated Trust for Art and Cultural Heritage

(*d*) Indian National Trust for Art and Cultural Heritage

52. While delivering lecture if there is some disturbance in the class, a teacher should
   (*a*) keep quiet for a while and then continue.
   (*b*) punish those causing disturbance.
   (*c*) motivate to teach those causing disturbance.
   (*d*) not bother of what is happening in the class.

53. Effective teaching is a function of
   (*a*) Teacher's satisfaction.
   (*b*) Teacher's honesty and commitment.
   (*c*) Teacher's making students learn and understand.
   (*d*) Teacher's liking for professional excellence.

54. The most appropriate meaning of learning is
   (*a*) Acquisition of skills
   (*b*) Modification of behaviour
   (*c*) Personal adjustment
   (*d*) Inculcation of knowledge

55. Arrange the following teaching process in order :
   (*i*) Relate the present knowledge with previous one
   (*ii*) Evaluation
   (*iii*) Reteaching
   (*iv*) Formulating instructional objectives
   (*v*) Presentation of instructional materials
   (*a*) (*i*), (*ii*), (*iii*), (*iv*), (*v*)
   (*b*) (*ii*), (*i*), (*iii*), (*iv*), (*v*)
   (*c*) (*v*), (*iv*), (*iii*), (*i*), (*ii*)
   (*d*) (*iv*), (*i*), (*v*), (*ii*), (*iii*)

56. CIET stands for
   (*a*) Centre for Integrated Education and Technology
   (*b*) Central Institute for Engineering and Technology
   (*c*) Central Institute for Education Technology
   (*d*) Centre for Integrated Evaluation Techniques.

57. Teacher's role at higher education level is to
   (*a*) provide information to students.
   (*b*) promote self learning in students.
   (*c*) encourage healthy competition among students.
   (*d*) help students to solve their problems.

58. The Verstehen School of Understanding was popularised by
   (*a*) German Social Scientists
   (*b*) American Philosophers
   (*c*) British Academicians
   (*d*) Italian Political Analysts

59. The sequential operations in scientific research are
   (*a*) Co-variation, Elimination of Spurious Relations, Generalisation, Theorisation
   (*b*) Generalisation, Co-variation, Theorisation, Elimination of Spurious Relations
   (*c*) Theorisation, Generalisation, Elimination of Spurious Relations, Co-variation
   (*d*) Elimination of Spurious Relations, Theorisation, Generalisation, Co-variation.

60. In sampling, the lottery method is used for
   (*a*) Interpretation (*b*) Theorisation
   (*c*) Conceptualisation (*d*) Randomisation

ANSWERS

1. (*d*)	**2.** (*b*)	**3.** (*b*)	**4.** (*b*)	**5.** (*d*)	**6.** (*b*)	**7.** (*c*)	**8.** (*c*)	**9.** (*c*)	**10.** (*a*)
11. (*c*)	**12.** (*d*)	**13.** (*c*)	**14.** (*c*)	**15.** (*c*)	**16.** (*b*)	**17.** (*a*)	**18.** (*c*)	**19.** (*c*)	**20.** (*a*)
21. (*b*)	**22.** (*a*)	**23.** (*c*)	**24.** (*d*)	**25.** (*)	**26.** (*a*)	**27.** (*b*)	**28.** (*a*)	**29.** (*d*)	**30.** (*b*)
31. (*b*)	**32.** (*a*)	**33.** (*b*)	**34.** (*c*)	**35.** (*d*)	**36.** (*c*)	**37.** (*a*)	**38.** (*b*)	**39.** (*d*)	**40.** (*d*)
41. (*c*)	**42.** (*a*)	**43.** (*c*)	**44.** (*d*)	**45.** (*d*)	**46.** (*a*)	**47.** (*b*)	**48.** (*c*)	**49.** (*a*)	**50.** (*b*)
51. (*d*)	**52.** (*c*)	**53.** (*c*)	**54.** (*b*)	**55.** (*d*)	**56.** (*c*)	**57.** (*b*)	**58.** (*a*)	**59.** (*a*)	**60.** (*d*)

[Note : "*" denotes marks given to all candidates.]

Solved Paper 2013 (September)

UGC NET

PAPER-I

Note :
- This paper contains **Sixty (60)** multiple choice questions, each question carrying **two (2)** marks.
- Candidate is expected to answer any **Fifty (50)** questions.
- In case more than **Fifty (50)** questions are attempted, only the first **Fifty (50)** questions will be evaluated.

1. The world population growth rate at a certain reference year was 3.5%. Assuming exponential growth of population, after how many years, the population of the world would have increased by a factor 16 ?

(*a*) ~ 80 years (*b*) ~ 40 years
(*c*) ~ 160 years (*d*) ~ 320 years

2. Telephone is an example of

(*a*) linear communication
(*b*) non-linear communication
(*c*) circular
(*d*) mechanised

3. Means of grapevine communication are

(*a*) formal (*b*) informal
(*c*) critical (*d*) corporate

4. Communication issues at the international level are addressed by

(*a*) ILO (*b*) ITU
(*c*) UNDP (*d*) UNESCO

5. Referential framing used by TV audience connects media with

(*a*) reality (*b*) falsity
(*c*) negativity (*d*) passivity

6. The communicated knowledge in a classroom is considered as

(*a*) non-pervasive treasure
(*b*) limited judgement
(*c*) autonomous virtue
(*d*) cultural capital

7. Classroom communication is normally considered as

(*a*) effective (*b*) affective
(*c*) cognitive (*d*) non-selective

8. A person writes all the numbers from 0 to 99. The number of times digit 3 will be written is

(*a*) 18 (*b*) 19
(*c*) 20 (*d*) 21

9. Starting from point A, Ajit walks 14 metres towards west, he then turns to his right and walks 14 metres and then turns to his left and walks 10 metres. He again turns to his left and walks 14 metres and reaches to the point E. The shortest distance between A and E is

(*a*) 38 (*b*) 42
(*c*) 52 (*d*) 24

10. A, B, C, D, E and F are sitting around a round table. A is between E and F. E is opposite to D and C is not in either of the neighbouring seats of E. The person opposite to B is

(*a*) C (*b*) D
(*c*) A (*d*) F

11. The missing term in the series

2, 7, 24, 77, ?, 723 is

(*a*) 238 (*b*) 432
(*c*) 542 (*d*) 320

12. In certain city the Taxi charges comprise of a fixed charge and the charge of the distance travelled. A person paid ₹ 156 for a journey of 16 km and another person paid ₹ 204 for the journey of 24 km. The amount paid by a passenger who has travelled 30 km is

(*a*) 236 (*b*) 240
(*c*) 248 (*d*) 256

13. In certain code HEALTH is written as KHDOWK. The code of NORTH will be

(*a*) QRUWK (*b*) RQWUK
(*c*) RWQUK (*d*) RWUKQ

14. Yadav, Arjun, Rajesh and Kamal play cricket. Rajesh and Kamal play tennis but do not play football. Yadav does not play Badminton but play golf. Arjun does not play tennis. Kamal sometimes plays Badminton. Who does play only cricket ?

(*a*) Yadav (*b*) Arjun
(*c*) Rajesh (*d*) Kamal

15. A deductive argument can not be valid :

(*a*) If its premise / premises is/are true and its conclusion is true.
(*b*) If its premise / premises is /are true and its conclusion is false.
(*c*) If its premise / premises is/are false and its conclusion is false.
(*d*) If its premise / premises is / are false and its conclusion is true.

16. An analogical argument is strengthened by

(*a*) making the claim bolder while its premises remain unchanged.
(*b*) reducing the claim made on the basis of the premises affirmed.
(*c*) remaining the claim unchanged while the evidence in its support is found to exhibit greater frailty.
(*d*) None of the above.

17. If two propositions cannot both be false but may both be true, what is the relation between the two propositions ?

(*a*) Contrary (*b*) Sub-contrary
(*c*) Sub-alternation (*d*) Contradictory

18. Given below are some codes of arrangements of three items in order of wider scope. Select the correct code.

(*a*) Garments, cloth and shirts
(*b*) Cloth, garments and shirts
(*c*) Shirts, garments and cloth
(*d*) Garments, shirts and cloth

19. What is equivalent of the statement 'All atheists are pessimists' ?

(*a*) All non-pessimists are nonatheists.
(*b*) All non-atheists are nonpessimists.
(*c*) All pessimists are atheists.
(*d*) None of the above.

Direction (Q. 20 – 23) : In the following table, trends in production of energy in India by primary sources are given. Study the table and answer question (Production in peta Joules)

Year	Coal & Lignite	Crude Petroleum	Natural Gas	Electricity (Hydro & Nuclear)	Total
2006-07	7459	1423	1223	4763	14,868
2007-08	7926	1429	1248	4944	15,547
2008-09	8476	1403	1265	5133	16,277
2009-10	9137	1411	1830	4511	16,889
2010-11	9207	1579	2012	5059	17,857

20. In which year primary sources recorded the lowest growth in total production of energy ?

(*a*) 2007–08 (*b*) 2008–09
(*c*) 2009–10 (*d*) 2010–11

21. Which source of energy has shown the highest growth rate in production during 2006-07 to 2010-11 ?

(*a*) Coal & lignite
(*b*) Crude petroleum
(*c*) Hydro & nuclear electricity
(*d*) Total production of energy

22. Which one of the following primary sources of energy has recorded the highest growth in production in 2008–09 ?

(*a*) Coal & lignite
(*b*) Crude petroleum
(*c*) Natural gas
(*d*) Hydro & nuclear electricity

23. In which year, production of hydro and nuclear electricity was almost double the production of crude petroleum and natural gas taken together ?

(*a*) 2006–07 (*b*) 2007–08
(*c*) 2008–09 (*d*) 2009–10

24. The Internet ethical protocol is called

(*a*) net protocol (*b*) netiquette
(*c*) net ethics (*d*) net morality

25. Commercial messages on the net are identified as

(*a*) Net ads
(*b*) Internet commercials
(*c*) Webmercials
(*d*) Viral advertisements

26. Manuel Castelle was the first to use the term
(*a*) Internet society
(*b*) Electronic society
(*c*) Network society
(*d*) Telematic society

27. GIF stands for
(*a*) Global Information Format
(*b*) Graphics Information Format
(*c*) Graphics Interchange File
(*d*) Graphics Interchange Format

28. Which one of the following is not an Operating System ?
(*a*) IBM AIX (*b*) Linux
(*c*) Sun Solaris (*d*) Firefox

29. Which of the following is/are a minority institution(s) ?
1. Punjabi University, Patiala
2. Osmania University, Hyderabad
3. Kashmir University, Srinagar
4. St. Stephens College, Delhi

Select the correct answer from the code given below :

Codes :
(*a*) 1 and 2 (*b*) 2 and 4
(*c*) 2 only (*d*) 4 only

30. Which of the following statements are correct about the National Advisory ouncil (NAC) ?
1. The National Advisory Council is a statutory body.
2. It is headed by the Prime Minister of India.
3. It facilitates constant interaction with the leaders of civil society.
4. It provides policy and legislative inputs to the Government of India.

Select the correct answer from the code given below :

Codes :
(*a*) 1, 2 and 3
(*b*) 2, 3 and 4
(*c*) 1, 3 and 4
(*d*) 3 and 4

31. Which of the following are voluntary provisions in the 73rd Constitutional Amendment Act (1992) ?
1. Minimum age of 21 for contesting elections to Panchayats.
2. Indirect elections to the post of Chairperson of Panchayats at the intermediate and district levels.
3. Representation of Members of Parliament and State Legislature on Panchayati Raj institutions.
4. Reservation of seats for backward classes.

Select the correct answer from the code given below :

Codes :
(*a*) 1, 2 and 4 (*b*) 2, 3 and 4
(*c*) 1, 2 and 3 (*d*) 3 and 4

32. In which of the following States the segment of population, which is in majority, enjoys the benefit of reservation of seats in the State Assembly ?
(*a*) Meghalaya and Mizoram
(*b*) Assam and Nagaland
(*c*) Madhya Pradesh and Assam
(*d*) Rajasthan and Arunachal Pradesh

33. Which of the following are the ways of acquiring Indian citizenship ?
1. Birth
2. Descent
3. Naturalisation
4. Incorporation of territory

Select the correct answer from the code given below :

Codes :
(*a*) 1 and 2 (*b*) 1 and 4
(*c*) 1, 2 and 3 (*d*) 1, 2, 3 and 4

34. Which of the following statements about the Union Public Service Commission are correct ?
1. UPSC is a Constitutional body.
2. It serves as an advisory body.
3. It is called upon to advise the Government in regard to representation of the Scheduled Castes and Scheduled Tribes in the Civil Service.

4. It is consulted on appointments of Chairman and members of Tribunals and Commissions.

Select the correct answer from the code given below :

Codes :

(*a*) 1, 2 and 3 (*b*) 1, 2 and 4

(*c*) 1, 3 and 4 (*d*) 1 and 2

Read the following passage carefully and answer Question Nos. from 35 to 40 :

I had occasion to work with her closely during the Women's International Year in 1975 when she was chairing a Steering Committee and made me the member in charge of publicity. Representatives from different political parties and women's organizations were on the committee and though the leftists claimed a sort of proprietary right over her, Aruna encouraged and treated all members alike. It was not her political affiliations or her involvement in a particular cause, which won her respect and recognition, but her utter honesty in public life, her integrity and her compassion for the oppressed which made her an adorable person. She had the courage to differ with and defy the mightiest in the land; yet her human spirit prompted her to work in the worst of slums to offer succour to the poor and the exploited.

In later years – around late eighties and early nineties – Aruna Asaf Ali's health began to deteriorate. Though her mind remained alert, she could not actively take up her pet causes – action for women's advancement, planning for economic justice, role of media, reaffirmation of values in public affairs etc. Slowly, her movements were restricted and Aruna who had drawn sustenance from common people, from her involvement in public life, became a lonely person. She passed away in July 1996.

35. Which Committee was chaired by Aruna ?

(*a*) Women's International Year's Committee

(*b*) Steering Committee of Women's International Year

(*c*) A Committee of Publicity

(*d*) Women's Organizations

36. Who were made the members of the Committee of Publicity ?

Choose the answer from codes given below :

(*i*) Representatives from different political parties.

(*ii*) Representatives from the leftist parties.

(*iii*) Representatives from the women's organizations.

(*iv*) None of the above.

Codes :

(*a*) (*i*), (*iii*)

(*b*) (*i*), (*ii*)

(*c*) (*i*), (*ii*), (*iii*)

(*d*) (*iv*)

37. Aruna earned respect because of

(*a*) she identified with the leftists

(*b*) she did not associate with any political party

(*c*) chairing a Steering Committee

(*d*) she identified with women's organizations

38. Who tried to monopolize Aruna as their proprietary right ?

(*a*) Women Organizations

(*b*) Leftists

(*c*) Steering Committee

(*d*) Some Political Parties

39. Aruna's health began to deteriorate from

(*a*) 1985 – 2002

(*b*) 1998 – 2000

(*c*) 1981 – 2000

(*d*) 1989 – 2001

40. Aruna's pet cause(s) in her life was/ were

(*a*) Role of media

(*b*) Economic justice

(*c*) Reaffirmation of values in public affairs

(*d*) All the above

41. A good teacher must be

(*a*) resourceful and autocratic

(*b*) resourceful and participative

(*c*) resourceful and authoritative

(*d*) resourceful and dominant

42. Which one of the following is the best method of teaching ?
(*a*) Lecture method
(*b*) Discussion method
(*c*) Demonstration method
(*d*) Question-Answer method

43. Successful Communication in classroom teaching is
(*a*) Circular (*b*) Reciprocal
(*c*) Directional (*d*) Influential

44. Which one of the following types of evaluation assesses the learning progress to provide continuous feedback to both teachers and students during instruction ?
(*a*) Placement evaluation
(*b*) Formative evaluation
(*c*) Diagnostic evaluation
(*d*) Summative

45. Which one of the following is a scaled down teaching situation ?
(*a*) Macro teaching
(*b*) Team teaching
(*c*) Cooperative teaching
(*d*) Micro teaching

46. CLASS stands for
(*a*) Complete Literacy and Studies in Schools
(*b*) Computer Literates and Students in Schools
(*c*) Computer Literacy and Studies in Schools
(*d*) Centre for Literacy and Studies in Schools

47. Which one of the following is not a type of experimental method ?
(*a*) Single group experiment
(*b*) Residual group experiment
(*c*) Parallel group experiment
(*d*) Rational group experiment

48. Which one of the following is not a non-parametric test ?
(*a*) t-test
(*b*) Sign test
(*c*) Chi-square test
(*d*) Run test

49. Read the following statements – one labelled as Assertion (A) and the other as Reason (R) :
Assertion (A) : Qualitative research in India has a long way to go to reach international standards.
Reason (R) : Because the funding agencies do not support qualitative research in academic institutions.
Find the correct answer from the codes given below :
(*a*) Both (A) and (R) are true and (R) is the correct explanation of (A).
(*b*) Both (A) and (R) are true, but (R) is not the correct explanation of (A).
(*c*) (A) is true, but (R) is false.
(*d*) Both (A) and (R) are false.

50. Identify the correct sequence of research steps :
(*a*) Selection of topic, review of literature, data collection, interpretation of findings
(*b*) Review of literature, selection of topic, data collection, interpretation of findings
(*c*) Selection of topic, data collection, review of literature, interpretation of findings
(*d*) Selection of topic, review of literature, interpretation of findings, data collection

51. Deconstruction is a popular method of research in
(*a*) Basic Science (*b*) Applied Science
(*c*) Social Science (*d*) Literature

52. With which one of the following techniques communality is associated ?
(*a*) Univariate analysis
(*b*) Factor analysis
(*c*) Case studies
(*d*) SWOT analysis

53. The variable which impacts the relationship between an independent variable and a dependent variable is known as
(*a*) antecedent variable
(*b*) precedent variable
(*c*) predictor variable
(*d*) control variable

54. Which one of the following is a nonprobability sampling method ?

(*a*) Simple Random Sampling

(*b*) Stratified Sampling

(*c*) Cluster Sampling

(*d*) Quota Sampling

55. By the year 2022, the Climate Change Action Plan of Government of India aims at installing

(*a*) 20,000 MW of wind power

(*b*) 25,000 MW of wind power

(*c*) 20,000 MW of solar power

(*d*) 10,000 MW of solar power

56. Which one of the following biosphere reserves has UNESCO recognition ?

(*a*) Manas

(*b*) Kanchenjunga

(*c*) Seshachalam Hills

(*d*) Greater Nicobar

57. Which activity contributes to water pollution more than any other throughout world ?

(*a*) Agriculture

(*b*) Hydroelectric power generation

(*c*) Industry

(*d*) Urbanisation

58. Match List – I with List – II and find the correct answer from the codes given below :

List – I	List – II
(Biosphere Reserve)	**(Area of Location)**
A. Nilgiri	*i.* Deccan Peninsula
B. Manas	*ii.* Chhattisgarh
C. Similipal	*iii.* Eastern Himalaya
D. Achankmar-Amarkantak	*iv.* Western Ghat

Codes :

	A	**B**	**C**	**D**
(*a*)	*i*	*ii*	*iii*	*iv*
(*b*)	*ii*	*iii*	*iv*	*i*
(*c*)	*iii*	*iv*	*ii*	*i*
(*d*)	*iv*	*iii*	*i*	*ii*

59. G5 are the five most important emerging economies of world. Which one of the following does not form part of G5 ?

(*a*) Mexico (*b*) Brazil

(*c*) China (*d*) Korea

60. Which of the following nations has the maximum per capita emissions of carbon dioxide ?

(*a*) China (*b*) Japan

(*c*) USA (*d*) India

ANSWERS

1. (*a*)	**2.** (*a*)	**3.** (*b*)	**4.** (*d*)	**5.** (*a*)	**6.** (*d*)	**7.** (*c*)	**8.** (*c*)	**9.** (*d*)	**10.** (*d*)
11. (*a*)	**12.** (*b*)	**13.** (*a*)	**14.** (*b*)	**15.** (*b*)	**16.** (*b*)	**17.** (*b*)	**18.** (*b*)	**19.** (*a*)	**20.** (*c*)
21. (*a*)	**22.** (*a*)	**23.** (*c*)	**24.** (*b*)	**25.** (*c*)	**26.** (*c*)	**27.** (*d*)	**28.** (*d*)	**29.** (*d*)	**30.** (*d*)
31. (*d*)	**32.** (*a*)	**33.** (*d*)	**34.** (*d*)	**35.** (*b*)	**36.** (*a*)	**37.** (*b*)	**38.** (*b*)	**39.** (*c*)	**40.** (*d*)
41. (*b*)	**42.** (*c*)	**43.** (*b*)	**44.** (*b*)	**45.** (*d*)	**46.** (*c*)	**47.** (*b*)	**48.** (*a*)	**49.** (*c*)	**50.** (*a*)
51. (*d*)	**52.** (*b*)	**53.** (*d*)	**54.** (*d*)	**55.** (*c*)	**56.** (*d*)	**57.** (*a*)	**58.** (*d*)	**59.** (*d*)	**60.** (*c*)

Solved Paper 2013 (June)

UGC NET

PAPER-I

Note : • This paper contains **Sixty (60)** multiple choice questions, each question carrying **two (2)** marks.

• Candidate is expected to answer any **Fifty (50)** questions.

• In case more than **Fifty (50)** questions are attempted, only the first **Fifty (50)** questions will be evaluated.

1. Which one of the following references is written as per Modern Language Association (MLA) format ?

(*a*) Hall, Donald. Fundamentals of Electronics, New Delhi : Prentice Hall of India, 2005

(*b*) Hall, Donald, Fundamentals of Electronics, New Delhi : Prentice Hall of India, 2005

(*c*) Hall, Donald, Fundamentals of Electronics, New Delhi – Prentice Hall of India, 2005

(*d*) Hall, Donald. Fundamentals of Electronics. New Delhi : Prentice Hall of India, 2005

2. A workshop is

(*a*) a conference for discussion on a topic.

(*b*) a meeting for discussion on a topic.

(*c*) a class at a college or a university in which a teacher and the students discuss a topic.

(*d*) a brief intensive course for a small group emphasizing the development of a skill or technique for solving a specific problem.

3. A working hypothesis is

(*a*) a proven hypothesis for an argument.

(*b*) not required to be tested.

(*c*) a provisionally accepted hypothesis for further research.

(*d*) a scientific theory.

Read the following passage carefully and answer the questions (4 to 9) :

The Taj Mahal has become one of the world's best known monuments. This domed white marble structure is situated on a high plinth at the southern end of a four-quartered garden, evoking the gardens of paradise, enclosed within walls measuring 305 by 549 metres. Outside the walls, in an area known as Mumtazabad, were living quarters for attendants, markets, serais and other structures built by local merchants and nobles. The tomb complex and the other imperial structures of Mumtazabad were maintained by the income of thirty villages given specifically for the tomb's support. The name Taj Mahal is unknown in Mughal chronicles, but it is used by contemporary Europeans in India, suggesting that this was the tomb's popular name. In contemporary texts, it is generally called simply the Illuminated Tomb (Rauza-i-Munavvara).

Mumtaz Mahal died shortly after delivering her fourteenth child in 1631. The Mughal court was then residing in Burhanpur. Her remains were temporarily buried by the griefstricken emperor in a spacious garden known as Zainabad on the bank of the river Tapti. Six months later her body was transported to Agra, where it was interred in land chosen for the mausoleum. This land, situated south of the Mughal city on the bank of the Jamuna, had belonged to the Kachhwaha rajas since the time of Raja Man Singh and was purchased from the then current raja, Jai Singh. Although contemporary chronicles indicate Jai Singh's willing cooperation in this exchange, extant farmans (imperial commands) indicate that the final price was not settled until almost two years after the mausoleum's commencement. Jai Singh's further cooperation was insured by imperial orders issued between 1632 and 1637 demanding that he provide stone masons and carts to transport marble from the mines at Makrana, within his "ancestral domain", to Agra where both the Taj Mahal and Shah Jahan's additions to the Agra fort were constructed concurrently.

Work on the mausoleum was commenced early in 1632. Inscriptional evidence indicates much of the tomb was completed by 1636. By 1643, when Shah Jahan most lavishly celebrated the 'Urs ceremony for Mumtaz Mahal', the entire complex was virtually complete.

4. Marble stone used for the construction of the Taj Mahal was brought from the ancestral domain of Raja Jai Singh. The name of the place where mines of marble is

(*a*) Burhanpur (*b*) Makrana

(*c*) Amber (*d*) Jaipur

5. The popular name Taj Mahal was given by

(*a*) Shah Jahan (*b*) Tourists

(*c*) Public (*d*) European travellers

6. Point out the true statement from the following :

(*a*) Marble was not used for the construction of the Taj Mahal.

(*b*) Red sand stone is non-visible in the Taj Mahal complex.

(*c*) The Taj Mahal is surrounded by a four-quartered garden known as Chahr Bagh.

(*d*) The Taj Mahal was constructed to celebrate the 'Urs ceremony for Mumtaz Mahal'.

7. In the contemporary texts the Taj Mahal is known

(*a*) Mumtazabad (*b*) Mumtaz Mahal

(*c*) Zainabad (*d*) Rauza-i-Munavvara

8. The construction of the Taj Mahal was completed between the period

(*a*) 1632 – 1636 A.D. (*b*) 1630 – 1643 A.D.

(*c*) 1632 – 1643 A.D. (*d*) 1636 – 1643 A.D.

9. The documents indicating the ownership of land, where the Taj Mahal was built, known as

(*a*) Farman

(*b*) Sale Deed

(*c*) Sale-Purchase Deed

(*d*) None of the above

10. In the process of communication, which one of the following is in the chronological order ?

(*a*) Communicator, Medium, Receiver, Effect, Message

(*b*) Medium, Communicator, Message, Receiver, Effect

(*c*) Communicator, Message, Medium, Receiver, Effect

(*d*) Message, Communicator, Medium, Receiver, Effect

11. Bengal Gazette, the first Newspaper in India was started in 1780 by

(*a*) Dr. Annie Besant

(*b*) James Augustus Hicky

(*c*) Lord Cripson

(*d*) A.O. Hume

12. Press censorship in India was imposed during the tenure of the Prime Minister

(*a*) Rajeev Gandhi (*b*) Narasimha Rao

(*c*) Indira Gandhi (*d*) Deve Gowda

13. Communication via New media such as computers, teleshopping, internet and mobile telephony is termed as

(*a*) Entertainment

(*b*) Interactive communication

(*c*) Developmental communication

(*d*) Communitarian

14. Classroom communication of a teacher rests on the principle of

(*a*) Infotainment (*b*) Edutainment

(*c*) Entertainment (*d*) Enlightenment

15. ________ is important when a teacher communicates with his/her student.

(*a*) Sympathy (*b*) Empathy

(*c*) Apathy (*d*) Antipathy

16. In a certain code GALIB is represented by HBMJC. TIGER will be represented by

(*a*) UJHFS (*b*) UHJSF

(*c*) JHUSF (*d*) HUJSF

17. In a certain cricket tournament 45 matches were played. Each team played once against each of the other teams. The number of teams participated in the tournament is

(*a*) 8 (*b*) 10

(*c*) 12 (*d*) 14

18. The missing number in the series

40, 120, 60, 180, 90, ?, 135 is

(*a*) 110 (*b*) 270

(*c*) 105 (*d*) 210

19. The odd numbers from 1 to 45 which are exactly divisible by 3 are arranged in an ascending order. The number at 6th position is

(*a*) 18 (*b*) 24

(*c*) 33 (*d*) 36

20. The mean of four numbers a, b, c, d is 100. If c = 70, then the mean of the remaining numbers is

(a) 30 (b) $\frac{85}{2}$

(c) $\frac{170}{3}$ (d) 110

21. If the radius of a circle is increased by 50%, the perimeter of the circle will increase by

(a) 20% (b) 30%

(c) 40% (d) 50%

22. If the statement 'some men are honest' is false, which among the following statements will be true.

Choose the correct code given below :

(i) All men are honest.

(ii) No men are honest.

(iii) Some men are not honest.

(iv) All men are dishonest.

Codes :

(a) (i), (ii) and (iii) (b) (ii), (iii) and (iv)

(c) (i), (iii) and (iv) (d) (ii), (i) and (iv)

23. Choose the proper alternative given in the codes to replace the question mark.

Bee – Honey, Cow – Milk, Teacher – ?

(a) Intelligence (b) Marks

(c) Lessons (d) Wisdom

24. P is the father of R and S is the son of Q and T is the brother of P. If R is the sister of S, how is Q related to T ?

(a) Wife (b) Sister-in-law

(c) Brother-in-law (d) Daughter-in-law

25. A definition put forward to resolve a dispute by influencing attitudes or stirring emotions is called

(a) Lexical (b) Persuasive

(c) Stipulative (d) Precisions

26. Which of the codes given below contains only the correct statements ?

Statements :

(i) Venn diagram is a clear method of notation.

(ii) Venn diagram is the most direct method of testing the validity of categorical syllogisms.

(iii) In Venn diagram method the premises and the conclusion of a categorical syllogism is diagrammed.

(iv) In Venn diagram method the three overlapping circles are drawn for testing a categorical syllogism.

Codes :

(a) (i), (ii) & (iii) (b) (i), (ii) & (iv)

(c) (ii), (iii) & (iv) (d) (i), (iii) & (iv)

27. Inductive reasoning presupposes

(a) unity in human nature

(b) integrity in human nature

(c) uniformity in human nature

(d) harmony in human nature

Read the table below and based on this table answer questions from 28 to 33 :

Area under Major Horticulture Crops

(in lakh hectares)

Year	Fruits	Vegetables	Flowers	Total Horticulture Area
2005-06	53	72	1	187
2006-07	56	75	1	194
2007-08	58	78	2	202
2008-09	61	79	2	207
2009-10	63	79	2	209

28. Which of the following two years have recorded the highest rate of increase in area under the total horticulture ?

(a) 2005–06 & 2006–07

(b) 2006–07 & 2008–09

(c) 2007–08 & 2008–09

(d) 2006–07 & 2007–08

29. Shares of the area under flowers, vegetables and fruits in the area under total horticulture are respectively :

(a) 1, 38 and 30 percent

(b) 30, 38 and 1 percent

(c) 38, 30 and 1 percent

(d) 35, 36 and 2 percent

30. Which of the following has recorded the highest rate of increase in area during 2005-06 to 2009-10 ?

(a) Fruits (b) Vegetables

(c) Flowers (d) Total horticulture

31. Find out the horticultural crop that has recorded an increase of area by around 10 percent from 2005-06 to 2009-10

(a) Fruits (b) Vegetables

(c) Flowers (d) Total horticulture

32. What has been the share of area under fruits, vegetables and flowers in the area under total horticulture in 2007- 08 ?

(a) 53 percent (b) 68 percent

(c) 79 percent (d) 100 percent

33. In which year, area under fruits has recorded the highest rate of increase ?

(a) 2006-07 (b) 2007-08

(c) 2008-09 (d) 2009-10

34. 'www' stands for

(a) work with web (b) word wide web

(c) world wide web (d) worth while web

35. A hard disk is divided into tracks which is further subdivided into

(a) Clusters (b) Sectors

(c) Vectors (d) Heads

36. A computer program that translates a program statement by statement into machine language is called a/an

(a) Compiler (b) Simulator

(c) Translator (d) Interpreter

37. A Gigabyte is equal to

(a) 1024 Megabytes

(b) 1024 Kilobytes

(c) 1024 Terabytes

(d) 1024 Bytes

38. A Compiler is a software which converts

(a) characters to bits

(b) high level language to machine language

(c) machine language to high level language

(d) words to bits

39. Virtual memory is

(a) an extremely large main memory.

(b) an extremely large secondary memory.

(c) an illusion of extremely large main memory.

(d) a type of memory used in super computers.

40. The phrase 'tragedy of commons' is in the context of

(a) tragic event related to damage caused by release of poisonous gases.

(b) tragic conditions of poor people.

(c) degradation of renewable free access resources.

(d) climate change.

41. Kyoto Protocol is related to

(a) Ozone depletion (b) Hazardous waste

(c) Climate change (d) Nuclear energy

42. Which of the following is a source of emissions leading to the eventual formation of surface ozone as a pollutant ?

(a) Transport sector

(b) Refrigeration and Airconditioning

(c) Wetlands

(d) Fertilizers

43. The smog in cities in India mainly consists of

(a) Oxides of sulphur

(b) Oxides of nitrogen and unburnt hydrocarbons

(c) Carbon monoxide and SPM

(d) Oxides of sulphur and ozone

44. Which of the following types of natural hazards have the highest potential to cause damage to humans ?

(a) Earthquakes

(b) Forest fires

(c) Volcanic eruptions

(d) Droughts and Floods

45. The percentage share of renewable energy sources in the power production in India is around

(a) 2-3% (b) 22-25%

(c) 10-12% (d) < 1%

46. In which of the following categories the enrolment of students in higher education in 2010-11 was beyond the percentage of seats reserved ?

(a) OBC students (b) SC students

(c) ST students (d) Woman students

47. Which one of the following statements is not correct about the University Grants Commission (UGC) ?

(*a*) It was established in 1956 by an Act of Parliament.

(*b*) It is tasked with promoting and coordinating higher education.

(*c*) It receives Plan and Non-Plan funds from the Central Government.

(*d*) It receives funds from State Governments in respect of State Universities.

48. Consider the statement which is followed by two arguments (I) and (II) :

Statement : Should India switch over to a two party system ?

Arguments :

(I) Yes, it will lead to stability of Government.

(II) No, it will limit the choice of voters.

(*a*) Only argument (I) is strong.

(*b*) Only argument (II) is strong.

(*c*) Both the arguments are strong.

(*d*) Neither of the arguments is strong.

49. Consider the statement which is followed by two arguments (I) and (II) :

Statement : Should persons with criminal background be banned from contesting elections ?

Arguments :

(I) Yes, it will decriminalise politics.

(II) No, it will encourage the ruling party to file frivolous cases against their political opponents.

(*a*) Only argument (I) is strong.

(*b*) Only argument (II) is strong.

(*c*) Both the arguments are strong.

(*d*) Neither of the arguments is strong.

50. Which of the following statement(s) is/are correct about a Judge of the Supreme Court of India ?

1. A Judge of the Supreme Court is appointed by the President of India.
2. He holds office during the pleasure of the President.
3. He can be suspended, pending an inquiry.
4. He can be removed for proven misbehaviour or incapacity.

Select the correct answer from the codes given below :

Codes :

(*a*) 1, 2 and 3 (*b*) 1, 3 and 4

(*c*) 1 and 3 (*d*) 1 and 4

51. In the warrant of precedence, the Speaker of the Lok Sabha comes next only to

(*a*) The President

(*b*) The Vice-President

(*c*) The Prime Minister

(*d*) The Cabinet Ministers

52. The black-board can be utilised best by a teacher for

(*a*) putting the matter of teaching in black and white

(*b*) making the students attentive

(*c*) writing the important and notable points

(*d*) highlighting the teacher himself

53. Nowadays the most effective mode of learning is

(*a*) self study

(*b*) face-to-face learning

(*c*) e-learning

(*d*) blended learning

54. At the primary school stage, most of the teachers should be women because they

(*a*) can teach children better than men.

(*b*) know basic content better than men.

(*c*) are available on lower salaries.

(*d*) can deal with children with love and affection.

55. Which one is the highest order of learning ?

(*a*) Chain learning

(*b*) Problem-solving learning

(*c*) Stimulus-response learning

(*d*) Conditioned-reflex learning

56. A person can enjoy teaching as a profession when he

(*a*) has control over students.

(*b*) commands respect from students.

(*c*) is more qualified than his colleagues.

(*d*) is very close to higher authorities.

57. "A diagram speaks more than 1000 words." The statement means that the teacher should
(*a*) use diagrams in teaching.
(*b*) speak more and more in the class.
(*c*) use teaching aids in the class.
(*d*) not speak too much in the class.

58. A research paper
(*a*) is a compilation of information on a topic.
(*b*) contains original research as deemed by the author.
(*c*) contains peer-reviewed original research or evaluation of research conducted by others.
(*d*) can be published in more than one journal.

59. Which one of the following belongs to the category of good eresearch ethics
(*a*) Publishing the same paper in two research journals without telling the editors.
(*b*) Conducting a review of the literature that acknowledges the contributions of other people in the relevant field or relevant prior work.
(*c*) Trimming outliers from a data set without discussing your reasons in a research paper.
(*d*) Including a colleague as an author on a research paper in return for a favour even though the colleague did not make a serious contribution to the paper.

60. Which of the following sampling methods is not based on probability ?
(*a*) Simple Random Sampling
(*b*) Stratified Sampling
(*c*) Quota Sampling
(*d*) Cluster Sampling

ANSWERS

1. (*d*)	**2.** (*d*)	**3.** (*c*)	**4.** (*b*)	**5.** (*d*)	**6.** (*c*)	**7.** (*d*)	**8.** (*c*)	**9.** (*a*)	**10.** (*c*)
11. (*b*)	**12.** (*c*)	**13.** (*b*)	**14.** (*b*)	**15.** (*b*)	**16.** (*a*)	**17.** (*b*)	**18.** (*b*)	**19.** (*c*)	**20.** (*d*)
21. (*d*)	**22.** (*b*)	**23.** (*d*)	**24.** (*b*)	**25.** (*b*)	**26.** (*b*)	**27.** (*c*)	**28.** (*d*)	**29.** (*a*)	**30.** (*c*)
31. (*b*)	**32.** (*b*)	**33.** (*a*)	**34.** (*c*)	**35.** (*b*)	**36.** (*d*)	**37.** (*a*)	**38.** (*b*)	**39.** (*c*)	**40.** (*c*)
41. (*c*)	**42.** (*a*)	**43.** (*b*)	**44.** (*d*)	**45.** (*c*)	**46.** (*a*)	**47.** (*d*)	**48.** (*c*)	**49.** (*a*)	**50.** (*d*)
51. (*c*)	**52.** (*c*)	**53.** (*c, d*)	**54.** (*d*)	**55.** (*d*)	**56.** (*b*)	**57.** (*c*)	**58.** (*c*)	**59.** (*b*)	**60.** (*c*)

Solved Paper 2012 (December)

UGC NET

PAPER-I

Note : • This paper contains **Sixty (60)** multiple choice questions, each question carrying **two (2)** marks.

• Candidate is expected to answer any **Fifty (50)** questions.

• In case more than **Fifty (50)** questions are attempted, only the first **Fifty (50)** questions will be evaluated.

1. The English word 'Communication' is derived from the words

(*a*) Communis and Communicare

(*b*) Communist and Commune

(*c*) Communism and Communalism

(*d*) Communion and Common sense

2. Chinese Cultural Revolution leader Mao Zedong used a type of communication to talk to the masses is known as

(*a*) Mass line communication

(*b*) Group communication

(*c*) Participatory communication

(*d*) Dialogue communication

3. Conversing with the spirits and ancestors is termed as

(*a*) Transpersonal communication

(*b*) Intrapersonal communication

(*c*) Interpersonal communication

(*d*) Face-to-face communication

4. The largest circulated daily newspaper among the following is

(*a*) The Times of India (*b*) The Indian Express

(*c*) The Hindu (*d*) The Deccan Herald

5. The pioneer of the silent feature film in India was

(*a*) K.A. Abbas (*b*) Satyajit Ray

(*c*) B.R. Chopra (*d*) Dada Sahib Phalke

6. Classroom communication of a teacher rests on the principle of

(*a*) Infotainment (*b*) Edutainment

(*c*) Entertainment (*d*) Power equation

7. The missing number in the series :

0, 6, 24, 60, 120, ?, 336, is

(*a*) 240 (*b*) 220

(*c*) 280 (*d*) 210

8. A group of 7 members having a majority of boys is to be formed out of 6 boys and 4 girls. The number of ways the group can be formed is

(*a*) 80 (*b*) 100

(*c*) 90 (*d*) 110

9. The number of observations in a group is 40. The average of the first 10 members is 4.5 and the average of the remaining 30 members is 3.5. The average of the whole group is

(*a*) 4 (*b*) 15/2

(*c*) 15/4 (*d*) 6

10. If MOHAN is represented by the code KMFYL, then COUNT will be represented by

(*a*) AMSLR (*b*) MSLAR

(*c*) MASRL (*d*) SAMLR

11. The sum of the ages of two persons A and B is 50. 5 years ago, the ratio of their ages was 5/3. The present age of A and B are

(*a*) 30, 20 (*b*) 35, 15

(*c*) 38, 12 (*d*) 40, 10

12. Let a means minus (–), b means multiplied by (×), C means divided by (÷) and D means plus (+). The value of 90 D 9 a 29 C 10 b 2 is

(*a*) 8 (*b*) 10

(*c*) 12 (*d*) 14

13. Consider the Assertion–I and Assertion–II and select the right code given below :

Assertion – I : Even Bank-lockers are not safe. Thieves can break them and take away your wealth. But thieves can not go to heaven. So you should keep your wealth in heaven.

Assertion – II : The difference of skincolour of beings is because of the distance from the sun and not because of some permanent traits. Skin-colour is the result of body's reaction to the sun and its rays.

Codes :

(*a*) Both the assertions-I and II are forms of argument.

(*b*) The assertion-I is an argument but the assertion-II is not.

(*c*) The assertion-II is an argument but the assertion-I is not.

(*d*) Both the assertions are explanations of facts.

14. By which of the following proposition, the proposition 'some men are not honest' is contradicted ?

(*a*) All men are honest.

(*b*) Some men are honest.

(*c*) No men are honest.

(*d*) All of the above.

15. A stipulative definition is

(*a*) always true

(*b*) always false

(*c*) sometimes true sometimes false

(*d*) neither true nor false

16. Choose the appropriate alternative given in the codes to replace the question mark.

Examiner – Examinee, Pleader – Client, Preceptor – ?

(*a*) Customer (*b*) Path-finder

(*c*) Perceiver (*d*) Disciple

17. If the statement 'most of the students are obedient' is taken to be true, which one of the following pair of statements can be claimed to be true ?

I. All obedient persons are students.

II. All students are obedient.

III. Some students are obedient.

IV. Some students are not disobedient.

Codes :

(*a*) I & II (*b*) II & III

(*c*) III & IV (*d*) II & IV

18. Choose the right code :

A deductive argument claims that :

I. The conclusion does not claim something more than that which is contained in the premises.

II. The conclusion is supported by the premise/premises conclusively.

III. If the conclusion is false, then premise/premises may be either true or false.

IV. If premise/combination of premises is true, then conclusion must be true.

Codes :

(*a*) I and II (*b*) I and III

(*c*) II and III (*d*) All the above

On the basis of the data given in the following table, give answers to questions from 19 to 24 :

Government Expenditures on Social Services

(As percent of total expenditure)

Sl. No.	Items	2007-08	2008-09	2009-10	2010-11
	Social Services	11.06	12.94	13.06	14.02
(a)	Education, sports & youth affairs	4.02	4.04	3.96	4.46
(b)	Health & family welfare	2.05	1.91	1.90	2.03
(c)	Water supply, housing, etc.	2.02	2.31	2.20	2.27
(d)	Information & broadcasting	0.22	0.22	0.20	0.22
(e)	Welfare to SC/ST & OBC	0.36	0.35	0.41	0.63
(f)	Labour and employment	0.27	0.27	0.22	0.25
(g)	Social welfare & nutrition	0.82	0.72	0.79	1.06
(h)	North-eastern areas	0.00	1.56	1.50	1.75
(i)	Other social services	1.29	1.55	1.87	1.34
	Total Government expenditure	100.00	100.00	100.00	100.00

19. How many activities in the social services are there where the expenditure has been less than 5 percent of the total expenditures incurred on the social services in 2008-09 ?
(a) One (b) Three
(c) Five (d) All the above

20. In which year, the expenditures on the social services have increased at the highest rate ?
(a) 2007-08 (b) 2008-09
(c) 2009-10 (d) 2010-11

21. Which of the following activities remains almost stagnant in terms of share of expenditures?
(a) North-eastern areas
(b) Welfare to SC/ST & OBC
(c) Information & broadcasting
(d) Social welfare and nutrition

22. Which of the following item's expenditure share is almost equal to the remaining three items in the given years ?
(a) Information & broadcasting
(b) Welfare to SC/ST and OBC
(c) Labour and employment
(d) Social welfare & nutrition

23. Which of the following items of social services has registered the highest rate of increase in expenditures during 2007-08 to 2010-11 ?
(a) Education, sports & youth affairs
(b) Welfare to SC/ST & OBC
(c) Social welfare & nutrition
(d) Overall social services

24. Which of the following items has registered the highest rate of decline in terms of expenditure during 2007-08 to 2009-10 ?
(a) Labour and employment
(b) Health & family welfare
(c) Social welfare & nutrition
(d) Education, sports & youth affairs

25. ALU stands for
(a) American Logic Unit
(b) Alternate Local Unit
(c) Alternating Logic Unit
(d) Arithmetic Logic Unit

26. A Personal Computer uses a number of chips mounted on a circuit board called
(a) Microprocessor (b) System Board
(c) Daughter Board (d) Mother Board

27. Computer Virus is a
(a) Hardware (b) Bacteria
(c) Software (d) None of these

28. Which one of the following is correct ?
(a) $(17)_{10} = (17)_{16}$ (b) $(17)_{10} = (17)_{8}$
(c) $(17)_{10} = (10111)_{2}$ (d) $(17)_{10} = (10001)_{2}$

29. The file extension of MS-Word document in Office 2007 is _______.
(a) .pdf (b) .doc
(c) .docx (d) .txt

30. _______ is a protocol used by e-mail clients to download e-mails to your computer.
(a) TCP (b) FTP
(c) SMTP (d) POP

31. Which of the following is a source of methane?
(a) Wetlands
(b) Foam Industry
(c) Thermal Power Plants
(d) Cement Industry

32. 'Minamata disaster' in Japan was caused by pollution due to
(a) Lead (b) Mercury
(c) Cadmium (d) Zinc

33. Biomagnification means increase in the
(a) concentration of pollutants in living organisms
(b) number of species
(c) size of living organisms
(d) biomass

34. Nagoya Protocol is related to
(a) Climate change (b) Ozone depletion
(c) Hazardous waste (d) Biodiversity

35. The second most important source after fossil fuels contributing to India's energy needs is
(a) Solar energy (b) Nuclear energy
(c) Hydropower (d) Wind energy

36. In case of earthquakes, an increase of magnitude 1 on Richter Scale implies

(*a*) a ten-fold increase in the amplitude of seismic waves.
(*b*) a ten-fold increase in the energy of the seismic waves.
(*c*) two-fold increase in the amplitude of seismic waves.
(*d*) two-fold increase in the energy of seismic waves.

37. Which of the following is not a measure of Human Development Index ?

(*a*) Literacy Rate (*b*) Gross Enrolment
(*c*) Sex Ratio (*d*) Life Expectancy

38. India has the highest number of students in colleges after

(*a*) the U.K. (*b*) the U.S.A.
(*c*) Australia (*d*) Canada

39. Which of the following statement(s) is/are not correct about the Attorney General of India ?

1. The President appoints a person, who is qualified to be a Judge of a High Court, to be the Attorney General of India.
2. He has the right of audience in all the Courts of the country.
3. He has the right to take part in the proceedings of the Lok Sabha and the Rajya Sabha.
4. He has a fixed tenure.

Select the correct answer from the codes given below :

Codes :

(*a*) 1 and 4 (*b*) 2, 3 and 4
(*c*) 3 and 4 (*d*) 3 only

40. Which of the following prefix President Pranab Mukherjee desires to be discontinued while interacting with Indian dignitaries as well as in official notings ?

1. His Excellency 2. Mahamahim
3. Hon'ble 4. Shri/Smt.

Select the correct answer from the codes given below :

Codes :

(*a*) 1 and 3 (*b*) 2 and 3
(*c*) 1 and 2 (*d*) 1, 2 and 3

41. Which of the following can be done under conditions of financial emergency ?

1. State Legislative Assemblies can be abolished.
2. Central Government can acquire control over the budget and expenditure of States.
3. Salaries of the Judges of the High Courts and the Supreme Court can be reduced.
4. Right to Constitutional Remedies can be suspended.

Select the correct answer from the codes given below :

Codes :

(*a*) 1, 2 and 3 (*b*) 2, 3 and 4
(*c*) 1 and 2 (*d*) 2 and 3

42. Match List – I with List – II and select the correct answer from the codes given below :

List – I	**List – II**
A. Poverty Reduction Programme	(*i*) Mid-day Meals
B. Human Development Scheme	(*ii*) Indira Awas Yojana (IAY)
C. Social Assistance Scheme	(*iii*) National Old Age Pension (NOAP)
D. Minimum Need Scheme	(*iv*) MNREGA

Codes :

	A	**B**	**C**	**D**
(*a*)	(*iv*)	(*i*)	(*iii*)	(*ii*)
(*b*)	(*ii*)	(*iii*)	(*iv*)	(*i*)
(*c*)	(*iii*)	(*iv*)	(*i*)	(*ii*)
(*d*)	(*iv*)	(*iii*)	(*ii*)	(*i*)

43. For an efficient and durable learning, learner should have

(*a*) ability to learn only
(*b*) requisite level of motivation only
(*c*) opportunities to learn only
(*d*) desired level of ability and motivation

44. Classroom communication must be

(*a*) Teacher centric (*b*) Student centric
(*c*) General centric (*d*) Textbook centric

45. The best method of teaching is to

(*a*) impart information
(*b*) ask students to read books
(*c*) suggest good reference material
(*d*) initiate a discussion and participate in it

46. Interaction inside the classroom should generate

(*a*) Argument (*b*) Information

(*c*) Ideas (*d*) Controversy

47. "Spare the rod and spoil the child", gives the message that

(*a*) punishment in the class should be banned.

(*b*) corporal punishment is not acceptable.

(*c*) undesirable behaviour must be punished.

(*d*) children should be beaten with rods.

48. The type of communication that the teacher has in the classroom, is termed as

(*a*) Interpersonal

(*b*) Mass communication

(*c*) Group communication

(*d*) Face-to-face communication

49. Which one of the following is an indication of the quality of a research journal ?

(*a*) Impact factor (*b*) h-index

(*c*) g-index (*d*) i10-index

50. Good 'research ethics' means

(*a*) Not disclosing the holdings of shares/stocks in a company that sponsors your research.

(*b*) Assigning a particular research problem to one Ph.D./research student only.

(*c*) Discussing with your colleagues confidential data from a research paper that you are reviewing for an academic journal.

(*d*) Submitting the same research manuscript for publishing in more than one journal.

51. Which of the following sampling methods is based on probability ?

(*a*) Convenience sampling

(*b*) Quota sampling

(*c*) Judgement sampling

(*d*) Stratified sampling

52. Which one of the following references is written according to American Psychological Association (APA) format ?

(*a*) Sharma, V. (2010). Fundamentals of Computer Science.

New Delhi : Tata McGraw Hill

(*b*) Sharma, V. 2010. Fundamentals of Computer Science.

New Delhi : Tata McGraw Hill

(*c*) Sharma.V. 2010. Fundamentals of Computer Science,

New Delhi : Tata McGraw Hill

(*d*) Sharma, V. (2010), Fundamentals of Computer Science,

New Delhi : Tata McGraw Hill

53. Arrange the following steps of research in correct sequence :

1. Identification of research problem
2. Listing of research objectives
3. Collection of data
4. Methodology
5. Data analysis
6. Results and discussion

(*a*) 1 – 2 – 3 – 4 – 5 – 6

(*b*) 1 – 2 – 4 – 3 – 5 – 6

(*c*) 2 – 1 – 3 – 4 – 5 – 6

(*d*) 2 – 1 – 4 – 3 – 5 – 6

54. Identify the incorrect statement :

(*a*) A hypothesis is made on the basis of limited evidence as a starting point for further investigations.

(*b*) A hypothesis is a basis for reasoning without any assumption of its truth.

(*c*) Hypothesis is a proposed explanation for a phenomenon.

(*d*) Scientific hypothesis is a scientific theory.

Read the following passage carefully and answer the questions (55 to 60) :

The popular view of towns and cities in developing countries and of urbanization process is that despite the benefits and comforts it brings, the emergence of such cities connotes environmental degradation, generation of slums and squatters, urban poverty, unemployment, crimes, lawlessness, traffic chaos etc. But what is the reality ? Given the unprecedental increase in urban population over the last 50 years from 300 million in 1950 to 2 billion in 2000 in developing countries, the wonder really is how well the world has coped, and not how badly.

In general, the urban quality of life has improved in terms of availability of water and sanitation, power, health and education, communication and transport. By way of illustration, a large number of urban residents have been provided with improved water in urban areas in Asia's largest countries such as China, India, Indonesia and Philippines. Despite that, the access to improved water in terms of percentage of total urban population seems to have declined during the last decade of 20th century, though in absolute numbers, millions of additional urbanites, have been provided improved services. These countries have made significant progress in the provision of sanitation services too, together, providing for an additional population of more than 293 million citizens within a decade (1990-2000). These improvements must be viewed against the backdrop of rapidly increasing urban population, fiscal crunch and strained human resources and efficient and quality-oriented public management.

55. The popular view about the process of urbanization in developing countries is
(*a*) Positive (*b*) Negative
(*c*) Neutral (*d*) Unspecified

56. The average annual increase in the number of urbanites in developing countries, from 1950 to 2000 A.D. was close to
(*a*) 30 million (*b*) 40 million
(*c*) 50 million (*d*) 60 million

57. The reality of urbanization is reflected in
(*a*) How well the situation has been managed.
(*b*) How badly the situation has gone out of control.
(*c*) How fast has been the tempo of urbanization.
(*d*) How fast the environment has degraded.

58. Which one of the following is not considered as an indicator of urban quality of life?
(*a*) Tempo of urbanization
(*b*) Provision of basic services
(*c*) Access to social amenities
(*d*) All the above

59. The author in this passage has tried to focus on
(*a*) Extension of Knowledge
(*b*) Generation of Environmental Consciousness
(*c*) Analytical Reasoning
(*d*) Descriptive Statement

60. In the above passage, the author intends to state
(*a*) The hazards of the urban life
(*b*) The sufferings of the urban life
(*c*) The awareness of human progress
(*d*) The limits to growth

ANSWERS

1. (*a*)	2. (*a*)	3. (*a*)	4. (*a*)	5. (*d*)	6. (*b*)	7. (*d*)	8. (*b*)	9. (*c*)	10. (*a*)
11. (*a*)	12. (*)	13. (*b*)	14. (*a*)	15. (*d*)	16. (*d*)	17. (*c*)	18. (*a*)	19. (*d*)	20. (*b*)
21. (*c*)	22. (*d*)	23. (*b*)	24. (*a*)	25. (*d*)	26. (*d*)	27. (*c*)	28. (*d*)	29. (*c*)	30. (*d*)
31. (*a*)	32. (*b*)	33. (*a*)	34. (*d*)	35. (*c*)	36. (*a*)	37. (*c*)	38. (*b*)	39. (*a*)	40. (*c*)
41. (*d*)	42. (*a*)	43. (*d*)	44. (*b*)	45. (*d*)	46. (*c*)	47. (*c*)	48. (*c*)	49. (*a*)	50. (*b*)
51. (*d*)	52. (*a*)	53. (*b*)	54. (*d*)	55. (*b*)	56. (*a*)	57. (*a*)	58. (*a*)	59. (*c*)	60. (*d*)

[Note : "*" denotes marks given to all candidates.]

■■

Solved Paper 2012 (June)

UGC NET

PAPER-I

Note : • This paper contains **Sixty (60)** multiple choice questions, each question carrying **two (2)** marks.

• Candidate is expected to answer any **Fifty (50)** questions.

• In case more than **Fifty (50)** questions are attempted, only the first **Fifty (50)** questions will be evaluated.

1. Video-Conferencing can be classified as one of the following types of communication :

(*a*) Visual one way

(*b*) Audio-Visual one way

(*c*) Audio-Visual two way

(*d*) Visual two way

2. MC National University of Journalism and Communication is located at

(*a*) Lucknow (*b*) Bhopal

(*c*) Chennai (*d*) Mumbai

3. All India Radio (A.I.R.) for broadcasting was named in the year

(*a*) 1926 (*b*) 1936

(*c*) 1946 (*d*) 1956

4. In India for broadcasting TV programmes which system is followed ?

(*a*) NTCS (*b*) PAL

(*c*) NTSE (*d*) SECAM

5. The term 'DAVP' stands for

(*a*) Directorate of Advertising & Vocal Publicity

(*b*) Division of Audio-Visual Publicity

(*c*) Department of Audio-Visual Publicity

(*d*) Directorate of Advertising & Visual Publicity

6. The term "TRP" is associated with TV shows stands for

(*a*) Total Rating Points

(*b*) Time Rating Points

(*c*) Thematic Rating Points

(*d*) Television Rating Points

7. Which is the number that comes next in the following sequence ?

2, 6, 12, 20, 30, 42, 56, ____

(*a*) 60 (*b*) 64

(*c*) 72 (*d*) 70

8. Find the next letter for the series YVSP ....

(*a*) N (*b*) M

(*c*) O (*d*) L

9. Given that in a code language, '645' means 'day is warm'; '42' means 'warm spring' and '634' means 'spring is sunny'; which digit represents 'sunny' ?

(*a*) 3 (*b*) 2

(*c*) 4 (*d*) 5

10. The basis of the following classification is : 'first President of India' 'author of Godan' 'books in my library', 'blue things' and 'students who work hard'

(*a*) Common names

(*b*) Proper names

(*c*) Descriptive phrases

(*d*) Indefinite description

11. In the expression 'Nothing is larger than itself' the relation 'is larger than' is

(*a*) antisymmetric (*b*) asymmetrical

(*c*) intransitive (*d*) irreflexive

12. Assertion (A) : There are more laws on the books today than ever before, and more crimes being committed than ever before.

Reason (R) : Because to reduce crime we must eliminate the laws.

Choose the correct answer from below :

(*a*) (A) is true, (R) is doubtful and (R) is not the correct explanation of (A).

(*b*) (A) is false, (R) is true and (R) is the correct explanation of (A).

(*c*) (A) is doubtful, (R) is doubtful and (R) is not the correct explanation of (A).

(*d*) (A) is doubtful, (R) is true and (R) is not the correct explanation of (A).

13. If the proposition "All men are not mortal" is true then which of the following inferences is correct ? Choose from the code given below :

1. "All men are mortal" is true.
2. "Some men are mortal" is false.
3. "No men are mortal" is doubtful.
4. "All men are mortal" is false.

Code :

(*a*) 1, 2 and 3 (*b*) 2, 3 and 4

(*c*) 1, 3 and 4 (*d*) 1 and 3

14. Determine the nature of the following definition :

"Abortion" means the ruthless murdering of innocent beings.

(*a*) Lexical (*b*) Persuasive

(*c*) Stipulative (*d*) Theoretical

15. Which one of the following is not an argument ?

(*a*) Devadutt does not eat in the day so he must be eating at night.

(*b*) If Devadutt is growing fat and if he does not eat during the day, he will be eating at night.

(*c*) Devadutt eats in the night so he does not eat during the day.

(*d*) Since Devadutt does not eat in the day, he must be eating in the night.

16. Venn diagram is a kind of diagram to

(*a*) represent and assess the validity of elementary inferences of syllogistic form.

(*b*) represent but not assess the validity of elementary inferences of syllogistic form.

(*c*) represent and assess the truth of elementary inferences of syllogistic form.

(*d*) assess but not represent the truth of elementary inferences of syllogistic form.

17. Reasoning by analogy leads to

(*a*) certainty

(*b*) definite conclusion

(*c*) predictive conjecture

(*d*) surety

18. Which of the following statements are false ? Choose from the code given below :

1. Inductive arguments always proceed from the particular to the general.
2. A cogent argument must be inductively strong.
3. A valid argument may have a false premise and a false conclusion.
4. An argument may legitimately be spoken of as 'true' or 'false'.

Code :

(*a*) 2, 3 and 4 (*b*) 1 and 3

(*c*) 2 and 4 (*d*) 1 and 2

19. Six persons A, B, C, D, E and F are standing in a circle. B is between F and C, A is between E and D, F is to the left of D. Who is between A and F ?

(*a*) B (*b*) C

(*c*) D (*d*) E

20. The price of petrol increases by 25%. By what percentage must a customer reduce the consumption so that the earlier bill on the petrol does not alter ?

(*a*) 20% (*b*) 25%

(*c*) 30% (*d*) 33.33%

21. If Ram knows that y is an integer greater than 2 and less than 7 and Hari knows that y is an integer greater than 5 and less than 10, then they may correctly conclude that

(*a*) y can be exactly determined

(*b*) y may be either of two values

(*c*) y may be any of three values

(*d*) there is no value of y satisfying these conditions

22. Four pipes can fill a reservoir in 15, 20, 30 and 60 hours respectively. The first one was opened at 6 AM, second at 7 AM, third at 8 AM and the fourth at 9 AM. When will the reservoir be filled ?

(*a*) 11 AM (*b*) 12 Noon

(*c*) 1 PM (*d*) 1 : 30 PM

The total electricity generation in a country is 97 GW. The contribution of various energy sources is indicated in percentage terms in the Pie Chart given below ;

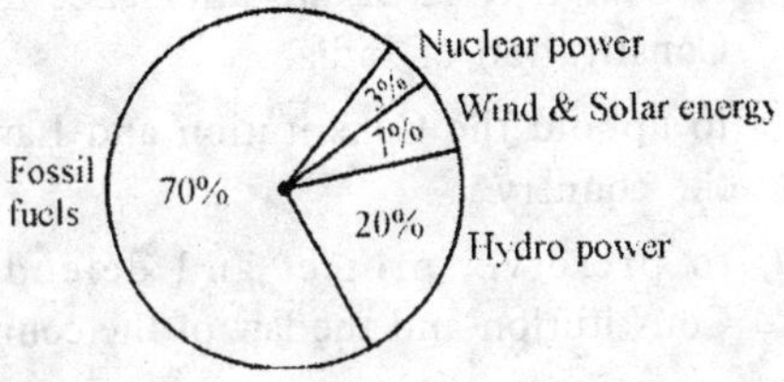

23. What is the contribution of wind and solar power in absolute terms in the electricity generation ?

(*a*) 6.79 GW (*b*) 19.4 GW

(*c*) 9.7 GW (*d*) 29.1 GW

24. What is the contribution of renewable energy sources in absolute terms in the electricity generation ?

(*a*) 29.1 GW (*b*) 26.19 GW

(*c*) 67.9 GW (*d*) 97 GW

25. TCP/IP is necessary if one is to connect to the

(*a*) Phone lines (*b*) LAN

(*c*) Internet (*d*) a Server

26. Each character on the keyboard of computer has an ASCII value which stands for

(*a*) American Stock Code for Information Interchange

(*b*) American Standard Code for Information Interchange

(*c*) African Standard Code for Information Interchange

(*d*) Adaptable Standard Code for Information Change

27. Which of the following is not a programming language ?

(*a*) Pascal (*b*) Microsoft Office

(*c*) Java (*d*) C++

28. Minimum number of bits required to store any 3 digit decimal number is equal to

(*a*) 3 (*b*) 5

(*c*) 8 (*d*) 10

29. Internet explorer is a type of

(*a*) Operating System

(*b*) Compiler

(*c*) Browser

(*d*) IP address

30. POP3 and IMAP are e-mail accounts in which

(*a*) One automatically gets one's mail everyday

(*b*) One has to be connected to the server to read or write one's mail

(*c*) One only has to be connected to the server to send and receive email

(*d*) One does not need any telephone lines

31. Irritation in eyes is caused by the pollutant

(*a*) Sulphur di-oxide (*b*) Ozone

(*c*) PAN (*d*) Nitrous oxide

32. Which is the source of chlorofluorocarbons ?

(*a*) Thermal power plants

(*b*) Automobiles

(*c*) Refrigeration and Airconditioning

(*d*) Fertilizers

33. Which of the following is not a renewable natural resource ?

(*a*) Clean air (*b*) Fertile soil

(*c*) Fresh water (*d*) Salt

34. Which of the following parameters is not used as a pollution indicator in water ?

(*a*) Total dissolved solids

(*b*) Coliform count

(*c*) Dissolved oxygen

(*d*) Density

35. S and P waves are associated with

(*a*) floods (*b*) wind energy

(*c*) earthquakes (*d*) tidal energy

36. Match Lists I and II and select the correct answer from the codes given below :

List – I	List – II
(*i*) Ozone hole	A. Tsunami
(*ii*) Greenhouse effect	B. UV radiations
(*iii*) Natural hazards	C. Methane
(*iv*) Sustainable development	D. Eco-centrism

Codes :

	(i)	(ii)	(iii)	(iv)
(a)	B	C	A	D
(b)	C	B	A	D
(c)	D	C	A	B
(d)	D	B	C	A

37. Indian Institute of Advanced Study is located at

(a) Dharmshala (b) Shimla

(c) Solan (d) Chandigarh

38. Indicate the number of Regional Offices of National Council of Teacher Education.

(a) 04 (b) 05

(c) 06 (d) 08

39. Which of the following rights was considered the "Heart and Soul" of the Indian Constitution by Dr. B.R. Ambedkar ?

(a) Freedom of Speech

(b) Right to Equality

(c) Right to Freedom of Religion

(d) Right to Constitutional Remedies

40. Who among the following created the office of the District Collector in India ?

(a) Lord Cornwallis

(b) Warren Hastings

(c) The Royal Commission on Decentralisation

(d) Sir Charles Metcalfe

41. The Fundamental Duties of a citizen include

1. Respect for the Constitution, the National Flag and the National Anthem
2. To develop the scientific temper.
3. Respect for the Government.
4. To protect Wildlife.

Choose the correct answer from the codes given below :

Codes :

(a) 1, 2 and 3

(b) 1, 2 and 4

(c) 2, 3 and 4

(d) 1, 3, 4 and 2

42. The President of India takes oath

(a) to uphold the sovereignty and integrity of India.

(b) to bear true faith and allegiance to the Constitution of India.

(c) to uphold the Constitution and Laws of the country.

(d) to preserve, protect and defend the Constitution and the law of the country.

43. If you get an opportunity to teach a visually challenged student along with normal students, what type of treatment would you like to give him in the class ?

(a) Not giving extra attention because majority may suffer.

(b) Take care of him sympathetically in the class- room.

(c) You will think that blindness is his destiny and hence you cannot do anything.

(d) Arrange a seat in the front row and try to teach at a pace convenient to him.

44. Which of the following is not a characteristic of a good achievement test ?

(a) Reliability

(b) Objectivity

(c) Ambiguity

(d) Validity

45. Which of the following does not belong to a projected aid ?

(a) Overhead projector

(b) Blackboard

(c) Epidiascope

(d) Slide projector

46. For a teacher, which of the following methods would be correct for writing on the blackboard?

(a) Writing fast and as clearly as possible.

(b) Writing the matter first and then asking students to read it.

(c) Asking a question to students and then writing the answer as stated by them.

(d) Writing the important points as clearly as possible.

47. A teacher can be successful if he/she

(*a*) helps students in becoming better citizens

(*b*) imparts subject knowledge to students

(*c*) prepares students to pass the examination

(*d*) presents the subject matter in a well organized manner

48. Dynamic approach to teaching means

(*a*) Teaching should be forceful and effective

(*b*) Teachers should be energetic and dynamic

(*c*) The topics of teaching should not be static, but dynamic

(*d*) The students should be required to learn through activities

49. The research that aims at immediate application is

(*a*) Action Research

(*b*) Empirical Research

(*c*) Conceptual Research

(*d*) Fundamental Research

50. When two or more successive footnotes refer to the same work which one of the following expressions is used ?

(*a*) ibid (*b*) et.al

(*c*) op.cit : (*d*) loc.cit.

51. Nine year olds are taller than seven year olds. This is an example of a reference drawn from

(*a*) Vertical study

(*b*) Cross-sectional study

(*c*) Time series study

(*d*) Experimental study

52. Conferences are meant for

(*a*) Multiple target groups

(*b*) Group discussions

(*c*) Show-casing new Research

(*d*) All the above

53. Ex Post Facto research means

(*a*) The research is carried out after the incident

(*b*) The research is carried out prior to the incident

(*c*) The research is carried out along with the happening of an incident.

(*d*) The research is carried out keeping in mind the possibilities of an incident.

54. Research ethics do not include

(*a*) Honesty (*b*) Subjectivity

(*c*) Integrity (*d*) Objectivity

Read the following passage carefully and answer the questions 55 to 60 :

James Madison said, "A people who mean to be their own governors must arm themselves with power that knowledge gives." In India, the Official Secrets Act, 1923 was a convenient smokescreen to deny members of the public access to information. Public functioning has traditionally been shrouded in secrecy. But in a democracy in which people govern themselves, it is necessary to have more openness. In the maturing of our democracy, right to information is a major step forward; it enables citizens to participate fully in the decision-making process that affects their lives so profoundly. It is in this context that the address of the Prime Minister in the Lok Sabha is significant. He said, "I would only like to see that everyone, particularly our civil servants, should see the Bill in a positive spirit; not as a draconian law for paralyzing Government, but as an instrument for improving Government-Citizen interface resulting in a friendly, caring and effective Government functioning for the good of our People." He further said, "This is an innovative Bill, where there will be scope to review its functioning as we gain experience. Therefore, this is a piece of legislation, whose working will be kept under constant reviews."

The Commission, in its Report, has dealt with the application of the Right to Information in Executive, Legislature and Judiciary. The judiciary could be a pioneer in implementing the Act in letter and spirit because much of the work that the Judiciary does is open to public scrutiny, Government of India has sanctioned an e-governance project in the Judiciary for about ₹ 700 crores which would bring about systematic classification, standardization and categorization of records. This would help the judiciary to fulfil its mandate under the Act. Similar capacity building would be required in all other public authorities. The transformation from nontransparency to transparency and public accountability is the responsibility of all three organs of State.

55. A person gets power
(*a*) by acquiring knowledge
(*b*) from the Official Secrets Act, 1923
(*c*) through openings
(*d*) by denying public information

56. Right to Information is a major step forward to
(*a*) enable citizens to participate fully in the decision making process
(*b*) to make the people aware of the Act
(*c*) to gain knowledge of administration
(*d*) to make the people Government friendly

57. The Prime Minister considered the Bill
(*a*) to provide power to the civil servants
(*b*) as an instrument for improving Government-citizen interface resulting in a friendly, caring and effective Government
(*c*) a draconian law against the officials
(*d*) to check the harassment of the people

58. The Commission made the Bill effective by
(*a*) extending power to the executive authorities
(*b*) combining the executive and legislative power
(*c*) recognizing Judiciary a pioneer in implementing the act in letter and spirit
(*d*) educating the people before its implementation

59. The Prime Minister considered the Bill innovative and hoped that
(*a*) It could be reviewed based on the experience gained on its functioning.
(*b*) The civil servants would see the Bill in a positive spirit.
(*c*) It would not be considered as a draconian law for paralyzing Government
(*d*) All the above

60. The transparency and public accountability is the responsibility of three organs of the State. These three organs are
(*a*) Lok Sabha, Rajya Sabha and Judiciary
(*b*) Lok Sabha, Rajya Sabha and Executive
(*c*) Judiciary, Legislature and the Commission
(*d*) Legislature, Executive and Judiciary

ANSWERS

1. (*c*)	**2.** (*b*)	**3.** (*b*)	**4.** (*b*)	**5.** (*d*)	**6.** (*d*)	**7.** (*c*)	**8.** (*b*)	**9.** (*a*)	**10.** (*c*)
11. (*d*)	**12.** (*a*)	**13.** (*b*)	**14.** (*b*)	**15.** (*b*)	**16.** (*a*)	**17.** (*c*)	**18.** (*c*)	**19.** (*c*)	**20.** (*a*)
21. (*a*)	**22.** (*c*)	**23.** (*a*)	**24.** (*b*)	**25.** (*c*)	**26.** (*b*)	**27.** (*b*)	**28.** (*d*)	**29.** (*c*)	**30.** (*c*)
31. (*c*)	**32.** (*c*)	**33.** (*d*)	**34.** (*d*)	**35.** (*c*)	**36.** (*a*)	**37.** (*b*)	**38.** (*a*)	**39.** (*d*)	**40.** (*b*)
41. (*b*)	**42.** (*d*)	**43.** (*d*)	**44.** (*c*)	**45.** (*b*)	**46.** (*d*)	**47.** (*d*)	**48.** (*d*)	**49.** (*a*)	**50.** (*a*)
51. (*b*)	**52.** (*d*)	**53.** (*a*)	**54.** (*b*)	**55.** (*a*)	**56.** (*a*)	**57.** (*b*)	**58.** (*c*)	**59.** (*d*)	**60.** (*d*)

Solved Paper 2011 (December)

UGC NET

PAPER-I

Note : • This paper contains **Sixty (60)** multiple choice questions, each question carrying **two** (2) marks.

• Candidate is expected to answer any **Fifty (50)** questions.

• In case more than **Fifty (50)** questions are attempted, only the first **Fifty (50)** questions will be evaluated.

1. Photo bleeding means

(*a*) Photo cropping

(*b*) Photo placement

(*c*) Photo cutting

(*d*) Photo colour adjustment

2. While designing communication strategy feed-forward studies are conducted by

(*a*) Audience (*b*) Communicator

(*c*) Satellite (*d*) Media

3. In which language the newspapers have highest circulation ?

(*a*) English (*b*) Hindi

(*c*) Bengali (*d*) Tamil

4. Aspect ratio of TV Screen is

(*a*) 4 : 3 (*b*) 3 : 4

(*c*) 2 : 3 (*d*) 2 : 4

5. Communication with oneself is known as

(*a*) Organisational Communication

(*b*) Grapewine Communication

(*c*) Interpersonal Communication

(*d*) Intrapersonal Communication

6. The term 'SITE' stands for

(*a*) Satellite Indian Television Experiment

(*b*) Satellite International Television Experiment

(*c*) Satellite Instructional Television Experiment

(*d*) Satellite Instructional Teachers Education

7. What is the number that comes next in the sequence ?

2, 5, 9, 19, 37, _____

(*a*) 76 (*b*) 74

(*c*) 75 (*d*) 50

8. Find the next letter for the series MPSV.....

(*a*) X (*b*) Y

(*c*) Z (*d*) A

9. If '367' means 'I am happy'; '748' means 'you are sad' and '469' means 'happy and sad' in a given code, then which of the following represents 'and' in that code ?

(*a*) 3 (*b*) 6

(*c*) 9 (*d*) 4

10. The basis of the following classification is 'animal', 'man', 'house', 'book', and 'student' :

(*a*) Definite descriptions

(*b*) Proper names

(*c*) Descriptive phrases

(*d*) Common names

11. Assertion (A) : The coin when flipped next time will come up tails.

Reason (R) : Because the coin was flipped five times in a row, and each time it came up heads.

Choose the correct answer from below :

(*a*) Both (A) and (R) are true, and (R) is the correct explanation of (A).

(*b*) Both (A) and (R) are false, and (R) is the correct explanation of (A).

(*c*) (A) is doubtful, (R) is true, and (R) is not the correct explanation of (A).

(*d*) (A) is doubtful, (R) is false, and (R) is the correct explanation of (A).

12. The relation 'is a sister of' is

(*a*) non-symmetrical (*b*) symmetrical

(*c*) asymmetrical (*d*) transitive

13. If the proposition "Vegetarians are not meat eaters" is false, then which of the following inferences is correct ? Choose from the codes given below :

1. "Some vegetarians are meateaters" is true.
2. "All vegetarians are meat eaters" is doubtful.
3. "Some vegetarians are not meat eaters" is true.
4. "Some vegetarians are not meat eaters" is doubtful.

Codes :

(*a*) 1, 2 and 3 (*b*) 2, 3 and 4

(*c*) 1, 3 and 4 (*d*) 1, 2 and 4

14. Determine the nature of the following definition :

'Poor' means having an annual income of ₹ 10,000.

(*a*) persuasive (*b*) precising

(*c*) lexical (*d*) stipulative

15. Which one of the following is not an argument?

(*a*) If today is Tuesday, tomorrow will be Wednesday.

(*b*) Since today is Tuesday, tomorrow will be Wednesday.

(*c*) Ram insulted me so I punched him in the nose.

(*d*) Ram is not at home, so he must have gone to town.

16. Venn diagram is a kind of diagram to

(*a*) represent and assess the truth of elementary inferences with the help of Boolean Algebra of classes.

(*b*) represent and assess the validity of elementary inferences with the help of Boolean Algebra of classes.

(*c*) represent but not assess the validity of elementary inferences with the help of Boolean Algebra of classes.

(*d*) assess but not represent the validity of elementary inferences with the help of Boolean Algebra of classes.

17. Inductive logic studies the way in which a premise may

(*a*) support and entail a conclusion

(*b*) not support but entail a conclusion

(*c*) neither support nor entail a conclusion

(*d*) support a conclusion without entailing it

18. Which of the following statements are true ? Choose from the codes given below.

1. Some arguments, while not completely valid, are almost valid.
2. A sound argument may be invalid.
3. A cogent argument may have a probably false conclusion.
4. A statement may be true or false.

Codes :

(*a*) 1 and 2 (*b*) 1, 3 and 4

(*c*) 4 alone (*d*) 3 and 4

19. If the side of the square increases by 40%, then the area of the square increases by

(*a*) 60 % (*b*) 40 %

(*c*) 196 % (*d*) 96 %

20. There are 10 lamps in a hall. Each one of them can be switched on independently. The number of ways in which hall can be illuminated is

(*a*) 10^2 (*b*) 1023

(*c*) 2^{10} (*d*) 10 !

21. How many numbers between 100 and 300 begin or end with 2 ?

(*a*) 100 (*b*) 110

(*c*) 120 (*d*) 180

22. In a college having 300 students, every student reads 5 newspapers and every newspaper is read by 60 students. The number of newspapers required is

(*a*) at least 30 (*b*) at most 20

(*c*) exactly 25 (*d*) exactly 5

The total CO_2 emissions from various sectors are 5 mmt. In the Pie Chart given below, the percentage contribution to CO_2 emissions from various sectors is indicated.

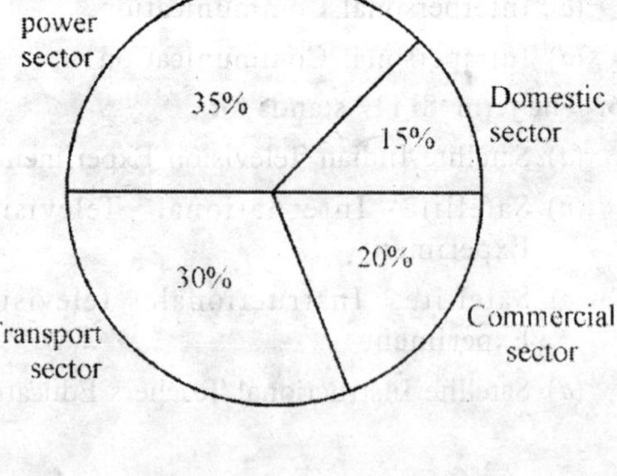

23. What is the absolute CO_2 emission from domestic sector ?

(a) 1.5 mmt (b) 2.5 mmt

(c) 1.75 mmt (d) 0.75 mmt

24. What is the absolute CO_2 emission for combined thermal power and transport sectors ?

(a) 3.25 mmt (b) 1.5 mmt

(c) 2.5 mmt (d) 4 mmt

23. Which of the following is not a measure of central tendency ?

(a) Mean (b) Median

(c) Mode (d) Range

24. In a normally distributed data set, what percentage of data points lie between mean ± standard deviation ?

(a) ~ 67 % (b) ~ 50%

(c) ~ 97 % (d) ~ 37%

25. Which of the following operating system is used on mobile phones ?

(a) Windows Vista (b) Android

(c) Windows XP (d) All of the above

26. If $(y)_x$ represents a number y in base x, then which of the following numbers is smallest of all ?

(a) $(1111)_2$ (b) $(1111)_8$

(c) $(1111)_{10}$ (d) $(1111)_{16}$

27. High level programming language can be converted to machine language using which of the following ?

(a) Oracle (b) Compiler

(c) Mat lab (d) Assembler

28. HTML is used to create

(a) machine language program

(b) high level program

(c) web page

(d) web server

29. The term DNS stands for

(a) Domain Name System

(b) Defense Nuclear System

(c) Downloadable New Software

(d) Dependent Name Server

30. IPv4 and IPv6 are addresses used to identify computers on the internet.

Find the correct statement out of the following:

(a) Number of bits required for IPv4 address is more than number of bits required for IPv6 address.

(b) Number of bits required for IPv4 address is same as number of bits required for IPv6 address.

(c) Number of bits required for IPv4 address is less than number of bits required for IPv6 address.

(d) Number of bits required for IPv4 address is 64.

31. Which of the following pollutants affects the respiratory tract in humans ?

(a) Carbon monoxide

(b) Nitric oxide

(c) Sulphur di-oxide

(d) Aerosols

32. Which of the following pollutants is not emitted from the transport sector ?

(a) Oxides of nitrogen

(b) Chlorofluorocarbons

(c) Carbon monoxide

(d) Poly aromatic hydrocarbons

33. Which of the following sources of energy has the maximum potential in India ?

(a) Solar energy

(b) Wind energy

(c) Ocean thermal energy

(d) Tidal energy

34. Which of the following is not a source of pollution in soil ?

(a) Transport sector

(b) Agriculture sector

(c) Thermal power plants

(d) Hydropower plants

35. Which of the following is not a natural hazard ?

(a) Earthquake (b) Tsunami

(c) Flash floods (d) Nuclear accident

36. Ecological footprint represents

(*a*) area of productive land and water to meet the resources requirement

(*b*) energy consumption

(*c*) CO_2 emissions per person

(*d*) forest cover

37. The aim of value education to inculcate in students is

(*a*) the moral values

(*b*) the social values

(*c*) the political values

(*d*) the economic values

38. Indicate the number of Regional Offices of University Grants Commission of India.

(*a*) 10 (*b*) 07

(*c*) 08 (*d*) 09

39. One-rupee currency note in India bears the signature of

(*a*) The President of India

(*b*) Finance Minister of India

(*c*) Governor, Reserve Bank of India

(*d*) Finance Secretary of Government of India

40. Match the List – I with the List – II and select the correct answer from the codes given below :

List–I (Commissions and Committees)

A. First Administrative Reforms Commission

B. Paul H. Appleby Committee I

C. K. Santhanam Committee

D. Second Administrative Reforms Commission

List – II (Year)

(*i*) 2005

(*ii*) 1962

(*iii*) 1966

(*iv*) 1953

Codes :

	A	B	C	D
(*a*)	(*i*)	(*iii*)	(*ii*)	(*iv*)
(*b*)	(*iii*)	(*iv*)	(*ii*)	(*i*)
(*c*)	(*iv*)	(*ii*)	(*iii*)	(*i*)
(*d*)	(*ii*)	(*i*)	(*iv*)	(*iii*)

41. Constitutionally the registration and recognition of political parties is the function performed by

(*a*) The State Election Commission of respective States

(*b*) The Law Ministry of Government of India

(*c*) The Election Commission of India

(*d*) Election Department of the State Governments

42. The members of Gram Sabha are

(*a*) Sarpanch, Upsarpanch and all elected Panchas

(*b*) Sarpanch, Upsarpanch and Village level worker

(*c*) Sarpanch, Gram Sevak and elected Panchas

(*d*) Registered voters of Village Panchayat

43. By which of the following methods the true evaluation of the students is possible?

(*a*) Evaluation at the end of the course.

(*b*) Evaluation twice in a year.

(*c*) Continuous evaluation.

(*d*) Formative evaluation.

44. Suppose a student wants to share his problems with his teacher and he visits the teacher's house for the purpose, the teacher should

(*a*) contact the student's parents and solve his problem.

(*b*) suggest him that he should never visit his house.

(*c*) suggest him to meet the principal and solve the problem.

(*d*) extend reasonable help and boost his morale.

45. When some students are deliberately attempting to disturb the discipline of the class by making mischief, what will be your role as a teacher ?

(*a*) Expelling those students.

(*b*) Isolate those students.

(*c*) Reform the group with your authority.

(*d*) Giving them an opportunity for introspection and improve their behaviour.

46. Which of the following belongs to a projected aid ?

(*a*) Blackboard (*b*) Diorama

(*c*) Epidiascope (*d*) Globe

47. A teacher is said to be fluent in asking questions, if he can ask
(*a*) meaningful questions
(*b*) as many questions as possible
(*c*) maximum number of questions in a fixed time
(*d*) many meaningful questions in a fixed time

48. Which of the following qualities is most essential for a teacher ?
(*a*) He should be a learned person.
(*b*) He should be a well dressed person.
(*c*) He should have patience.
(*d*) He should be an expert in his subject.

49. A hypothesis is a
(*a*) law (*b*) canon
(*c*) postulate (*d*) supposition

50. Suppose you want to investigate the working efficiency of nationalised bank in India, which one of the following would you follow ?
(*a*) Area Sampling
(*b*) Multi-stage Sampling
(*c*) Sequential Sampling
(*d*) Quota Sampling

51. Controlled group condition is applied in
(*a*) Survey Research
(*b*) Historical Research
(*c*) Experimental Research
(*d*) Descriptive Research

52. Workshops are meant for
(*a*) giving lectures
(*b*) multiple target groups
(*c*) showcase new theories
(*d*) hands on training/experience

53. Which one of the following is a research tool ?
(*a*) Graph (*b*) Illustration
(*c*) Questionnaire (*d*) Diagram

54. Research is not considered ethical if it
(*a*) tries to prove a particular point.
(*b*) does not ensure privacy and anonymity of the respondent.
(*c*) does not investigate the data scientifically.
(*d*) is not of a very high standard.

Read the following passage carefully and answer the questions (Qn. Nos. 55 to 60) :

The catalytic fact of the twentieth century is uncontrollable development, consumerist society, political materialism, and spiritual devaluation. This inordinate development has led to the transcendental 'second reality' of sacred perception that biologically transcendence is a part of human life. As the century closes, it dawns with imperative vigour that the 'first reality' of enlightened rationalism and the 'second reality' of the Beyond have to be harmonised in a worthy state of man. The *de facto* values describe what we are, they portray the 'is' of our ethic, they are *est* values (Latin *est* means is). The ideal values tell us what we ought to be, they are *esto* values (Latin *esto* 'ought to be'). Both have to be in the ebb and flow of consciousness. The ever new science and technology and the ever-perennial faith are two modes of one certainty, that is the wholeness of man, his courage to be, his share in Being.

The materialistic foundations of science have crumbled down. Science itself has proved that matter is energy, processes are as valid as facts, and affirmed the non-materiality of the universe. The encounter of the 'two cultures', the scientific and the humane, will restore the normal vision, and will be the bedrock of a 'science of understanding' in the new century. It will give new meaning to the ancient perception that quantity (measure) and quality (value) coexist at the root of nature. Human endeavours cannot afford to be humanistically irresponsible.

55. The problem raised in the passage reflects overall on
(*a*) Consumerism
(*b*) Materialism
(*c*) Spiritual devaluation
(*d*) Inordinate development

56. The '*de facto*' values in the passage means
(*a*) What is
(*b*) What ought to be
(*c*) What can be
(*d*) Where it is

57. According to the passage, the 'first reality' constitutes

(*a*) Economic prosperity

(*b*) Political development

(*c*) Sacred perception of life

(*d*) Enlightened rationalism

58. Encounter of the 'two cultures', the scientific and the human implies

(*a*) Restoration of normal vision

(*b*) Universe is both material and non-material

(*c*) Man is superior to nature

(*d*) Co-existence of quantity and quality in nature

59. The contents of the passage are

(*a*) Descriptive

(*b*) Prescriptive

(*c*) Axiomatic

(*d*) Optional

60. The passage indicates that science has proved that

(*a*) universe is material

(*b*) matter is energy

(*c*) nature has abundance

(*d*) humans are irresponsible

ANSWERS

1. (*d*)	**2.** (*b*)	**3.** (*b*)	**4.** (*a*)	**5.** (*d*)	**6.** (*c*)	**7.** (*c*)	**8.** (*b*)	**9.** (*c*)	**10.** (*d*)
11. (*d*)	**12.** (*b*)	**13.** (*a*)	**14.** (*d*)	**15.** (*d*)	**16.** (*b*)	**17.** (*d*)	**18.** (*c*)	**19.** (*d*)	**20.** (*d*)
21. (*b*)	**22.** (*d*)	**23.** (*d*)	**24.** (*a*)	**25.** (*d*)	**26.** (*c*)	**27.** (*b*)	**28.** (*c*)	**29.** (*a*)	**30.** (*c*)
31. (*a*)	**32.** (*b*)	**33.** (*a*)	**34.** (*a*)	**35.** (*d*)	**36.** (*a*)	**37.** (*a*)	**38.** (*b*)	**39.** (*d*)	**40.** (*b*)
41. (*c*)	**42.** (*d*)	**43.** (*c*)	**44.** (*d*)	**45.** (*d*)	**46.** (*c*)	**47.** (*d*)	**48.** (*d*)	**49.** (*d*)	**50.** (*b*)
51. (*c*)	**52.** (*d*)	**53.** (*c*)	**54.** (*c*)	**55.** (*d*)	**56.** (*a*)	**57.** (*d*)	**58.** (*a*)	**59.** (*a*)	**60.** (*b*)

Solved Paper 2011 (June)

UGC NET

PAPER-I

Note : • This paper contains **Sixty (60)** multiple choice questions, each question carrying **two (2)** marks.

• Candidate is expected to answer any **Fifty (50)** questions.

• In case more than **Fifty (50)** questions are attempted, only the first **Fifty (50)** questions will be evaluated.

1. A research paper is a brief report of research work based on

(*a*) Primary Data only

(*b*) Secondary Data only

(*c*) Both Primary and Secondary Data

(*d*) None of the above

2. Newton gave three basic laws of motion. This research is categorized as

(*a*) Descriptive Research

(*b*) Sample Survey

(*c*) Fundamental Research

(*d*) Applied Research

3. A group of experts in a specific area of knowledge assembled at a place and prepared a syllabus for a new course. The process may be termed as

(*a*) Seminar

(*b*) Workshop

(*c*) Conference

(*d*) Symposium

4. In the process of conducting research 'Formulation of Hypothesis" is followed by

(*a*) Statement of Objectives

(*b*) Analysis of Data

(*c*) Selection of Research Tools

(*d*) Collection of Data

Read the following passage carefully and answer questions 5 to 10 :

All historians are interpreters of text if they be private letters, Government records or parish birthlists or whatever. For most kinds of historians, these are only the necessary means to understanding something other than the texts themselves, such as a political action or a historical trend, whereas for the intellectual historian, a full understanding of his chosen texts is itself the aim of his enquiries. Of course, the intellectual history is particularly prone to draw on the focus of other disciplines that are habitually interpreting texts for purposes of their own, probing the reasoning that ostensibly connects premises and conclusions. Furthermore, the boundaries with adjacent subdisciplines are shifting and indistinct : the history of art and the history of science both claim a certain autonomy, partly just because they require specialised technical skills, but both can also be seen as part of a wider intellectual history, as is evident when one considers, for example, the common stock of knowledge about cosmological beliefs or moral ideals of a period.

Like all historians, the intellectual historian is a consumer rather than a producer of 'methods'. His distinctiveness lies in which aspect of the past he is trying to illuminate, not in having exclusive possession of either a corpus of evidence or a body of techniques. That being said, it does seem that the label 'intellectual history' attracts a disproportionate share of misunderstanding.

It is alleged that intellectual history is the history of something that never really mattered. The long dominance of the historical profession by political historians bred a kind of philistinism, an unspoken belief that power and its exercise was 'what mattered'. The prejudice was reinforced by the assertion that political action was never really the outcome of principles or ideas that were 'more flapdoodle'. The legacy of this precept is still discernible in the tendency to require ideas to have 'licensed' the political class before they can be deemed worthy of intellectual attention, as if there were some reasons why the history of art or science, of philosophy or literature, were somehow of interest and significance than the history of Parties or Parliaments. Perhaps in recent years the mirror-image of this philistinism has been more common in the claim that ideas of any one is of systematic expression or sophistication do not matter, as if they were only held by a minority.

Answer the following questions :

5. An intellectual historian aims to fully understand
   (*a*) the chosen texts of his own
   (*b*) political actions
   (*c*) historical trends
   (*d*) his enquiries

6. Intellectual historians do not claim exclusive possession of
   (*a*) conclusions
   (*b*) any corpus of evidence
   (*c*) distinctiveness
   (*d*) habitual interpretation

7. The misconceptions about intellectual history stem from
   (*a*) a body of techniques
   (*b*) the common stock of knowledge
   (*c*) the dominance of political historians
   (*d*) cosmological beliefs

8. What is philistinism ?
   (*a*) Reinforcement of prejudice
   (*b*) Fabrication of reasons
   (*c*) The hold of land-owning classes
   (*d*) Belief that power and its exercise matter

9. Knowledge of cosmological beliefs or moral ideas of a period can be drawn as part of
   (*a*) literary criticism
   (*b*) history of science
   (*c*) history of philosophy
   (*d*) intellectual history

10. The claim that ideas of any one is of systematic expression do not matter, as if they were held by a minority, is
   (*a*) to have a licensed political class
   (*b*) a political action
   (*c*) a philosophy of literature
   (*d*) the mirror-image of philistinism

11. Public communication tends to occur within a more
   (*a*) complex structure
   (*b*) political structure
   (*c*) convenient structure
   (*d*) formal structure

12. Transforming thoughts, ideas and messages into verbal and non-verbal signs is referred to as
   (*a*) channelisation (*b*) mediation
   (*c*) encoding (*d*) decoding

13. Effective communication needs a supportive
   (*a*) economic environment
   (*b*) political environment
   (*c*) social environment
   (*d*) multi-cultural environment

14. A major barrier in the transmission of cognitive data in the process of communication is an individual's
   (*a*) personality (*b*) expectation
   (*c*) social status (*d*) coding ability

15. When communicated, institutionalised stereotypes become
   (*a*) myths
   (*b*) reasons
   (*c*) experiences
   (*d*) convictions

16. In mass communication, selective perception is dependent on the receiver's
   (*a*) competence
   (*b*) pre-disposition
   (*c*) receptivity
   (*d*) ethnicity

17. Determine the relationship between the pair of words NUMERATOR : DENOMINATOR and then select the pair of words from the following which have a similar relationship :
(*a*) fraction : decimal
(*b*) divisor : quotient
(*c*) top : bottom
(*d*) dividend : divisor

18. Find the wrong number in the sequence
125, 127, 130, 135, 142, 153, 165
(*a*) 130 (*b*) 142
(*c*) 153 (*d*) 165

19. If HOBBY is coded as IOBY and LOBBY is coded as MOBY; then BOBBY is coded as
(*a*) BOBY (*b*) COBY
(*c*) DOBY (*d*) OOBY

20. The letters in the first set have certain relationship. On the basis of this relationship, make the right choice for the second set :
K/T : 11/20 :: J/R : ?
(*a*) 10/8 (*b*) 10/18
(*c*) 11/19 (*d*) 10/19

21. If A = 5, B = 6, C = 7, D = 8 and so on, what do the following numbers stand for?
17, 19, 20, 9, 8
(*a*) Plane (*b*) Moped
(*c*) Motor (*d*) Tonga

22. The price of oil is increased by 25%. If the expenditure is not allowed to increase, the ratio between the reduction in consumption and the original consumption is
(*a*) 1 : 3 (*b*) 1 : 4
(*c*) 1 : 5 (*d*) 1 : 6

23. How many 8's are there in the following sequence which are preceded by 5 but not immediately followed by 3 ?
5 8 3 7 5 8 6 3 8 5 4 5 8 4 7 6
5 5 8 3 5 8 7 5 8 2 8 5
(*a*) 4 (*b*) 5
(*c*) 7 (*d*) 3

24. If a rectangle were called a circle, a circle a point, a point a triangle and a triangle a square, the shape of a wheel is
(*a*) Rectangle
(*b*) Circle
(*c*) Point
(*d*) Triangle

25. Which one of the following methods is best suited for mapping the distribution of different crops as provided in the standard classification of crops in India ?
(*a*) Pie diagram
(*b*) Chorochromatic technique
(*c*) Isopleth technique
(*d*) Dot method

26. Which one of the following does not come under the methods of data classification?
(*a*) Qualitative (*b*) Normative
(*c*) Spatial (*d*) Quantitative

27. Which one of the following is not a source of data ?
(*a*) Administrative records
(*b*) Population census
(*c*) GIS
(*d*) Sample survey

28. If the statement 'some men are cruel' is false, which of the following statements/statement are/is true ?
(*i*) All men are cruel.
(*ii*) No men are cruel.
(*iii*) Some men are not cruel.
(*a*) (*i*) and (*iii*)
(*b*) (*i*) and (*ii*)
(*c*) (*ii*) and (*iii*)
(*d*) (*iii*) only

29. The octal number system consists of the following symbols :
(*a*) 0 – 7
(*b*) 0 – 9
(*c*) 0 – 9, A – F
(*d*) None of the above

30. The binary equivalent of $(-19)_{10}$ in signed magnitude system is

(*a*) 11101100

(*b*) 11101101

(*c*) 10010011

(*d*) None of these

31. DNS in internet technology stands for

(*a*) Dynamic Name System

(*b*) Domain Name System

(*c*) Distributed Name System

(*d*) None of these

32. HTML stands for

(*a*) Hyper Text Markup Language

(*b*) Hyper Text Manipulation Language

(*c*) Hyper Text Managing Links

(*d*) Hyper Text Manipulating Links

33. Which of the following is type of LAN ?

(*a*) Ethernet

(*b*) Token Ring

(*c*) FDDI

(*d*) All of the above

34. Which of the following statements is true?

(*a*) Smart cards do not require an operating system.

(*b*) Smart cards and PCs use some operating system.

(*c*) COS is smart card operating system.

(*d*) The communication between reader and card is in full duplex mode.

35. The Ganga Action Plan was initiated during the year

(*a*) 1986 (*b*) 1988

(*c*) 1990 (*d*) 1992

36. Identify the correct sequence of energy sources in order of their share in the power sector in India :

(*a*) Thermal > nuclear > hydro > wind

(*b*) Thermal > hydro > nuclear > wind

(*c*) Hydro > nuclear > thermal > wind

(*d*) Nuclear > hydro > wind > thermal

37. Chromium as a contaminant in drinking water in excess of permissible levels, causes

(*a*) Skeletal damage

(*b*) Gastrointestinal problem

(*c*) Dermal and nervous problems

(*d*) Liver/Kidney problems

38. The main precursors of winter smog are

(*a*) N_2O and hydrocarbons

(*b*) NO_X and hydrocarbons

(*c*) SO_2 and hydrocarbons

(*d*) SO_2 and ozone

39. Flash floods are caused when

(*a*) the atmosphere is convectively unstable and there is considerable vertical wind shear

(*b*) the atmosphere is stable

(*c*) the atmosphere is convectively unstable with no vertical windshear

(*d*) winds are catabatic

40. In mega cities of India, the dominant source of air pollution is

(*a*) transport sector

(*b*) thermal power

(*c*) municipal waste

(*d*) commercial sector

41. The first Open University in India was set up in the State of

(*a*) Andhra Pradesh

(*b*) Delhi

(*c*) Himachal Pradesh

(*d*) Tamil Nadu

42. Most of the Universities in India are funded by

(*a*) the Central Government

(*b*) the State Governments

(*c*) the University Grants Commission

(*d*) Private bodies and Individuals

43. Which of the following organizations looks after the quality of Technical and Management education in India ?

(*a*) NCTE (*b*) MCI

(*c*) AICTE (*d*) CSIR

44. Consider the following statements :

Identify the statement which implies natural justice.

(*a*) The principle of natural justice is followed by the Courts.

(*b*) Justice delayed is justice denied.

(*c*) Natural justice is an inalienable right of a citizen

(*d*) A reasonable opportunity of being heard must be given.

45. The President of India is

(*a*) the Head of State

(*b*) the Head of Government

(*c*) both Head of the State and the Head of the Government

(*d*) None of the above

46. Who among the following holds office during the pleasure of the President of India?

(*a*) Chief Election Commissioner

(*b*) Comptroller and Auditor General of India

(*c*) Chairman of the Union Public Service Commission

(*d*) Governor of a State

Questions 47 to 49 are based upon the following diagram in which there are three interlocking circles A, P and S where A stands for Artists, circle P for Professors and circle S for Sportspersons.

Different regions in the figure are lettered from a to f :

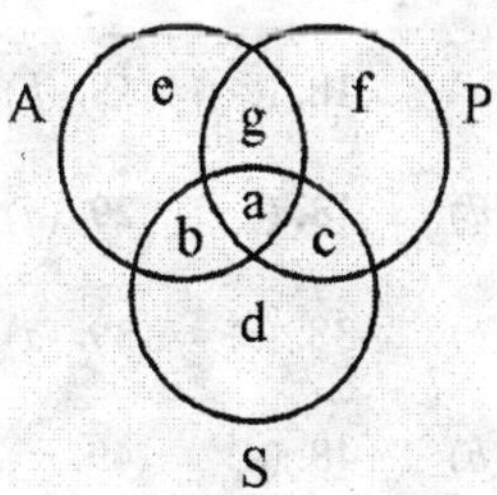

47. The region which represents artists who are neither sportsmen nor professors.

(*a*) d (*b*) e

(*c*) b (*d*) g

48. The region which represents professors, who are both artists and sportspersons.

(*a*) a (*b*) c

(*c*) d (*d*) g

49. The region which represents professors, who are also sportspersons, but not artists.

(*a*) e (*b*) f

(*c*) c (*d*) g

Questions 50 to 52 are based on the following data :

Measurements of some variable X were made at an interval of 1 minute from 10 A.M. to 10:20 A.M. The data, thus, obtained is as follows :

X : 60, 62, 65, 64, 63, 61, 66, 65, 70, 68
63, 62, 64, 69, 65, 64, 66, 67, 66, 64

50. The value of X, which is exceeded 10% of the time in the duration of measurement, is

(*a*) 69 (*b*) 68

(*c*) 67 (*d*) 66

51. The value of X, which is exceeded 90% of the time in the duration of measurement, is

(*a*) 63 (*b*) 62

(*c*) 61 (*d*) 60

52. The value of X, which is exceeded 50% of the time in the duration of measurement, is

(*a*) 66 (*b*) 65

(*c*) 64 (*d*) 63

53. For maintaining an effective discipline in the class, the teacher should

(*a*) Allow students to do what they like.

(*b*) Deal with the students strictly.

(*c*) Give the students some problem to solve.

(*d*) Deal with them politely and firmly.

54. An effective teaching aid is one which

(*a*) is colourful and good looking

(*b*) activates all faculties

(*c*) is visible to all students

(*d*) easy to prepare and use

55. Those teachers are popular among students who

(*a*) develop intimacy with them

(*b*) help them solve their problems

(*c*) award good grades

(*d*) take classes on extra tuition fee

56. The essence of an effective classroom environment is
(*a*) a variety of teaching aids
(*b*) lively student-teacher interaction
(*c*) pin-drop silence
(*d*) strict discipline

57. On the first day of his class, if a teacher is asked by the students to introduce himself, he should
(*a*) ask them to meet after the class
(*b*) tell them about himself in brief
(*c*) ignore the demand and start teaching
(*d*) scold the student for this unwanted demand

58. Moral values can be effectively inculcated among the students when the teacher
(*a*) frequently talks about values
(*b*) himself practices them
(*c*) tells stories of great persons
(*d*) talks of Gods and Goddesses

59. The essential qualities of a researcher are
(*a*) spirit of free enquiry
(*b*) reliance on observation and evidence
(*c*) systematization or theorizing of knowledge
(*d*) all the above

60. Research is conducted to
I. Generate new knowledge
II. Not to develop a theory
III. Obtain research degree
IV. Reinterpret existing knowledge
Which of the above are correct ?
(*a*) I, III & II
(*b*) III, II & IV
(*c*) II, I & III
(*d*) I, III & IV

ANSWERS

1. (*c*)	**2.** (*c*)	**3.** (*c*)	**4.** (*c*)	**5.** (*a*)	**6.** (*b*)	**7.** (*a*)	**8.** (*d*)	**9.** (*d*)	**10.** (*d*)
11. (*c*)	**12.** (*c*)	**13.** (*c*)	**14.** (*d*)	**15.** (*d*)	**16.** (*c*)	**17.** (*d*)	**18.** (*c*)	**19.** (*b*)	**20.** (*b*)
21. (*b*)	**22.** (*c*)	**23.** (*a*)	**24.** (*c*)	**25.** (*a*)	**26.** (*c*)	**27.** (*d*)	**28.** (*b*)	**29.** (*a*)	**30.** (*d*)
31. (*b*)	**32.** (*a*)	**33.** (*d*)	**34.** (*d*)	**35.** (*a*)	**36.** (*a*)	**37.** (*c*)	**38.** (*c*)	**39.** (*a*)	**40.** (*a*)
41. (*a*)	**42.** (*c*)	**43.** (*c*)	**44.** (*b*)	**45.** (*c*)	**46.** (*b*)	**47.** (*b*)	**48.** (*a*)	**49.** (*c*)	**50.** (*b*)
51. (*c*)	**52.** (*c*)	**53.** (*d*)	**54.** (*b*)	**55.** (*b*)	**56.** (*b*)	**57.** (*b*)	**58.** (*b*)	**59.** (*d*)	**60.** (*d*)

Solved Paper 2010 (December)

UGC NET

PAPER-I

Note : • This paper contains **Sixty (60)** multiple choice questions, each question carrying **two (2)** marks.

• Candidate is expected to answer any **Fifty (50)** questions.

• In case more than **Fifty (50)** questions are attempted, only the first **Fifty (50)** questions will be evaluated.

1. Which of the following variables cannot be expressed in quantitative terms ?
   (*a*) Socio-economic Status
   (*b*) Marital Status
   (*c*) Numerical Aptitude
   (*d*) Professional Attitude
2. A doctor studies the relative effectiveness of two drugs of dengue fever. His research would be classified as
   (*a*) Descriptive Survey
   (*b*) Experimental Research
   (*c*) Case Study
   (*d*) Ethnography
3. The term 'phenomenology' is associated with the process of
   (*a*) Qualitative Research
   (*b*) Analysis of Variance
   (*c*) Correlational Study
   (*d*) Probability Sampling
4. The 'Sociogram' technique is used to study
   (*a*) Vocational Interest
   (*b*) Professional Competence
   (*c*) Human Relations
   (*d*) Achievement Motivation

Read the following passage carefully and answer questions from 5 to 10 :

It should be remembered that the nationalist movement in India, like all nationalist movements, was essentially a bourgeois movement. It represented the natural historical stage of development, and to consider it or to criticise it as a working-class movement is wrong. Gandhi represented that movement and the Indian masses in relation to that movement to a supreme degree, and he became the voice of Indian people to that extent. The main contribution of Gandhi to India and the Indian masses has been through the powerful movements which he launched through the National Congress. Through nation-wide action he sought to mould the millions, and largely succeeded in doing so, and changing them from a demoralised, timid and hopeless mass, bullied and crushed by every dominant interest, and incapable of resistance, into a people with self-respect and self-reliance, resisting tyranny, and capable of united action and sacrifice for a larger cause.

Gandhi made people think of political and economic issues and every village and every bazaar hummed with argument and debate on the new ideas and hopes that filled the people. That was an amazing psychological change. The time was ripe for it, of course, and circumstances and world conditions worked for this change. But a great leader is necessary to take advantage of circumstances and conditions. Gandhi was that leader, and he released many of the bonds that imprisoned and disabled our minds, and none of us who experienced it can ever forget that great feeling of release and exhilaration that came over the Indian people.

Gandhi has played a revolutionary role in India of the greatest importance because he knew how to make the most of the objective conditions and could reach the heart of the masses, while groups with a more advanced ideology functioned largely in the air because they did not fit in with those conditions and could therefore not evoke any substantial response from the masses.

It is perfectly true that Gandhi, functioning in the nationalist plane, does not think in terms of the conflict of classes, and tries to compose their differences. But the action he has indulged and taught the people has inevitably raised mass consciousness tremendously and made social issues vital. Gandhi and the Congress must be judged by the policies they pursue and the action they indulge in. But behind this, personality counts and colours those policies and activities. In the case of very exceptional person like Gandhi the question of personality becomes especially important in order to understand and appraise him. To us he has represented the spirit and honour of India, the yearning of her sorrowing millions to be rid of their innumerable burdens, and an insult to him by the British Government or others has been an insult to India and her people.

5. Which one of the following is true of the given passage ?
   (*a*) The passage is a critique of Gandhi's role in Indian movement for independence.
   (*b*) The passage hails the role of Gandhi in India's freedom movement.
   (*c*) The author is neutral on Gandhi's role in India's freedom movement.
   (*d*) It is an account of Indian National Congress's support to the working-class movement.
6. The change that the Gandhian movement brought among the Indian masses was
   (*a*) Physical (*b*) Cultural
   (*c*) Technological (*d*) Psychological
7. To consider the nationalist movement or to criticise it as a working-class movement was wrong because it was a
   (*a*) historical movement
   (*b*) voice of the Indian people
   (*c*) bourgeois movement
   (*d*) movement represented by Gandhi
8. Gandhi played a revolutionary role in India because he could
   (*a*) preach morality
   (*b*) reach the heart of Indians
   (*c*) see the conflict of classes
   (*d*) lead the Indian National Congress
9. Groups with advanced ideology functioned in the air as they did not fit in with
   (*a*) objective conditions of masses
   (*b*) the Gandhian ideology
   (*c*) the class consciousness of the people
   (*d*) the differences among masses
10. The author concludes the passage by
   (*a*) criticising the Indian masses
   (*b*) the Gandhian movement
   (*c*) pointing out the importance of the personality of Gandhi
   (*d*) identifying the sorrows of millions of Indians
11. Media that exist in an interconnected series of communication – points are referred to as
   (*a*) Networked media
   (*b*) Connective media
   (*c*) Nodal media
   (*d*) Multimedia
12. The information function of mass communication is described as
   (*a*) diffusion (*b*) publicity
   (*c*) surveillance (*d*) diversion
13. An example of asynchronous medium is
   (*a*) Radio (*b*) Television
   (*c*) Film (*d*) Newspaper
14. In communication, connotative words are
   (*a*) explicit (*b*) abstract
   (*c*) simple (*d*) cultural
15. A message beneath a message is labelled as
   (*a*) embedded text
   (*b*) internal text
   (*c*) inter-text
   (*d*) sub-text
16. In analog mass communication, stories are
   (*a*) static
   (*b*) dynamic
   (*c*) interactive
   (*d*) exploratory

17. Determine the relationship between the pair of words ALWAYS : NEVER and then select from the following pair of words which have a similar relationship :

(*a*) often : rarely

(*b*) frequently : occasionally

(*c*) constantly : frequently

(*d*) intermittently : casually

18. Find the wrong number in the sequence : 52, 51, 48, 43, 34, 27, 16

(*a*) 27 (*b*) 34

(*c*) 43 (*d*) 48

19. In a certain code, PAN is written as 31 and PAR as 35, then PAT is written in the same code as

(*a*) 30 (*b*) 37

(*c*) 39 (*d*) 41

20. The letters in the first set have certain relationship. On the basis of this relationship, make the right choice for the second set :

AF : IK : : LQ : ?

(*a*) MO (*b*) NP

(*c*) OR (*d*) TV

21. If 5472 = 9, 6342 = 6, 7584 = 6, what is 9236 ?

(*a*) 2 (*b*) 3

(*c*) 4 (*d*) 5

22. In an examination, 35% of the total students failed in Hindi, 45% failed in English and 20% in both. The percentage of those who passed in both subjects is

(*a*) 10 (*b*) 20

(*c*) 30 (*d*) 40

23. Two statements I and II given below are followed by two conclusions (A) and (B). Supposing the statements are true, which of the following conclusions can logically follow?

Statements :

I. Some flowers are red.

II. Some flowers are blue.

Conclusions :

A. Some flowers are neither red nor blue.

B. Some flowers are both red and blue.

(*a*) Only (A) follows.

(*b*) Only (B) follows.

(*c*) Both (A) and (B) follow.

(*d*) Neither (A) nor (B) follows.

24. If the statement 'all students are intelligent' is true, which of the following statements are false ?

(*i*) No students are intelligent.

(*ii*) Some students are intelligent.

(*iii*) Some students are not intelligent.

(*a*) (*i*) and (*ii*) (*b*) (*i*) and (*iii*)

(*c*) (*ii*) and (*iii*) (*d*) (*i*) only

25. A reasoning where we start with certain particular statements and conclude with a universal statement is called

(*a*) Deductive Reasoning

(*b*) Inductive Reasoning

(*c*) Abnormal Reasoning

(*d*) Transcendental Reasoning

26. What is the smallest number of ducks that could swim in this formation – two ducks in front of a duck, two ducks behind a duck and a duck between two ducks ?

(*a*) 5 (*b*) 7

(*c*) 4 (*d*) 3

27. Mr. A, Miss B, Mr. C and Miss D are sitting around a table and discussing their trades.

(*i*) Mr. A sits opposite to the cook.

(*ii*) Miss B sits right to the barber

(*iii*) The washerman sits right to the barber

(*iv*) Miss D sits opposite to Mr. C

What are the trades of A and B ?

(*a*) Tailor and barber

(*b*) Barber and cook

(*c*) Tailor and cook

(*d*) Tailor and washerman

28. Which one of the following methods serve to measure correlation between two variables ?

(*a*) Scatter Diagram

(*b*) Frequency Distribution

(*c*) Two-way table

(*d*) Coefficient of Rank Correlation

29. Which one of the following is not an Internet Service Provider (ISP) ?

(*a*) MTNL (*b*) BSNL

(*c*) ERNET India (*d*) Infotech India Ltd.

30. The hexadecimal number system consists of the symbols

(*a*) 0 – 7 (*b*) 0 – 9 , A – F

(*c*) 0 – 7, A – F (*d*) None of these

31. The binary equivalent of $(-15)_{10}$ is (2's complement system is used)

(*a*) 11110001 (*b*) 11110000

(*c*) 10001111 (*d*) None of these

32. 1 GB is equal to

(*a*) 2^{30} bits (*b*) 2^{30} bytes

(*c*) 2^{20} bits (*d*) 2^{20} bytes

33. The set of computer programs that manage the hardware/software of a computer is called

(*a*) Compiler system

(*b*) Operation system

(*c*) Operating system

(*d*) None of these

34. S/MIME in Internet technology stands for

(*a*) Secure Multipurpose Internet Mail Extension

(*b*) Secure Multimedia Internet Mail Extension

(*c*) Simple Multipurpose Internet Mail Extension

(*d*) Simple Multimedia Internet Mail Extension

35. Which of the following is not covered in 8 missions under the Climate Action Plan of Government of India ?

(*a*) Solar power

(*b*) Waste to energy conversion

(*c*) Afforestation

(*d*) Nuclear energy

36. The concentration of Total Dissolved Solids (TDS) in drinking water should not exceed

(*a*) 500 mg/L (*b*) 400 mg/L

(*c*) 300 mg/L (*d*) 200 mg/L

37. 'Chipko' movement was first started by

(*a*) Arundhati Roy

(*b*) Medha Patkar

(*c*) Ila Bhatt

(*d*) Sunderlal Bahuguna

38. The constituents of photochemical smog responsible for eye irritation are

(*a*) SO_2 and O_3 (*b*) SO_2 and NO_2

(*c*) HCHO and PAN (*d*) SO_2 and SPM

39. **Assertion (A) :** Some carbonaceous aerosols may be carcinogenic.

Reason (R) : They may contain polycyclic aromatic hydrocarbons (PAHs).

(*a*) Both (A) and (R) are correct and (R) is the correct explanation of (A).

(*b*) Both (A) and (R) are correct but (R) is not the correct explanation of (A).

(*c*) (A) is correct, but (R) is false.

(*d*) (A) is false, but (R) is correct.

40. Volcanic eruptions affect

(*a*) atmosphere and hydrosphere

(*b*) hydrosphere and biosphere

(*c*) lithosphere, biosphere and atmosphere

(*d*) lithosphere, hydrosphere and atmosphere

41. India's first Defence University is in the State of

(*a*) Haryana (*b*) Andhra Pradesh

(*c*) Uttar Pradesh (*d*) Punjab

42. Most of the Universities in India

(*a*) conduct teaching and research only

(*b*) affiliate colleges and conduct examinations

(*c*) conduct teaching/research and examinations

(*d*) promote research only

43. Which one of the following is not a Constitutional Body ?

(*a*) Election Commission

(*b*) Finance Commission

(*c*) Union Public Service Commission

(*d*) Planning Commission

44. Which one of the following statements is not correct ?

(*a*) Indian Parliament is supreme.

(*b*) The Supreme Court of India has the power of judicial review.

(*c*) There is a division of powers between the Centre and the States.

(*d*) There is a Council of Ministers to aid and advise the President.

45. Which one of the following statements reflects the republic character of Indian democracy ?

(*a*) Written Constitution

(*b*) No State religion

(*c*) Devolution of power to local Government institutions

(*d*) Elected President and directly or indirectly elected Parliament

46. Who among the following appointed by the Governor can be removed by only the President of India ?

(*a*) Chief Minister of a State

(*b*) A member of the State Public Service Commission

(*c*) Advocate-General

(*d*) Vice-Chancellor of a State University

47. If two small circles represent the class of the 'men' and the class of the 'plants' and the big circle represents 'mortality', which one of the following figures represent the proposition 'All men are mortal.' ?

(*a*) 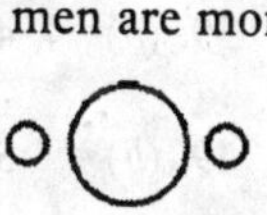

(*b*) 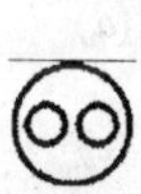

(*c*) 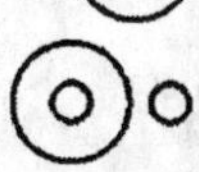

(*d*) 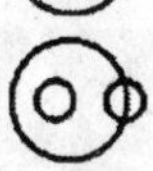

The following table presents the production of electronic items (TVs and LCDs) in a factory during the period from 2006 to 2010. Study the table carefully and answer the questions from 48 to 52 :

Year	2006	2007	2008	2009	2010
TVs	6000	9000	13000	11000	8000
LCDs	7000	9400	9000	10000	12000

48. In which year, the total production of electronic items is maximum ?

(*a*) 2006 (*b*) 2007

(*c*) 2008 (*d*) 2010

49. What is the difference between averages of production of LCDs and TVs from 2006 to 2008 ?

(*a*) 3000 (*b*) 2867

(*c*) 3015 (*d*) 2400

50. What is the year in which production of TVs is half the production of LCDs in the year 2010 ?

(*a*) 2007 (*b*) 2006

(*c*) 2009 (*d*) 2008

51. What is the ratio of production of LCDs in the years 2008 and 2010 ?

(*a*) 4 : 3 (*b*) 3 : 4

(*c*) 1 : 3 (*d*) 2 : 3

52. What is the ratio of production of TVs in the years 2006 and 2007 ?

(*a*) 6 : 7 (*b*) 7 : 6

(*c*) 2 : 3 (*d*) 3 : 2

53. Some students in a class exhibit great curiosity for learning. It may be because such children

(*a*) Are gifted

(*b*) Come from rich families

(*c*) Show artificial behaviour

(*d*) Create indiscipline in the class

54. The most important quality of a good teacher is

(*a*) Sound knowledge of subject matter

(*b*) Good communication skills

(*c*) Concern for students' welfare

(*d*) Effective leadership qualities

55. Which one of the following is appropriate in respect of teacher-student relationship?

(*a*) Very informal and intimate

(*b*) imited to classroom only

(*c*) Cordial and respectful

(*d*) Indifferent

56. The academic performance of students can be improved if parents are encouraged to

(*a*) supervise the work of their wards

(*b*) arrange for extra tuition

(*c*) remain unconcerned about it

(*d*) interact with teachers frequently

57. In a lively classroom situation, there is likely to be
(*a*) occasional roars of laughter
(*b*) complete silence
(*c*) frequent teacher-student dialogue
(*d*) loud discussion among students

58. If a parent approaches the teacher to do some favour to his/her ward in the examination, the teacher should
(*a*) try to help him
(*b*) ask him not to talk in those terms
(*c*) refuse politely and firmly
(*d*) ask him rudely to go away

59. Which of the following phrases is not relevant to describe the meaning of research as a process ?
(*a*) Systematic Activity
(*b*) Objective Observation
(*c*) Trial and Error
(*d*) Problem Solving

60. Which of the following is not an example of a continuous variable ?
(*a*) Family size (*b*) Intelligence
(*c*) Height (*d*) Attitude

ANSWERS

1. (*a*)	2. (*b*)	3. (*c*)	4. (*b*)	5. (*b*)	6. (*d*)	7. (*a*)	8. (*b*)	9. (*c*)	10. (*c*)
11. (*a*)	12. (*c*)	13. (*d*)	14. (*d*)	15. (*d*)	16. (*a*)	17. (*b*)	18. (*b*)	19. (*b*)	20. (*d*)
21. (*a*)	22. (*d*)	23. (*b*)	24. (*b*)	25. (*a*)	26. (*d*)	27. (*c*)	28. (*b*)	29. (*d*)	30. (*b*)
31. (*a*)	32. (*b*)	33. (*a*)	34. (*a*)	35. (*d*)	36. (*a*)	37. (*d*)	38. (*b*)	39. (*b*)	40. (*c*)
41. (*a*)	42. (*c*)	43. (*d*)	44. (*a*)	45. (*d*)	46. (*b*)	47. (*c*)	48. (*c*)	49. (*b*)	50. (*b*)
51. (*b*)	52. (*c*)	53. (*a*)	54. (*a*)	55. (*c*)	56. (*a*)	57. (*c*)	58. (*c*)	59. (*d*)	60. (*b*)

■■

Solved Paper 2010 (June)

UGC NET

PAPER-I

Note : • This paper contains **Sixty (60)** multiple choice questions, each question carrying **two (2)** marks.

• Candidate is expected to answer any **Fifty (50)** questions.

• In case more than **Fifty (50)** questions are attempted, only the first **Fifty (50)** questions will be evaluated.

1. Which one of the following is the most important quality of a good teacher ?

(*a*) Punctuality and sincerity

(*b*) Content mastery

(*c*) Content mastery and reactive

(*d*) Content mastery and sociable

2. The primary responsibility for the teacher's adjustment lies with

(*a*) The children

(*b*) The principal

(*c*) The teacher himself

(*d*) The community

3. As per the NCTE norms, what should be the staff strength for a unit of 100 students at B.Ed. level?

(*a*) 1 + 7 (*b*) 1 + 9

(*c*) 1 + 10 (*d*) 1 + 5

4. Research has shown that the most frequent symptom of nervous instability among teachers is

(*a*) Digestive upsets

(*b*) Explosive behaviour

(*c*) Fatigue

(*d*) Worry

5. Which one of the following statements is correct?

(*a*) Syllabus is an annexure to the curriculum.

(*b*) Curriculum is the same in all educational institutions.

(*c*) Curriculum includes both formal, and informal education.

(*d*) Curriculum does not include methods of evaluation.

6. A successful teacher is one who is

(*a*) Compassionate and disciplinarian

(*b*) Quite and reactive

(*c*) Tolerant and dominating

(*d*) Passive and active

Read the following passage carefully and answer the questions 7 to 12.

The phrase "What is it like ?" stands for a fundamental thought process. How does one go about observing and reporting on things and events that occupy segments of earth space ? Of all the infinite variety of phenomena on the face of the earth, how does one decide what phenomena to observe ? There is no such thing as a complete description of the earth or any part of it, for every microscopic point on the earth's surface differs from every other such point. Experience shows that the things observed are already familiar, because they are like phenomena that occur at home or because they resemble the abstract images and models developed in the human mind.

How are abstract images formed ? Humans alone among the animals possess language; their words symbolize not only specific things but also mental images of classes of things. People can remember what they have seen or experienced because they attach a word symbol to them.

During the long record of our efforts to gain more and more knowledge about the face of the earth as the human habitat, there has been a continuing interplay between things and events. The direct observation through the senses is described as a percept; the mental image is described as a concept. Percepts are what some people describe as reality, in contrast to mental images, which are theoretical, implying that they are not real.

The relation of Percept to Concept is not as simple as the definition implies. It is now quite clear that people of different cultures or even individuals in the same culture develop different mental images of reality and what they perceive is a reflection of these preconceptions. The direct observation of things and events on the face of the earth is so clearly a function of the mental images of the mind of the observer that the whole idea of reality must be reconsidered.

Concepts determine what the observer perceives, yet concepts are derived from the generalizations of previous percepts. What happens is that the educated observer is taught to accept a set of concepts and then sharpens or changes these concepts during a professional career. In any one field of scholarship, professional opinion at one time determines what concepts and procedures are acceptable, and these form a kind of model of scholarly behaviour.

7. The problem raised in the passage reflects on
   (*a*) thought process
   (*b*) human behaviour
   (*c*) cultural perceptions
   (*d*) professional opinion

8. According to the passage, human beings have mostly in mind
   (*a*) Observation of things
   (*b*) Preparation of mental images
   (*c*) Expression through language
   (*d*) To gain knowledge

9. Concept means
   (*a*) A mental image
   (*b*) A reality
   (*c*) An idea expressed in language form
   (*d*) All the above

10. The relation of Percept to Concept is
    (*a*) Positive (*b*) Negative
    (*c*) Reflective (*d*) Absolute

11. In the passage, the earth is taken as
    (*a*) The Globe
    (*b*) The Human Habitat
    (*c*) A Celestial Body
    (*d*) A Planet

12. Percept means
    (*a*) Direct observation through the senses
    (*b*) A conceived idea
    (*c*) Ends of a spectrum
    (*d*) An abstract image

13. Action research means
    (*a*) A longitudinal research
    (*b*) An applied research
    (*c*) A research initiated to solve an immediate problem
    (*d*) A research with socioeconomic objective

14. Research is
    (*a*) Searching again and again
    (*b*) Finding solution to any problem
    (*c*) Working in a scientific way to search for truth of any problem
    (*d*) None of the above

15. A common test in research demands much priority on
    (*a*) Reliability (*b*) Useability
    (*c*) Objectivity (*d*) All of the above

16. Which of the following is the first step in starting the research process ?
    (*a*) Searching sources of information to locate problem.
    (*b*) Survey of related literature
    (*c*) Identification of problem
    (*d*) Searching for solutions to the problem

17. If a researcher conducts a research on finding out which administrative style contributes more to institutional effectiveness ? This will be an example of
    (*a*) Basic Research (*b*) Action Research
    (*c*) Applied Research (*d*) None of the above

18. Normal Probability Curve should be
    (*a*) Positively skewed
    (*b*) Negatively skewed
    (*c*) Leptokurtic skewed
    (*d*) Zero skewed

19. In communication, a major barrier to reception of messages is
    (*a*) audience attitude
    (*b*) audience knowledge
    (*c*) audience education
    (*d*) audience income

20. Post-modernism is associated with
    (*a*) newspapers (*b*) magazines
    (*c*) radio (*d*) television

21. Didactic communication is

(*a*) intra-personal

(*b*) inter-personal

(*c*) organisational

(*d*) relational

22. In communication, the language is

(*a*) the non-verbal code

(*b*) the verbal code

(*c*) the symbolic code

(*d*) the iconic code

23. Identify the correct sequence of the following:

(*a*) Source, channel, message, receiver

(*b*) Source, receiver, channel, message

(*c*) Source, message, receiver, channel

(*d*) Source, message, channel, receiver

24. **Assertion (A) :** Mass media promote a culture of violence in the society.

Reason (R) : Because violence sells in the market as people themselves are violent in character.

(*a*) Both (A) and (R) are true and (R) is the correct explanation of (A).

(*b*) Both (A) and (R) are true, but (R) is not the correct explanation of (A).

(*c*) (A) is true, but (R) is false.

(*d*) Both (A) and (R) are false.

25. When an error of 1% is made in the length of a square, the percentage error in the area of a square will be

(*a*) 0 (*b*) 1/2

(*c*) 1 (*d*) 2

26. On January 12, 1980, it was a Saturday. The day of the week on January 12, 1979 was

(*a*) Thursday (*b*) Friday

(*c*) Saturday (*d*) Sunday

27. If water is called food, food is called tree, tree is called earth, earth is called world, which of the following grows a fruit ?

(*a*) Water (*b*) Tree

(*c*) World (*d*) Earth

28. E is the son of A, D is the son of B, E is married to C, C is the daughter of B. How is D related to E ?

(*a*) Brother (*b*) Uncle

(*c*) Father-in-law (*d*) Brother-in-law

29. If INSURANCE is coded as ECNARUSNI, how HINDRANCE will be coded ?

(*a*) CADNIHWCE (*b*) HANODEINR

(*c*) AENIRHDCN (*d*) ECNARDNIH

30. Find the next number in the following series:

2, 5, 10, 17, 26, 37, 50, ?

(*a*) 63 (*b*) 65

(*c*) 67 (*d*) 69

31. Which of the following is an example of circular argument ?

(*a*) God created man in his image and man created God in his own image.

(*b*) God is the source of a scripture and the scripture is the source of our knowledge of God.

(*c*) Some of the Indians are great because India is great.

(*d*) Rama is great because he is Rama.

32. Lakshmana is a morally good person because

(*a*) he is religious (*b*) he is educated

(*c*) he is rich (*d*) he is rational

33. Two statements I and II given below are followed by two conclusions (A) and (B). Supposing the statements are true, which of the following conclusions can logically follow?

I. Some religious people are morally good.

II. Some religious people are rational.

Conclusions :

A. Rationally religious people are good morally.

B. Non-rational religious persons are not morally good.

(*a*) Only (A) follows.

(*b*) Only (B) follows.

(*c*) Both (A) and (B) follow.

(*d*) Neither (A) nor (B) follows.

34. Certainty is

(*a*) an objective fact

(*b*) emotionally satisfying

(*c*) logical

(*d*) ontological

Questions from 35 to 36 : are based on the following diagram in which there are three intersecting circles I, S and P where circle I stands for Indians, circle S stands for scientists and circle P for politicians. Different regions of the figure are lettered from a to g.

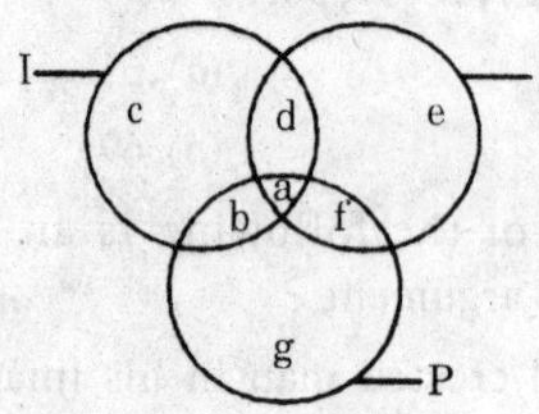

35. The region which represents non- Indian scientists who are politicians.

(*a*) f (*b*) d

(*c*) a (*d*) c

36. The region which represents politicians who are Indians as well as scientists.

(*a*) b (*b*) c

(*c*) a (*d*) d

37. The population of a city is plotted as a function of time (years) in graphic form below :

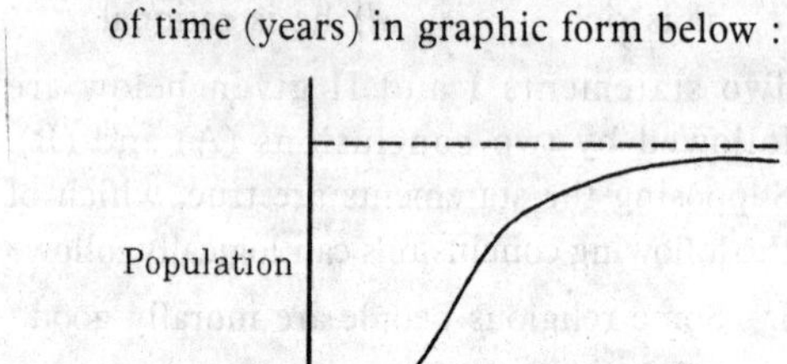

Which of the following inference can be drawn from above plot ?

(*a*) The population increases exponentially.

(*b*) The population increases in parabolic fashion.

(*c*) The population initially increases in a linear fashion and then stabilizes.

(*d*) The population initially increases exponentially and then stabilizes.

In the following chart, the price of logs is shown in per cubic metre and that of Plywood and Saw Timber in per tonnes. Study the chart and answer the following questions **38, 39 and 40.**

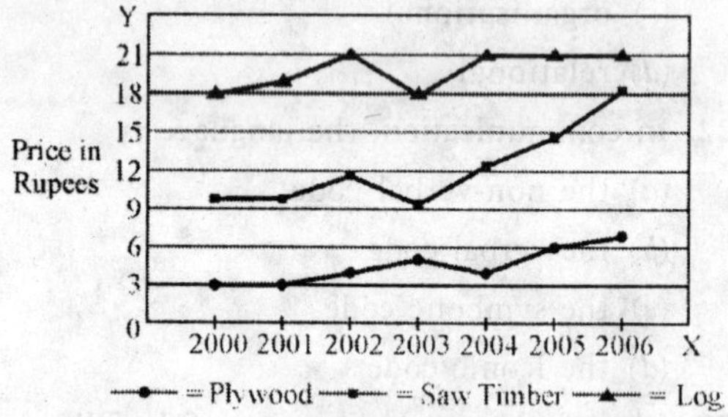

38. Which product shows the maximum percentage increase in price over the period ?

(*a*) Saw timber (*b*) Plywood

(*c*) Log (*d*) None of the above

39. What is the maximum percentage increase in price per cubic metre of log ?

(*a*) 6 (*b*) 12

(*c*) 18 (*d*) 20

40. In which year the prices of two products increased and that of the third increased?

(*a*) 2000 (*b*) 2002

(*c*) 2003 (*d*) 2006

41. Which one of the following is the oldest Archival source of data in India ?

(*a*) National Sample Surveys

(*b*) Agricultural Statistics

(*c*) Census

(*d*) Vital Statistics

42. In a large random data set following normal distribution, the ratio (%) of number of data points which are in the range of (mean ± standard deviation) to the total number of data points, is

(*a*) ~ 50% (*b*) ~ 67%

(*c*) ~ 97% (*d*) ~ 47%

43. Which number system is usually followed in a typical 32-bit computer ?

(*a*) 2 (*b*) 8

(*c*) 10 (*d*) 16

44. Which one of the following is an example of Operating System ?

(*a*) Microsoft Word
(*b*) Microsoft Excel
(*c*) Microsoft Access
(*d*) Microsoft Windows

45. Which one of the following represent the binary equivalent of the decimal number 23 ?

(*a*) 01011 (*b*) 10111
(*c*) 10011 (*d*) None of the above

46. Which one of the following is different from other members ?

(*a*) Google (*b*) Windows
(*c*) Linux (*d*) Mac

47. Where does a computer add and compare its data ?

(*a*) CPU (*b*) Memory
(*c*) Hard disk (*d*) Floppy disk

48. Computers on an internet are identified by

(*a*) e-mail address (*b*) street address
(*c*) IP address (*d*) None of the above

49. The Right to Information Act, 2005 makes the provision of

(*a*) Dissemination of all types of information by all Public authorities to any person.
(*b*) Establishment of Central, State and District Level Information Commissions as an appellate body.
(*c*) Transparency and accountability in Public authorities.
(*d*) All of the above

50. Which type of natural hazards cause maximum damage to property and lives?

(*a*) Hydrological
(*b*) Hydro-meteorological
(*c*) Geological
(*d*) Geo-chemical

51. Dioxins are produced from

(*a*) Wastelands
(*b*) Power plants
(*c*) Sugar factories
(*d*) Combustion of plastics

52. The slogan "A tree for each child" was coined for

(*a*) Social forestry programme
(*b*) Clean Air programme
(*c*) Soil conservation programme
(*d*) Environmental protection programme

53. The main constituents of biogas are

(*a*) Methane and Carbon di-oxide
(*b*) Methane and Nitric oxide
(*c*) Methane, Hydrogen and Nitric oxide
(*d*) Methane and Sulphur di-oxide

54. Assertion (A) : In the world as a whole, the environment has degraded during past several decades.

Reason (R) : The population of the world has been growing significantly.

(*a*) (A) is correct, (R) is correct and (R) is the correct explanation of (A).
(*b*) (A) is correct, (R) is correct and (R) is not the correct explanation of (A).
(*c*) (A) is correct, but (R) is false.
(*d*) (A) is false, but (R) is correct.

55. Climate change has implications for

1. soil moisture 2. forest fires
3. biodiversity 4. ground water

Identify the correct combination according to the code :

Codes :

(*a*) 1 and 3 (*b*) 1, 2 and 3
(*c*) 1, 3 and 4 (*d*) 1, 2, 3 and 4

56. The accreditation process by National Assessment and Accreditation Council (NAAC) differs from that of National Board of Accreditation (NBA) in terms of

(*a*) Disciplines covered by both being the same, there is duplication of efforts.
(*b*) One has institutional grading approach and the other has programme grading approach.
(*c*) Once get accredited by NBA or NAAC, the institution is free from renewal of grading, which is not a progressive decision.
(*d*) This accreditation amounts to approval of minimum standards in the quality of education in the institution concerned.

57. Which option is not correct ?

(*a*) Most of the educational institutions of National repute in scientific and technical sphere fall under 64th entry of Union list.

(*b*) Education, in general, is the subject of concurrent list since 42nd Constitutional Amendment Act 1976.

(*c*) Central Advisory Board on Education (CABE) was first established in 1920.

(*d*) India had implemented the right to Free and Compulsory Primary Education in 2002 through 86th Constitutional Amendment.

58. Which statement is not correct about the "National Education Day" of India ?

(*a*) It is celebrated on 5th September every year.

(*b*) It is celebrated on 11th November every year.

(*c*) It is celebrated in the memory of India's first Union Minister of Education, Dr. Abul Kalam Azad.

(*d*) It is being celebrated since 2008.

59. Match List-I with List-II and select the correct answer from the codes given below :

List – I (Articles of the Constitution)	**List – II (Institutions)**
A. Article 280	(*i*) Administrative Tribunals
B. Article 324	(*ii*) Election Commission of India
C. Article 323	(*iii*) Finance Commission at Union level
D. Article 315	(*iv*) Union Public Service Commission

Codes :

	A	**B**	**C**	**D**
(*a*)	(*i*)	(*ii*)	(*iii*)	(*iv*)
(*b*)	(*iii*)	(*ii*)	(*i*)	(*iv*)
(*c*)	(*ii*)	(*iii*)	(*iv*)	(*i*)
(*d*)	(*ii*)	(*iv*)	(*iii*)	(*i*)

60. Deemed Universities declared by UGC under Section 3 of the UGC Act 1956, are **not** permitted to

(*a*) offer programmes in higher education and issue degrees.

(*b*) give affiliation to any institute of higher education.

(*c*) open off-campus and off-shore campus anywhere in the country and overseas respectively without the permission of the UGC.

(*d*) offer distance education programmes without the approval of the Distance Education Council.

ANSWERS

1. (*d*)	**2.** (*c*)	**3.** (*c*)	**4.** (*b*)	**5.** (*a*)	**6.** (*a*)	**7.** (*a*)	**8.** (*c*)	**9.** (*a*)	**10.** (*c*)
11. (*b*)	**12.** (*a*)	**13.** (*c*)	**14.** (*c*)	**15.** (*c*)	**16.** (*a*)	**17.** (*c*)	**18.** (*d*)	**19.** (*a*)	**20.** (*d*)
21. (*d*)	**22.** (*c*)	**23.** (*d*)	**24.** (*d*)	**25.** (*d*)	**26.** (*b*)	**27.** (*d*)	**28.** (*d*)	**29.** (*d*)	**30.** (*b*)
31. (*b*)	**32.** (*a*)	**33.** (*a*)	**34.** (*b*)	**35.** (*a*)	**36.** (*c*)	**37.** (*d*)	**38.** (*b*)	**39.** (*c*)	**40.** (*b*)
41. (*c*)	**42.** (*b*)	**43.** (*a*)	**44.** (*d*)	**45.** (*d*)	**46.** (*a*)	**47.** (*a*)	**48.** (*c*)	**49.** (*a*)	**50.** (*a*)
51. (*d*)	**52.** (*d*)	**53.** (*a*)	**54.** (*a*)	**55.** (*d*)	**56.** (*b*)	**57.** (*b*)	**58.** (*a*)	**59.** (*b*)	**60.** (*c*)

■■

Solved Paper 2009 (December)

UGC NET

PAPER-I

Note : This paper contains **Fifty (50)** multiple choice questions, each question carrying **two (2)** marks.

1. The quotation "Where is the Wisdom, We Lost in Knowledge..." is by
   (*a*) John Keats
   (*b*) M. P. Carter
   (*c*) T. S. Eliot
   (*d*) Marshall McLuhan

2. Entropy is a measure of
   (*a*) Degree of relevance of information
   (*b*) Quantity of irrelevant information
   (*c*) Degree of uncertainty in information
   (*d*) Degree of certainty in information

3. CONPOLIS (India) was set up in the year
   (*a*) 1985 (*b*) 1986
   (*c*) 1987 (*d*) 1988

4. First time efforts for the development of libraries in India were made
   (*a*) S. R. Ranganathan
   (*b*) S. Radhakrishnan
   (*c*) Sayaji Rao Gaekwad I
   (*d*) Sayaji Rao Gaekwad III

5. An E-book which does not require an internet connection to access its contents is
   (*a*) Web book
   (*b*) Palm book
   (*c*) Electronic Ink e-book
   (*d*) Digital book

6. Emerald full text Database is published from
   (*a*) USA (*b*) Germany
   (*c*) France (*d*) U.K.

7. Who propounded "Conservative, moderate and liberal theories of reference service"?
   (*a*) William A Katz
   (*b*) S. R. Ranganathan
   (*c*) James I. Wyer
   (*d*) R. Emery

8. The input Centre for INIS in India is
   (*a*) DRDO (*b*) DSIR
   (*c*) TFIR (*d*) BARC

9. The provision of phase relations in DDC was made available from
   (*a*) 14th edition (*b*) 2nd edition
   (*c*) 7th edition (*d*) 11th edition

10. RDA stands for
    (*a*) Resource Description Agency
    (*b*) Reference Description and Access
    (*c*) Reference Description Agency
    (*d*) Resource Description and Access

11. Cost benefit analysis means
    (*a*) Value for money
    (*b*) Performance evaluation based on cost
    (*c*) Finding out unit cost
    (*d*) Performance evaluation based on inputs

12. Which national agency in India is assigning the ISBN?
    (*a*) Raja Ram Mohan Roy National Education Resource Centre
    (*b*) Delhi Public Library
    (*c*) Federation of Publishers in India
    (*d*) National Library of India

13. The term 'Cyberspace' was first used by
    (*a*) Andrew Pollock
    (*b*) William Gibson
    (*c*) John Postal
    (*d*) Joe Flower

14. RFID Technology is used in
    (*a*) Acquisition
    (*b*) Serial Control
    (*c*) Circulation Control
    (*d*) OPAC

15. The Boolean operator 'AND' is related to

(*a*) Productive

(*b*) Additive

(*c*) Logical Difference

(*d*) None of the above

16. The process of configuring the disks into tracks and sectors is called

(*a*) Booting

(*b*) Formatting

(*c*) Labelling

(*d*) All the above

17. A research design is

(*a*) A series of guide posts

(*b*) A series of sampling

(*c*) A hypothetical statement

(*d*) A controller of variance

18. In a questionnaire, questionnaire on age, income and gender are the examples of

(*a*) Dependent variables

(*b*) Intervening variables

(*c*) Independent variables

(*d*) Manipulation variables

19. The simple Dublin Core Metadata Element Set (DCMES) consists of

(*a*) 10 elements

(*b*) 15 elements

(*c*) 14 elements

(*d*) 18 elements

20. 'Libraries as Gateways to Knowledge' is the title of the document

(*a*) National Information Policy, 1986

(*b*) Information Technology Act, 2000

(*c*) National Knowledge Commission on Libraries, 2007

(*d*) None of the above

21. Assertion (A) : INDEST conceived J-Gate as a customized gate for e-journals subscribed by the member libraries.

Reason (R) : J-Gate provides a common access platform for all its members to search and share resources subscribed by the member libraries.

(*a*) Both (A) and (R) are true and (R) is the correct explanation.

(*b*) Both (A) and (R) are true but (R) is not the correct explanation.

(*c*) (A) is true but (R) is false.

(*d*) (A) is false but (R) is true.

22. Assertion (A) : XML, just like HTML is a meta language that is capable of containing extendable elements.

Reason (R) : XML develop and deploy new specific mark up, enabling automatic authoring and processing of networked information.

(*a*) (A) is false but (R) is true.

(*b*) Both (A) and (R) are true and (R) is not the correct explanation.

(*c*) (A) is true but (R) is false.

(*d*) Both (A) and (R) are true.

23. Assertion (A) : Measuring the Internet and in particular the web is a difficult task.

Reason (R) : Web is considered as a new publishing medium with inadequate editorial process.

(*a*) Both (A) and (R) are true and (R) is the correct explanation.

(*b*) Both (A) and (R) are true and (R) is not the correct explanation.

(*c*) (A) is true but (R) is false.

(*d*) (A) is false but (R) is true.

24. Assertion (A) : An indexing language is an artificial language as it uses controlled vocabulary.

Reason (R) : It provides different relationships between terms.

(*a*) Both (A) and (R) are false.

(*b*) Both (A) and (R) are true.

(*c*) (A) is true but (R) is false.

(*d*) (A) is false but (R) is true.

25. Assertion (A) : With large collection of documents, recall can be measured properly.

Reason (R) : The proper estimation of maximum recall for a query requires detailed knowledge of all the documents in the collection.

(*a*) Both (A) and (R) are true.

(*b*) Both (A) and (R) are true and (R) is not the correct explanation.

(*c*) (A) is true but (R) is false.

(*d*) (A) is false but (R) is true.

26. Assertion (A) : In contemporary digital environment, IPR become the focal point.

Reason (R) : Many fold increase of unfair use of I.P.

(*a*) (A) and (R) are true.

(*b*) (A) and (R) are false.

(*c*) (A) is true and (R) is false.

(*d*) (A) is false and (R) is true.

27. Assertion (A) : Library automation is at a slow pace in Indian Libraries.

Reason (R) : Lack of U.G.C. (India) support lead to this situation.

(*a*) Both (A) and (R) are true.

(*b*) Both (A) and (R) are false.

(*c*) (A) is true but (R) is false.

(*d*) (A) is false but (R) is true.

28. Assertion (A) : The development of Institutional Repositories in India is at a slow pace.

Reason (R) : This can be attributed to the non-availability of open source software and lack of interest among the LIS professionals.

(*a*) Both (A) and (R) are true.

(*b*) Both (A) and (R) are false.

(*c*) (A) is true but (R) is partially true.

(*d*) (A) is false and (R) is true.

29. Assertion (A) : Subject gateways offer the users an alternative to 'Vacuum Cleaner' type of search engines, such as Google, Infoseek, Alta Vista etc.

Reason (R) : Subject Gateways hold manually created records, rich resource description containing relevant information.

(*a*) Both (A) and (R) are true.

(*b*) Both (A) and (R) are true and (R) is not the correct explanation.

(*c*) (A) is true but (R) is false.

(*d*) (A) is false but (R) is true.

30. Assertion (A) : Para-professional staff supports the professional staff in Library routines.

Reason (R) : Para-professional staffs acquire skill by experience.

(*a*) (A) is false, but (R) is true.

(*b*) (A) is true, but (R) is false.

(*c*) Both (A) and (R) are false.

(*d*) Both (A) and (R) are true.

31. Public Library Law has already been passed in the following States. Identify the correct chronological order in which they were enacted.

(*i*) Uttaranchal (Uttarakhand)

(*ii*) Orissa

(*iii*) Gujarat

(*iv*) Haryana

Codes :

(*a*) (*i*) (*ii*) (*iii*) (*iv*) (*b*) (*iv*) (*ii*) (*i*) (*iii*)

(*c*) (*ii*) (*iii*) (*iv*) (*i*) (*d*) (*iii*) (*ii*) (*i*) (*iv*)

32. Arrange in chronological order the following persons who were associated with computing history :

(*i*) J. Presper Eckart (*ii*) John W Mauchly

(*iii*) August Ada (*iv*) Charles Babbage

Codes :

(*a*) (*iii*) (*ii*) (*i*) (*iv*) (*b*) (*ii*) (*i*) (*iii*) (*iv*)

(*c*) (*i*) (*iv*) (*iii*) (*ii*) (*d*) (*iv*) (*iii*) (*ii*) (*i*)

33. Arrange the following events of Public Library movement in chronological order:

(*i*) Enactment of Press and Registration of Books Act

(*ii*) Establishment of the Punjab Library, Lahore

(*iii*) Constitution of Fyzee Committee

(*iv*) Declaration of Imperial Library (Calcutta) as National Library of India

Codes :

(*a*) (*i*) (*iii*) (*iv*) (*ii*)

(*b*) (*i*) (*ii*) (*iii*) (*iv*)

(*c*) (*ii*) (*iii*) (*iv*) (*i*)

(*d*) (*iv*) (*i*) (*iii*) (*ii*)

34. Arrange the following layers of OSI model in the sequence in which they function :

(*i*) Network Layer (*ii*) Physical Layer

(*iii*) Transport Layer (*iv*) Data Link Layer

Codes :

(*a*) (*iii*) (*iv*) (*ii*) (*i*) (*b*) (*iv*) (*ii*) (*i*) (*iii*)

(*c*) (*ii*) (*iv*) (*i*) (*iii*) (*d*) (*i*) (*ii*) (*iii*) (*iv*)

35. Arrange the following four quadrants of spiral of scientific method in their logical order :

(*i*) Ascendant (*ii*) Nadir

(*iii*) Zenith (*iv*) Descendent

Codes :

(*a*) (*iv*) (*i*) (*iii*) (*ii*) (*b*) (*i*) (*iii*) (*iv*) (*ii*)

(*c*) (*iii*) (*ii*) (*i*) (*iv*) (*d*) (*ii*) (*i*) (*iii*) (*iv*)

36. Arrange the following books in order of their publication :

(*i*) Classified Catalogue Code

(*ii*) Prolegamena to Library Classification

(*iii*) Five Laws of Library Science

(*iv*) Colon Classification

Codes :

(*a*) (*i*) (*iv*) (*iii*) (*ii*) (*b*) (*iii*) (*ii*) (*iv*) (*i*)

(*c*) (*iii*) (*iv*) (*i*) (*ii*) (*d*) (*iv*) (*i*) (*ii*) (*iii*)

37. Arrange the following bibliographies according to their date of origin :

(*i*) Indian National Bibliography

(*ii*) Cumulative Book Index

(*iii*) Book In Print

(*iv*) British National Bibliography

Codes :

(*a*) (*iii*) (*iv*) (*i*) (*ii*)

(*b*) (*ii*) (*iii*) (*iv*) (*i*)

(*c*) (*i*) (*ii*) (*iii*) (*iv*)

(*d*) (*iv*) (*ii*) (*i*) (*iii*)

38. Arrange the following schemes of classification according to their year of origin :

(*i*) Colon Classification

(*ii*) Expansive Classification

(*iii*) Universal Decimal Classification

(*iv*) Dewey Decimal Classification

Codes :

(*a*) (*ii*) (*iii*) (*iv*) (*i*)

(*b*) (*iii*) (*iv*) (*i*) (*ii*)

(*c*) (*iv*) (*ii*) (*iii*) (*i*)

(*d*) (*i*) (*ii*) (*iv*) (*iii*)

39. Arrange the following principles and canons according to their levels as enunciated by Dr. S. R. Ranganathan :

(*i*) Principles of Cataloguing

(*ii*) General Normative Principles

(*iii*) Laws of Library Science

(*iv*) Canons of Cataloguing

Codes :

(*a*) (*i*) (*iv*) (*iii*) (*ii*)

(*b*) (*ii*) (*iii*) (*iv*) (*i*)

(*c*) (*ii*) (*i*) (*iv*) (*iii*)

(*d*) (*i*) (*iv*) (*ii*) (*iii*)

40. Arrange the following Associations according to their year of formation :

(*i*) ASLIB (*ii*) LA

(*iii*) ALA (*iv*) SLA

Codes :

(*a*) (*iii*) (*ii*) (*iv*) (*i*)

(*b*) (*ii*) (*iv*) (*i*) (*iii*)

(*c*) (*iii*) (*i*) (*iv*) (*ii*)

(*d*) (*iv*) (*i*) (*iii*) (*ii*)

41. Match the following :

List – I	List – II
A. Little Science, Big Science	(*i*) S.C. Bradfold
B. Documentation	(*ii*) William Martin
C. The Third Wave	(*iii*) Eric J de Solla Price
D. The Information Society	(*iv*) Alwin Toffler

Codes :

	A	B	C	D
(*a*)	(*i*)	(*ii*)	(*iii*)	(*iv*)
(*b*)	(iii)	(i)	(iv)	(ii)
(*c*)	(*iv*)	(*iii*)	(*ii*)	(*i*)
(*d*)	(*ii*)	(*i*)	(*iv*)	(*iii*)

42. Match the following :

List – I	List – II
A. Key Word Indexing	(*i*) J. R. Sharp
B. Citation Indexing	(*ii*) H. P. Luhn
C. Uniterm Indexing	(*iii*) E. Garfield
D. SLIC Indexing	(*iv*) M. Taube

Codes :

	A	B	C	D
(*a*)	(*ii*)	(*iii*)	(*iv*)	(*i*)
(*b*)	(*iii*)	(*iv*)	(*i*)	(*ii*)
(*c*)	(*iv*)	(*i*)	(*iii*)	(*ii*)
(*d*)	(*i*)	(*iii*)	(*ii*)	(*iv*)

43. Match the following :

List – I	List – II
A. Web Navigation Element	(*i*) Telecommunication
B. Shift + Tab	(*ii*) SQL
C. ANSI Standard	(*iii*) Hyperlink
D. TELNET	(*iv*) Select the previous link

Codes :

	A	B	C	D
(*a*)	(*i*)	(*ii*)	(*iii*)	(*iv*)
(*b*)	(*iv*)	(*iii*)	(*ii*)	(*i*)
(*c*)	(*iii*)	(*iv*)	(*ii*)	(*i*)
(*d*)	(*ii*)	(*iii*)	(*i*)	(*iv*)

44. Match the following :

List –I	List – II
A. Mcfee	(*i*) DOAJ
B. Directory	(*ii*) Antivirus
C. Personal Web pages	(*iii*) Vendor on Internet
D. Amazon.com	(*iv*) Blogs

Codes :

	A	B	C	D
(*a*)	(*ii*)	(*i*)	(*iv*)	(*iii*)
(*b*)	(*i*)	(*iv*)	(*iii*)	(*ii*)
(*c*)	(*ii*)	(*iii*)	(*iv*)	(*i*)
(*d*)	(*iv*)	(*iii*)	(*ii*)	(*i*)

45. Match the following :

List – I	List – II
A. Theory of Knowledge	(*i*) Farmington Plan
B. IS : 1553-1960	(*ii*) Metadata Format
C. Resource Sharing	(*iii*) Library Building
D. TEI	(*iv*) Epistomology

Codes :

	A	B	C	D
(*a*)	(*i*)	(*iii*)	(*ii*)	(*iv*)
(*b*)	(*ii*)	(*iii*)	(*i*)	(*iv*)
(*c*)	(*iv*)	(*iii*)	(*i*)	(*ii*)
(*d*)	(*iii*)	(*i*)	(*ii*)	(*iv*)

Read the passage given below, and answer the questions based on your understanding of the passage :

Rolland Munro describes accountability as an informal giving that is part of everyday conversation, as well as more formal transactions generally involving some sort of documentary artifact (what we archivists refer to as a "record"). He notes that the authors move "between accounts as stories, explanations and reasons for conduct on the one hand and accounts as coded representations, records, often in the form of numbers, on the other hand". Each of these modes mediates the other in what he refers to as "accountability relationships." "Distributions of materials and devices are as much as effect of the giving and calling for accounts, as they are integral to the business of producing and consuming accounts". Records are both intermediaries in the accountability process and evidence of it.

In our daily language we often refer to accountability as something that must be achieved, rather than as something that is done informally yet continuously. The difference here is between viewing accountability as a thing represented by an artifact, such as a record, and thinking about accountability as a process in which people and records must interact to achieve accountability. In this latter view, the focus on accountability becomes an analysis of the methods people use to engage in accountability relations.

46. Rolland Munro described accountability as

(*a*) Classified documentary artifacts

(*b*) Formal artifacts only

(*c*) Unpublished and published documents

(*d*) Informal, formal and documentary records

47. The phrase 'record keeping' is associated with
   (*a*) Computer programmers
   (*b*) Archivists
   (*c*) Chartered Accountants
   (*d*) Office Managers

48. What integral components Munro has identified for accounting in the business?
   (*a*) Records and Codes
   (*b*) Documentary archives
   (*c*) Materials and devices
   (*d*) Legal Regulations

49. In general usage accountability means
   (*a*) Something done informally
   (*b*) Something achieved
   (*c*) Something done continuously
   (*d*) All of the above

50. Accountability, which is represented by an artifact, includes
   (*a*) Process, Records, People
   (*b*) Theory, Practice, Records
   (*c*) Theory, Practice, People
   (*d*) People, Records, Accounts

ANSWERS

1. (*c*)	**2.** (*c*)	**3.** (*a*)	**4.** (*d*)	**5.** (*d*)	**6.** (*d*)	**7.** (*c*)	**8.** (*d*)	**9.** (*d*)	**10.** (*d*)
11. (*b*)	**12.** (*a*)	**13.** (*b*)	**14.** (*c*)	**15.** (*b*)	**16.** (*b*)	**17.** (*a*)	**18.** (*c*)	**19.** (*b*)	**20.** (*c*)
21. (*a*)	**22.** (*b*)	**23.** (*a*)	**24.** (*b*)	**25.** (*c*)	**26.** (*a*)	**27.** (*c*)	**28.** (*c*)	**29.** (*b*)	**30.** (*d*)
31. (*b*)	**32.** (*d*)	**33.** (*a*)	**34.** (*c*)	**35.** (*d*)	**36.** (*c*)	**37.** (*a*)	**38.** (*c*)	**39.** (*b*)	**40.** (*a*)
41. (*b*)	**42.** (*a*)	**43.** (*c*)	**44.** (*a*)	**45.** (*c*)	**46.** (*d*)	**47.** (*b*)	**48.** (*c*)	**49.** (*b*)	**50.** (*d*)

■■

Solved Paper 2009 (June)

UGC NET

PAPER-I

Note : This paper contains **Fifty (50)** multiple choice questions, each question carrying **two (2)** marks.

1. Good evaluation of written material should not be based on:
   (*a*) Linguistic expression
   (*b*) Logical presentation
   (*c*) Ability to reproduce whatever is read
   (*d*) Comprehension of subject

2. Why do teachers use teaching aid?
   (*a*) To make teaching fun-filled
   (*b*) To teach within understanding level of students
   (*c*) For students' attention
   (*d*) To make students attentive

3. Attitudes, concepts, skills and knowledge are products of:
   (*a*) Learning (*b*) Research
   (*c*) Heredity (*d*) Explanation

4. Which among the following gives more freedom to the learner to interact?
   (*a*) Use of film
   (*b*) Small group discussion
   (*c*) Lectures by experts
   (*d*) Viewing country-wide classroom programme on TV

5. Which of the following is not a product of learning?
   (*a*) Attitudes (*b*) Concepts
   (*c*) Knowledge (*d*) Maturation

6. How can the objectivity of the research be enhanced?
   (*a*) Through its impartiality
   (*b*) Through its reliability
   (*c*) Through its validity
   (*d*) All of these

7. Action-research is:
   (*a*) An applied research
   (*b*) A research carried out to solve immediate problems
   (*c*) A longitudinal research
   (*d*) All the above

8. The basis on which assumptions are formulated :
   (*a*) Cultural background of the country
   (*b*) Universities
   (*c*) Specific characteristics of the castes
   (*d*) All of these

9. Which of the following is classified in the category of the developmental research ?
   (*a*) Philosophical research
   (*b*) Action research
   (*c*) Descriptive research
   (*d*) All the above

10. We use Factorial Analysis:
    (*a*) To know the relationship between two variables
    (*b*) To test the Hypothesis
    (*c*) To know the difference between two variables
    (*d*) To know the difference among the many variables

Read the following passage and answer the questions 11 to 15 :

While the British rule in India was detrimental to the economic development of the country, it did help in starting of the process of modernizing Indian society and formed several progressive institutions during that process. One of the most beneficial institutions, which were initiated by the British, was democracy. Nobody can dispute that despite its many shortcomings; democracy was and is far better alternative to the arbitrary rule of the rajas and nawabs, which prevailed in India in the pre-British days.

However, one of the harmful traditions of British democracy inherited by India was that of conflict instead of cooperation between elected members. This was its essential feature. The party, which got the support of the majority of elected members, formed the Government while the others constituted a standing opposition. The existence of the opposition to those in power was and is regarded as a hallmark of democracy.

In principle, democracy consists of rule by the people; but where direct rule is not possible, it's rule by persons elected by the people. It is natural that there would be some differences of opinion among the elected members as in the rest of the society.

Normally, members of any organizations have differences of opinion between themselves on different issues but they manage to work on the basis of a consensus and they do not normally form a division between some who are in majority and are placed in power, while treating the others as in opposition.

The members of an organization usually work on consensus. Consensus simply means that after an adequate discussion, members agree that the maiority opinion may prevail for the time being. Thus persons who form a majority on one issue and whose opinion is allowed to prevail may not be on the same side if there is a difference on some other issue.

It was largely by accident that instead of this normal procedure, a two party system came to prevail in Britain and that is now being generally taken as the best method of democratic rule.

Many democratically inclined persons in India regret that such a two party system was not brought about in the country. It appears that to have two parties in India – of more or less equal strength - is a virtual impossibility. Those who regret the absence of a two-party system should take the reasons into consideration.

When the two party system got established in Britain, there were two groups among the rules (consisting of a limited electorate) who had the same economic interests among themselves and who therefore formed two groups within the selected members of Parliament.

There were members of the British aristocracy (which landed interests and consisting of lord, barons etc) and members of the new commercial class consisting of merchants and artisans. These groups were more or less of equal strength and they were able to establish their separate rule at different times.

Answer the following questions :

11. In pre-British period, when India was ruled by the independent rulers :

(*a*) Peace and prosperity prevailed in the society

(*b*) People were isolated from political affairs

(*c*) Public opinion was inevitable for policy making

(*d*) Law was equal for one and all

12. What is the distinguishing feature of the democracy practiced in Britain?

(*a*) End to the rule of might is right.

(*b*) Rule of the people, by the people and for the people.

(*c*) It has stood the test of time.

(*d*) Cooperation between elected members.

13. Democracy is practiced where:

(*a*) Elected members form a uniform opinion regarding policy matter.

(*b*) Opposition is more powerful than the ruling combine.

(*c*) Representatives of masses.

(*d*) None of these.

14. Which of the following is true about the British rule in India?

(*a*) It was behind the modernization of the Indian society.

(*b*) India gained economically during that period.

(*c*) Various establishments were formed for the purpose of progress.

(*d*) None of these.

15. Who became the members of the new commercial class during that time ?
(*a*) British Aristocrats
(*b*) Lord and barons
(*c*) Political Persons
(*d*) Merchants and artisans

16. Which one of the following Telephonic Conferencing with a radio link is very popular throughout the world ?
(*a*) TPS
(*b*) Telepresence
(*c*) Video conference
(*d*) Video teletext

17. Which is not 24 hours news channel?
(*a*) NDTV24x7
(*b*) ZEE News
(*c*) Aajtak
(*d*) Lok Sabha channel

18. The main objective of F.M. station in radio is :
(*a*) Information, Entertainment and Tourism
(*b*) Entertainment, Information and Interaction
(*c*) Tourism, Interaction and Entertainment
(*d*) Entertainment only

19. In communication chatting in internet is :
(*a*) Verbal communication
(*b*) Non verbal communication
(*c*) Parallel communication
(*d*) Grapevine communication

20. Match List-I with List-II and select the correct answer using the codes given below :

List-I (Artists)	List-II (Art)
A. Pandit Jasraj	(*i*) Hindustani vocalist
B. Kishan Maharaj	(*ii*) Sitar
C. Ravi Shankar	(*iii*) Tabla
D. Udai Shankar	(*iv*) Dance

Codes :

	A	B	C	D
(*a*)	(*i*)	(*ii*)	(*iii*)	(*iv*)
(*b*)	(*i*)	(*iii*)	(*iv*)	(*ii*)
(*c*)	(*i*)	(*iii*)	(*ii*)	(*iv*)
(*d*)	(*iii*)	(*ii*)	(*i*)	(*iv*)

21. Insert the missing number in the following :
3, 8, 18, 23, 33, ?, 48
(*a*) 37 (*b*) 40
(*c*) 38 (*d*) 45

22. In a certain code, CLOCK is written as KCOLC. How would STEPS be written in that code ?
(*a*) SPEST
(*b*) SPSET
(*c*) SPETS
(*d*) SEPTS

23. The letters in the first set have a certain relationship. On the basis of this relationship mark the right choice for the second set:
BDFH : OMKI : : GHIK : ?
(*a*) FHJL
(*b*) RPNL
(*c*) LNPR
(*d*) LJHF

24. What was the day of the week on 1st January 2001 ?
(*a*) Friday
(*b*) Tuesday
(*c*) Sunday
(*d*) Wednesday

25. Find out the wrong number in the sequence.
52, 51, 48, 43, 34, 27, 16
(*a*) 27 (*b*) 34
(*c*) 43 (*d*) 48

26. In a deductive argument conclusion is :
(*a*) Summing up of the premises
(*b*) Not necessarily based on premises
(*c*) Entailed by the premises
(*d*) Additional to the premises

27. 'No man are mortal' is contradictory of:
(*a*) Some man are mortal
(*b*) Some man are not mortal
(*c*) All men are mortal
(*d*) No mortal is man

28. A deductive argument is valid if:

(*a*) premises are false and conclusion true

(*b*) premises are false and conclusion is also false

(*c*) premises are true and conclusion is false

(*d*) premises are true and conclusion is true

29. Structure of logical argument is based on:

(*a*) Formal validity

(*b*) Material truth

(*c*) Linguistic expression

(*d*) Aptness of examples

30. Two ladies and two men are playing bridge and seated at North, East, South and West of a table. No lady is facing East. Persons sitting opposite to each other are not of the same sex. One man is facing South. Which direction are the ladies facing to?

(*a*) East and West

(*b*) North and West

(*c*) South and East

(*d*) None of these

Questions 31 and 32 are based on the following venn diagram in which there are three intersecting circles representing Hindi knowing persons, English knowing persons and persons who are working as teachers. Different regions so obtained in the figure are marked as a, b, c, d, e, f and g.

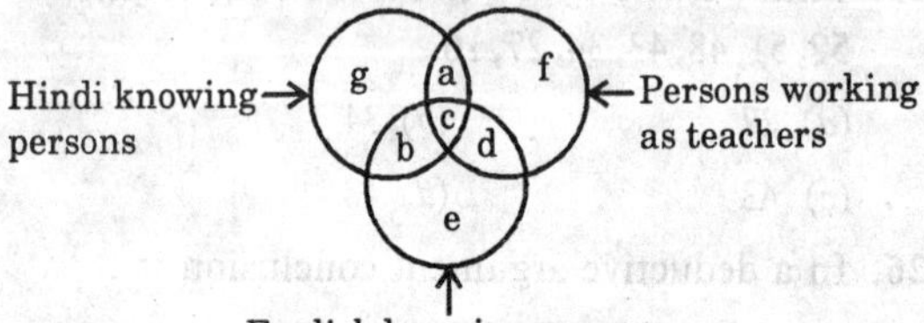

31. If you want to select Hindi and English knowing teachers, which of the following is to be selected ?

(*a*) g (*b*) b

(*c*) c (*d*) e

32. If you want to select persons, who do not know English and are not teachers, which of the region is to be selected ?

(*a*) e (*b*) g

(*c*) b (*d*) a

Study the following graph carefully and answer questions **33 to 35.**

Export of Engineering Goods

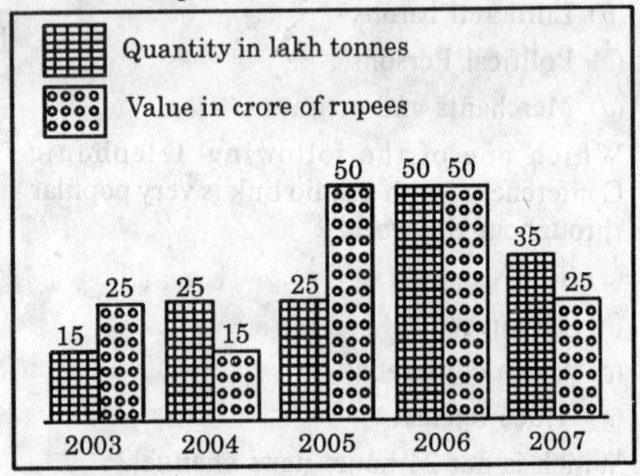

33. In which year the quantity of engineering goods' exports was maximum ?

(*a*) 2005

(*b*) 2006

(*c*) 2004

(*d*) 2007

34. In which year the value of engineering goods decreased by 50 percent compared to the previous year ?

(*a*) 2004

(*b*) 2007

(*c*) 2005

(*d*) 2006

35. In which year the quantity of exports was 100 percent higher than the quantity of previous year ?

(*a*) 2004

(*b*) 2005

(*c*) 2006

(*d*) 2007

36. What do you need to put your web pages on the www ?

(*a*) a connection to internet

(*b*) a web browser

(*c*) a web server

(*d*) all of the above

37. Which was the first company to launch mobile phone services in India ?

(*a*) Essar

(*b*) BPL

(*c*) Hutchison

(*d*) Airtel

38. Chandrayan I was launched on 22nd October, 2008 in India from :

(*a*) Bangalore

(*b*) Sri Harikota

(*c*) Chennai

(*d*) Ahmedabad

39. What is blog ?

(*a*) Online music

(*b*) Intranet

(*c*) A personal or corporate website in the form of an online journal

(*d*) A personal or corporate Google search

40. Which is not online Indian Matrimonial website ?

(*a*) www.jeevansathi.com

(*b*) www.bharatmatrimony.com

(*c*) www.shaadi.com

(*d*) www.u.k.singlemuslim.com

41. Environmental impact assessment is an objective analysis of the probable changes in:

(*a*) physical characteristics of the environment

(*b*) biophysical characteristics of the environment

(*c*) socio-economic characteristics of the environment

(*d*) all the above

42. Bog is a wetland that receives water from:

(*a*) nearby water bodies

(*b*) melting

(*c*) rain fall only

(*d*) sea only

43. Which of the following region is in the very high risk zone of earthquakes?

(*a*) Central Indian Highland

(*b*) Coastal region

(*c*) Himalayan region

(*d*) Indian desert

44. Match List-I with List-II and select the correct answer using the codes given below:

List – I (Institutes)	**List – II** (Cities)
A. Central Arid Zone Institute	(*i*) Kolkata
B. Space Application Centre	(*ii*) New Delhi
C. Indian Institute of Public Administration	(*iii*) Ahmedabad
D. Headquarters of Indian Science Congress	(*iv*) Jodhpur

Codes :

	A	B	C	D
(*a*)	(*iv*)	(*iii*)	(*ii*)	(*i*)
(*b*)	(*iv*)	(*ii*)	(*i*)	(*iii*)
(*c*)	(*iii*)	(*i*)	(*ii*)	(*iv*)
(*d*)	(*i*)	(*ii*)	(*iv*)	(*iii*)

45. Indian coastal areas experienced Tsunami disaster in the year :

(*a*) 2005

(*b*) 2004

(*c*) 2006

(*d*) 2007

46. The Kothari Commission's report was entitled on :

(*a*) Education and National Development

(*b*) Learning to be adventure

(*c*) Diversification of Education

(*d*) Education and socialization in democracy

47. Which of the following is not a Dualmode University ?

(*a*) Delhi University

(*b*) Bangalore University

(*c*) Madras University

(*d*) Indira Gandhi National Open University

48. Which part of the Constitution of India is known as "Code of Administrators"?

(*a*) Part I

(*b*) Part II

(*c*) Part III

(*d*) Part IV

49. Which article of the constitution provides safeguards to Naga Customary and their social practices against any act of Parliament ?

(*a*) Article 371 A

(*b*) Article 371 B

(*c*) Article 371 C

(*d*) Article 263

50. Which one of the following is not the tool of good governance ?

(*a*) Right to information

(*b*) Citizens' Charter

(*c*) Social Auditing

(*d*) Judicial Activism

ANSWERS

1. (*d*)	**2.** (*b*)	**3.** (*a*)	**4.** (*b*)	**5.** (*d*)	**6.** (*d*)	**7.** (*b*)	**8.** (*a*)	**9.** (*d*)	**10.** (*c*)
11. (*b*)	**12.** (*b*)	**13.** (*b*)	**14.** (*a*)	**15.** (*d*)	**16.** (*c*)	**17.** (*d*)	**18.** (*b*)	**19.** (*c*)	**20.** (*c*)
21. (*c*)	**22.** (*c*)	**23.** (*c*)	**24.** (*)	**25.** (*b*)	**26.** (*c*)	**27.** (*a*)	**28.** (*d*)	**29.** (*a*)	**30.** (*b*)
31. (*c*)	**32.** (*b*)	**33.** (*b*)	**34.** (*b*)	**35.** (*c*)	**36.** (*d*)	**37.** (*b*)	**38.** (*b*)	**39.** (*c*)	**40.** (*d*)
41. (*b*)	**42.** (*c*)	**43.** (*c*)	**44.** (*a*)	**45.** (*b*)	**46.** (*a*)	**47.** (*d*)	**48.** (*d*)	**49.** (*a*)	**50.** (*d*)

Solved Paper 2008 (December)

UGC NET

PAPER-I

Note : This paper contains **Fifty (50)** multiple choice questions, each question carrying **two (2)** marks.

1. According to Swami Vivekananda, teacher's success depends on:
   (*a*) His renunciation of personal gain and service to others
   (*b*) His professional training and creativity
   (*c*) His concentration on his work and duties with a spirit of obedience to God
   (*d*) His mastery on the subject and capacity in controlling the students

2. Which of the following teacher, will be liked most?
   (*a*) A teacher of high idealistic attitude
   (*b*) A loving teacher
   (*c*) A teacher who is disciplined
   (*d*) A teacher who often amuses his students

3. A teacher's most important challenge is:
   (*a*) To make students do their home work
   (*b*) To make teaching-learning process enjoyable
   (*c*) To maintain discipline in the class room
   (*d*) To prepare the question paper

4. Value-education stands for:
   (*a*) making a student healthy
   (*b*) making a student to get a job
   (*c*) inculcation of virtues
   (*d*) all-round development of personality

5. When a normal student behaves in an erratic manner in the class, you would:
   (*a*) pull up the student then and there
   (*b*) talk to the student after the class
   (*c*) ask the student to leave the class
   (*d*) ignore the student

6. The research is always -
   (*a*) verifying the old knowledge
   (*b*) exploring new knowledge
   (*c*) filling the gap between knowledge
   (*d*) all of these

7. The research that applies the laws at the time of field study to draw more and more clear ideas about the problem is:
   (*a*) Applied research
   (*b*) Action research
   (*c*) Experimental research
   (*d*) None of these

8. When a research problem is related to heterogeneous population, the most suitable sampling method is:
   (*a*) Cluster Sampling
   (*b*) Stratified Sampling
   (*c*) Convenient Sampling
   (*d*) Lottery Method

9. The process not needed in experimental research is:
   (*a*) Observation
   (*b*) Manipulation and replication
   (*c*) Controlling
   (*d*) Reference collection

10. A research problem is not feasible only when:
    (*a*) it is researchable
    (*b*) it is new and adds something to knowledge
    (*c*) it consists of independent and dependent variables
    (*d*) it has utility and relevance

Directions (Q.11-15): *Read the following passage carefully and answer the questions.*

Radically changing monsoon patterns, reduction in the winter rice harvest and a quantum increase in respiratory diseases all part of the environmental doomsday scenario which is reportedly playing out in South Asia. According to a United Nations Environment Programme report, a deadly three-kilometer deep blanket of pollution comprising a fearsome, cocktail of ash, acids, aerosols and other particles has enveloped in this region. For India, already struggling to cope with a drought, the implication of this are devastating and further crop failure will amount to a life and death question for many Indians. The increase in premature deaths will have adverse social and economic consequences and a rise in morbidities will place an unbearable burden on our crumbling health system. And there is no one to blame but ourselves. Both official and corporate India has always been allergic to any mention of clean technology. Most mechanical two wheelers roll of the assembly line without proper pollution control system. Little effort is made for R&D on simple technologies, which could make a vital difference to people's lives and the environment.

However, while there is no denying that South Asia must clean up its act, skeptics might question the timing of the haze report. The Kyoto meet on climate change is just two weeks away and the stage is set for the usual battle between the developing world and the West, particularly the Unites States of America. President Mr. Bush has adamantly refused to sign any protocol, which would mean a change in American consumption level. U.N. environment report will likely find a place in the U.S. arsenal as it plants an accusing finger towards controls like India and China. Yet the U.S.A. can hardly deny its own dubious role in the matter of erasing trading quotas.

Richer countries can simply buy up excess credits from poorer countries and continue to pollute. Rather than try to get the better of developing countries, who undoubtedly have taken up environmental shortcuts in their bid to catch up with the West, the USA should take a look at the environmental profigacy, which is going on within. From opening up virgin territories for oil exploration to relaxing the standards for drinking water, Mr. Bush's policies are not exactly beneficial, not even to America's interests. We realize that we are all in this together and that pollution anywhere should be a global concern otherwise there will only be more tunnels at the end of the tunnel.

11. Both official and corporate India is allergic to:

(*a*) Failure of Monsoon
(*b*) Poverty and Inequality
(*c*) Slowdown in Industrial Production
(*d*) Mention of Clean Technology

12. If the rate of premature death increases it will:

(*a*) Exert added burden on the crumbling economy
(*b*) Have adverse social and economic consequences
(*c*) Make positive effect on our effort to control population
(*d*) Have less job aspirants in the society

13. According to the passage, the two wheeler industry is not adequately concerned about:

(*a*) Passenger safety on the roads
(*b*) Life cover insurance of the vehicle owner
(*c*) Pollution control system in the vehicle
(*d*) Rising cost of the two wheelers

14. What could be the reason behind timing of the haze report just before the Kyoto meet?

(*a*) United Nations is working hand-in-glove with U.S.A.
(*b*) Organizers of the forthcoming meet to teach a lesson to the U.S.A.
(*c*) Drawing attention of the world towards devastating effects of environment degradation.
(*d*) U.S.A. wants to use it as a handle against the developing countries in the forthcoming meet

15. Which of the following is the indication of environmental degradation in South Asia?

(*a*) Social and economic inequality
(*b*) Crumbling health care system
(*c*) Inadequate pollution control system
(*d*) Radically changing monsoon pattern

16. Community Radio is a type of radio service that caters to the interest of:

(*a*) Local audience
(*b*) Education
(*c*) Entertainment
(*d*) News

17. Orcut is a part of:

(*a*) Intra personal Communication
(*b*) Mass Communication
(*c*) Group Communication
(*d*) Interpersonal Communication

18. Match List-I with List-II and select the correct answer using the codes given below:

List-I (Artists)	List - II (Art)
A. Amrita Shergill	(*i*) Flute
B. T. Swaminathan Pillai	(*ii*) Classical Song
C. Bhimsenjoshi	(*iii*) Painting
D. Padma Subramaniyam	(*iv*) Bharat Natyam

Codes:

	A	B	C	D
(*a*)	(*iii*)	(*i*)	(*ii*)	(iv)
(*b*)	(*ii*)	(*iii*)	(*i*)	(*iv*)
(*c*)	(*iv*)	(*ii*)	(*iii*)	(*i*)
(*d*)	(*i*)	(*iv*)	(*ii*)	(*iii*)

19. Which is not correct in latest communication award?

(*a*) Salman Rushdie - Booker's Prize - July 20, 2008

(*b*) Dilip Sanghavi - Business Standard CEO Award July 22, 2008

(*c*) Tapan Sinha - Dada Saheb Falke Award, July 21, 2008

(*d*) Gautam Ghosh - Osians Lifetime Achievement Award July 11, 2008

20. Firewalls are used to protect a communication network system against:

(*a*) Unauthorized attacks

(*b*) Virus attacks

(*c*) Data-driven attacks

(*d*) Fire-attacks

21. Insert the missing number in the following:

2/3, 4/7, ?, 11/21, 16/31

(*a*) 10/8 (*b*) 6/10

(*c*) 5/10 (*d*) 7/13

22. In a certain code, GAMESMAN is written as AGMEMSAN. How would DISCLOSE be written in that code?

(*a*) IDSCOLSE

(*b*) IDCSOLES

(*c*) IDSCOLES

(*d*) IDSCLOSE

23. The letters in the first set have a certain relationship. On the basis of this relationship mark the right choice for the second set:

AST : BRU : : NQV : ?

(*a*) ORW (*b*) MPU

(*c*) MRW (*d*) OPW

24. On what dates of April 1994 did SUNDAY fall?

(*a*) 2, 9, 16, 23, 30 (*b*) 3, 10, 17, 24

(*c*) 4, 11, 18, 25 (*d*) 1, 8, 15, 22, 29

25. Find out the wrong number in the sequence:

125, 127, 130, 135, 142, 153, 165

(*a*) 130 (*b*) 142

(*c*) 153 (*d*) 165

26. There are five books A, B, C, D and E. The book C lies above D, the book E is below A and B is below E. Which is at the bottom?

(*a*) E (*b*) B

(*c*) A (*d*) C

27. Logical reasoning is based on:

(*a*) Truth of involved propositions

(*b*) Valid relation among the involved propositions

(*c*) Employment of symbolic language

(*d*) Employment of ordinary language

28. Two propositions with the same subject and predicate terms but different in quality are:

(*a*) Contradictory (*b*) Contrary

(*c*) Subaltern (*d*) Identical

29. The premises of a valid deductive argument:

(*a*) Provide some evidence for its conclusion

(*b*) Provide no evidence for its conclusion

(*c*) Are irrelevant for its conclusion

(*d*) Provide conclusive evidence for its conclusion

30. Syllogistic reasoning is:

(*a*) Deductive

(*b*) Inductive

(*c*) Experimental

(*d*) Hypothetical

Directions (Q.31-33): *Study the following Venn diagram and answer questions.*

Three circles representing GRADUATES, CLERKS and GOVERNMENT EMPLOYEES are intersecting. The intersections are marked A, B, C, e, f, g and h. Which part best represents the statements in questions 31 to 33?

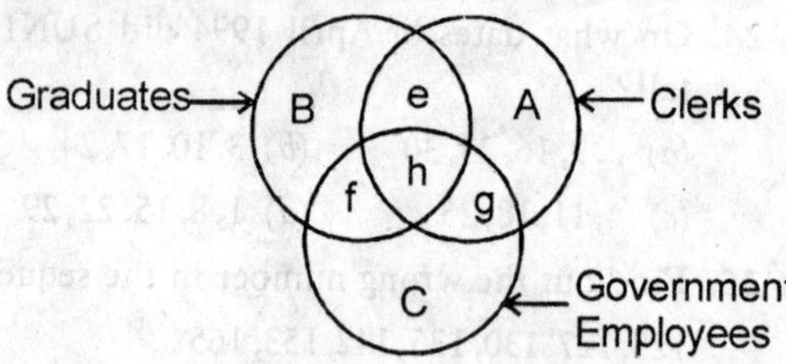

31. Some Graduates are Government employees but not as Clerks.

(*a*) h (*b*) g
(*c*) f (*d*) e

32. Clerks who are graduates as well as government employees:

(*a*) e (*b*) f
(*c*) g (*d*) h

33. Some graduates are Clerks but not Government employees.

(*a*) f (*b*) g
(*c*) h (*d*) e

Directions (Q.34-35): *Study the following graph and answer questions numbered from 34 to 35*

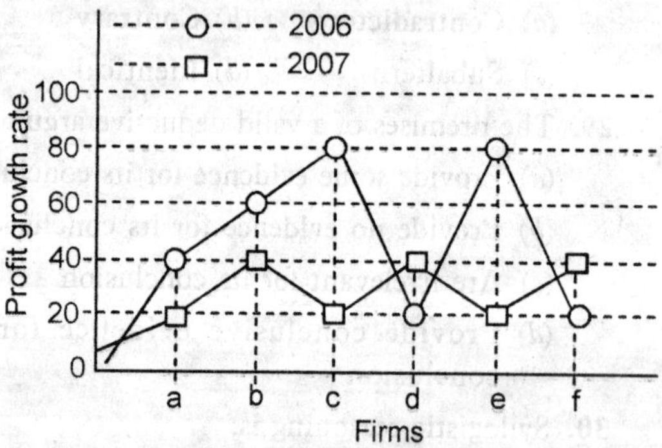

34. Which of the firms got maximum profit growth rate in the year 2006?

(*a*) ab (*b*) ce
(*c*) cd (*d*) ef

35. Which of the firms got maximum profit growth rate in the year 2007?

(*a*) bdf (*b*) acf
(*c*) bed (*d*) ace

36. The accounting software 'Tally' was developed by:

(*a*) HCL (*b*) TCS
(*c*) Infosys (*d*) Wipro

37. Errors in computer programmes are called:

(*a*) Follies (*b*) Mistakes
(*c*) Bugs (*d*) Spam

38. HTML is basically used to design:

(*a*) Web-page
(*b*) Web-site
(*c*) Graphics
(*d*) Tables and Frames

39. 'Micro Processing'is made for:

(*a*) Computer
(*b*) Digital System
(*c*) Calculator
(*d*) Electronic Goods

40. Information, a combination of graphics, text, sound, video and animation is called:

(*a*) Multiprogramme
(*b*) Multifacet
(*c*) Multimedia
(*d*) Multiprocess

41. Which of the following pairs regarding typical composition of hospital wastes is incorrect?

(*a*) Plastic- 9-12%
(*b*) Metals- 1-2%
(*c*) Ceramic- 8-10%
(*d*) Biodegradable- 35-40%

42. Fresh water achieves its greatest density at:

(*a*) -4° C (*b*) 0° C
(*c*) 4° C (*d*) -2.5° C

43. Which one of the following is not associated with earthquakes?

(*a*) Focus (*b*) Epicenter
(*c*) Seismograph (*d*) Swells

44. The tallest trees in the world are found in the region :

(*a*) Equatorial region

(*b*) Temperate region

(*c*) Monsoon region

(*d*) Mediterranean region

45. Match List-I with List-II and select the correct answer from the codes given below:

List-I (National Parks)	**List - II (States)**
A. Periyar	(*i*) Orissa
B. Nandan Kanan	(*ii*) Kerala
C. Corbett National Park	(*iii*) Rajasthan
D. Sariska Tiger Reserve	(*iv*) Uttarakhand

Codes :

	A	**B**	**C**	**D**
(*a*)	(*ii*)	(*i*)	(*iv*)	(*iii*)
(*b*)	(*i*)	(*ii*)	(*iv*)	(*iii*)
(*c*)	(*iii*)	(*ii*)	(*i*)	(*iv*)
(*d*)	(*i*)	(*ii*)	(*iii*)	(*iv*)

46. According to Radhakrishnan Commission, the aim of Higher Education is:

(*a*) To develop the democratic values, peace and harmony

(*b*) To develop great personalities who can give their contributions in politics, administration, industry and commerce

(*c*) Both (*a*) and (*b*)

(*d*) None of these

47. The National Museum at New Delhi is attached to:

(*a*) Delhi University

(*b*) a Deemed University

(*c*) a Subordinate Office of the JNU

(*d*) Part of Ministry of Tourism and Culture

48. Match List-I with List-II and select the correct answer from the code given below:

List-I (Institutions)

A. National Law Institute

B. Indian Institute of Advanced Studies

C. National Judicial Academy

D. National Savings Institute

List-II (Locations)

(*i*) Shimla

(*ii*) Bhopal

(*iii*) Hyderabad

(*iv*) Nagpur

Codes :

	A	**B**	**C**	**D**
(*a*)	(*iii*)	(*ii*)	(*iv*)	(*i*)
(*b*)	(*i*)	(*ii*)	(*iii*)	(*iv*)
(*c*)	(*iv*)	(*iii*)	(*i*)	(*ii*)
(*d*)	(*iii*)	(*i*)	(*ii*)	(*iv*)

49. Election of Rural and Urban local bodies are conducted and ultimately supervised by:

(*a*) Election Commission of India

(*b*) State Election Commission

(*c*) District Collector and District Magistrate

(*d*) Concerned Returning Officer

50. Which opinion is not correct?

(*a*) Education is a subject of concurrent list of VII schedule of Constitution of India

(*b*) University Grants Commission is a statutory body

(*c*) Patent, inventions, design, copyright and trademarks are the subject of concurrent list

(*d*) Indian Council of Social Science Research is a statutory body related to research in social sciences

ANSWERS

1. (*a*)	**2.** (*b*)	**3.** (*b*)	**4.** (*c*)	**5.** (*b*)	**6.** (*d*)	**7.** (*c*)	**8.** (*b*)	**9.** (*a*)	**10.** (*c*)
11. (*d*)	**12.** (*c*)	**13.** (*b*)	**14.** (*d*)	**15.** (*d*)	**16.** (*a*)	**17.** (*d*)	**18.** (*a*)	**19.** (*d*)	**20.** (*a*)
21. (*d*)	**22.** (*a*)	**23.** (*d*)	**24.** (*b*)	**25.** (*d*)	**26.** (*b*)	**27.** (*b*)	**28.** (*c*)	**29.** (*d*)	**30.** (*a*)
31. (*c*)	**32.** (*d*)	**33.** (*d*)	**34.** (*b*)	**35.** (*a*)	**36.** (*b*)	**37.** (*c*)	**38.** (*a*)	**39.** (*b*)	**40.** (*c*)
41. (*a*)	**42.** (*c*)	**43.** (*d*)	**44.** (*b*)	**45.** (*a*)	**46.** (*c*)	**47.** (*d*)	**48.** (*d*)	**49.** (*b*)	**50.** (*c*)

Solved Paper 2008 (June)

UGC NET

PAPER-I

Note : This paper contains **Fifty (50)** multiple choice questions, each question carrying **two (2)** marks.

1. The teacher has been glorified by the phrase "Friend, philosopher and guide" because:
   (*a*) He has to play all vital roles in the context of society
   (*b*) He transmits the high value of humanity to students
   (*c*) He is the great reformer of the society
   (*d*) He is a great patriot

2. The most important cause of failure for teacher lies in the area of:
   (*a*) inter personal relationship
   (*b*) lack of command over the knowledge of the subject
   (*c*) verbal ability
   (*d*) strict handling of the students

3. A teacher can establish rapport with his students by:
   (*a*) becoming a figure of authority
   (*b*) impressing students with knowledge and skill
   (*c*) playing the role of a guide
   (*d*) becoming a friend to the students

4. Education is a powerful instrument of:
   (*a*) Social transformation
   (*b*) Personal transformation
   (*c*) Cultural transformation
   (*d*) All the above

5. A teacher's major contribution towards the maximum self-realization of the student is affected through:
   (*a*) Constant fulfilment of the students' needs
   (*b*) Strict control of class-room activities
   (*c*) Sensitivity to students' needs, goals and purposes
   (*d*) Strict reinforcement of academic standards

6. Research problem is selected from the stand point of:
   (*a*) Researcher's interest
   (*b*) Financial support
   (*c*) Social relevance
   (*d*) Availability of relevant literature

7. Which one is called non-probability sampling?
   (*a*) Cluster sampling
   (*b*) Quota sampling
   (*c*) Systematic sampling
   (*d*) Stratified random sampling

8. Formulation of hypothesis may NOT be required in:
   (*a*) Survey method
   (*b*) Historical studies
   (*c*) Experimental studies
   (*d*) Normative studies

9. Field-work based research is classified as:
   (*a*) Empirical
   (*b*) Historical
   (*c*) Experimental
   (*d*) Biographical

10. Which of the following sampling method is appropriate to study the prevalence of AIDS amongst male and female in India in 1976, 1986, 1996 and 2006?
    (*a*) Cluster sampling
    (*b*) Systematic sampling
    (*c*) Quota sampling
    (*d*) Stratified random sampling

Directions (Q.11-15) : *Read the following passage and answer the questions*

The fundamental principle is that Article 14 forbids class legislation but permits reasonable classification for the purpose of legislation which classification must satisfy the twin tests of classification being founded on an intelligible differentia which distinguishes persons or things that are grouped together from those that are left out of the group and that differentia must have a rational nexus to the object sought to be achieved by the Statute in question. The thrust of Article 14 is that the citizen is entitled to equality before law and equal protection of laws. In the very nature of things the society being composed of unequals a welfare State will have to strive by both executive and legislative action to help the less fortunate in society to ameliorate their condition so that the social and economic inequality in the society may be bridged. This would necessitate a legislative application to a group of citizens otherwise unequal and amelioration of whose lot is the object of state affirmative action. In the absence of the doctrine of classification such legislation is likely to flounder on the bed rock of equality enshrined in Article 14. The Court realistically appraising the social and economic inequality and keeping in view the guidelines on which the State action must move as constitutionally laid down in Part IV of the Constitution evolved the doctrine of classification. The doctrine was evolved to sustain a legislation or State action designed to help weaker sections of the society or some such segments of the society in need of succour. Legislative and executive action may accordingly be sustained if it satisfies the twin tests of reasonable classification and the rational principle correlated to the object sought to be achieved.

The concept of equality before the law does not involve the idea of absolute equality among human beings which is a physical impossibility. All that Article 14 guarantees is a similarity of treatment contra-distinguished from identical treatment. Equality before law means that among equals the law should be equal and should be equally administered and that the likes should be treated alike. Equality before the law does not mean that things which are different shall be as though they are the same. It of course means denial of any special privilege by reason of birth, creed or the like. The legislation as well as the executive government, while dealing with diverse problems arising out of an infinite variety of human relations must of necessity have the power of making special laws, to attain any particular object and to achieve that object it must have the power of selection or classification of persons and things upon which such laws are to operate.

11. Right to equality, one of the fundamental rights, is enunciated in the constitution under Part III, Article:

(*a*) 12 (*b*) 13

(*c*) 14 (*d*) 15

12. The main thrust of Right to equality is that it permits:

(*a*) class legislation

(*b*) equality before law and equal protection under the law

(*c*) absolute equality

(*d*) special privilege by reason of birth

13. The social and economic inequality in the society can be bridged by:

(*a*) executive and legislative action

(*b*) universal suffrage

(*c*) identical treatment

(*d*) none of the above

14. The doctrine of classification is evolved to:

(*a*) Help weaker sections of the society

(*b*) Provide absolute equality

(*c*) Provide identical treatment

(*d*) None of the above

15. While dealing with diverse problems arising out of an infinite variety of human relations, the government
(*a*) must have the power of making special laws
(*b*) must not have any power to make special laws
(*c*) must have power to withdraw equal rights
(*d*) none of the above

16. Communication with oneself is known as:
(*a*) Group communication
(*b*) Grapevine communication
(*c*) Interpersonal communication
(*d*) Intrapersonal communication

17. Which broadcasting system for TV is followed in India?
(*a*) NTSE (*b*) PAL
(*c*) SECAM (*d*) NTCS

18. All India Radio before 1936 was known as:
(*a*) Indian Radio Broadcasting
(*b*) Broadcasting Service of India
(*c*) Indian Broadcasting Service
(*d*) All India Broadcasting Service

19. The biggest news agency of India is:
(*a*) PTI
(*b*) UNI
(*c*) NANAP
(*d*) Samachar Bharati

20. Prasar Bharati was launched in the year:
(*a*) 1995
(*b*) 1997
(*c*) 1999
(*d*) 2001

21. A statistical measure based upon the entire population is called parameter while measure based upon a sample is known as:
(*a*) Sample parameter
(*b*) Inference
(*c*) Statistics
(*d*) None of these

22. The importance of the correlation co-efficient lies in the fact that:
(*a*) There is a linear relationship between the correlated variables.
(*b*) It is one of the most valid measure of statistics.
(*c*) It allows one to determine the degree or strength of the association between two variables.
(*d*) It is a non-parametric method of statistical analysis.

23. The F-test:
(*a*) is essentially a two tailed test.
(*b*) is essentially a one tailed test.
(*c*) can be one tailed as well as two tailed depending on the hypothesis.
(*d*) can never be a one tailed test.

24. What will be the next letter in the following series?
DCXW, FGVU, HGTS
(*a*) AKPO (*b*) JBYZ
(*c*) JIRQ (*d*) LMRS

25. The following question is based on the diagram given below. If the two small circles represent formal class-room education and distance education and the big circle stands for university system of education, which figure represents the university systems?

(*a*)  (*b*) 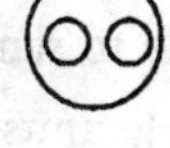

(*c*) 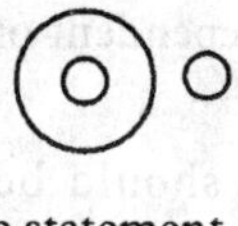 (*d*) 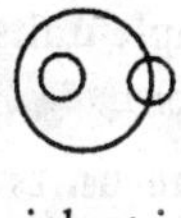

26. The statement, 'To be non-violent is good' is a:
(*a*) Moral judgement
(*b*) Factual judgement
(*c*) Religious judgement
(*d*) Value judgement

27. **Assertion (A) :** Man is a rational being.

Reason (R) : Man is a social being.

(*a*) Both (A) and (R) are true and (R) is the correct explanation of (A)

(*b*) Both (A) and (R) are true but (R) is not the correct explanation of (A)

(*c*) (A) is true but (R) is false

(*d*) (A) is false but (R) is true

28. Value Judgements are:

(*a*) Factual Judgements

(*b*) Ordinary Judgements

(*c*) Normative Judgements

(*d*) Expression of public opinion

29. Deductive reasoning proceeds from:

(*a*) general to particular

(*b*) particular to general

(*c*) one general conclusion to another general conclusion

(*d*) one particular conclusion to another particular conclusion

30. AGARTALA is written in code as 14168171, the code for AGRA is:

(*a*) 1641 (*b*) 1416

(*c*) 1441 (*d*) 1461

31. Which one of the following is the most comprehensive source of population data?

(*a*) National Family Health Surveys

(*b*) National Sample Surveys

(*c*) Census

(*d*) Demographic Health Surveys

32. Which one of the following principles is not applicable to sampling?

(*a*) Sample units must be clearly defined

(*b*) Sample units must be dependent on each other

(*c*) Same units of sample should be used throughout the study

(*d*) Sample units must be chosen in a systematic and objective manner

33. If January 1st, 2007 is Monday, what was the day on 1st January 1995?

(*a*) Sunday

(*b*) Monday

(*c*) Friday

(*d*) Saturday

34. Insert the missing number in the following series:

4 16 8 64 ? 256

(*a*) 16 (*b*) 24

(*c*) 32 (*d*) 20

35. If an article is sold for ₹ 178 at a loss of 11%; what would be its selling price in order to earn a profit of 11%?

(*a*) ₹ 222.50 (*b*) ₹ 267

(*c*) ₹ 222 (*d*) ₹ 220

36. WYSIWYG - describes the display of a document on screen as it will actually print:

(*a*) What you state is what you get

(*b*) What you see is what you get

(*c*) What you save is what you get

(*d*) What you suggest is what you get

37. Which of the following is not a Computer language?

(*a*) PASCAL (*b*) UNIX

(*c*) FORTRAN (*d*) COBOL

38. A key-board has at least:

(*a*) 91 keys

(*b*) 101 keys

(*c*) 111 keys

(*d*) 121 keys

39. An E-mail address is composed of:

(*a*) two parts

(*b*) three parts

(*c*) four parts

(*d*) five parts

40. Corel Draw is a popular:

(*a*) Illustration programme

(*b*) Programming language

(*c*) Text programme

(*d*) None of the above

41. Human ear is most sensitive to noise in which of the following ranges:

(*a*) 1 – 2 KHz (*b*) 100 – 500 Hz

(*c*) 10 – 12 KHz (*d*) 13 – 16 KHz

42. Which one of the following units is used to measure intensity of noise?

(*a*) decibel

(*b*) Hz

(*c*) Phon

(*d*) Watts/m2

43. If the population growth follows a logistic curve, the maximum sustainable yield:

(*a*) is equal to half the carrying capacity.

(*b*) is equal to the carrying capacity.

(*c*) depends on growth rates.

(*d*) depends on the initial population.

44. Chemical weathering of rocks is largely dependent upon:

(*a*) high temperature

(*b*) strong wind action

(*c*) heavy rainfall

(*d*) glaciation

45. Structure of earth's system consists of the following:

Match List-I with List-II and give the correct answer.

	List-I (Zone)	List-II (Chemical Character)
A	Atmosphere	(*i*) Inert gases
B	Biosphere	(*ii*) Salt, fresh water, snow and ice
C	Hydrosphere	(*iii*) Organic substances skeleton matter
D	Lithosphere	(*iv*) Light silicates

Codes:

	A	B	C	D
(*a*)	(*ii*)	(*iii*)	(*i*)	(*iv*)
(*b*)	(*i*)	(*iii*)	(*ii*)	(*iv*)
(c)	(*ii*)	(*i*)	(*iii*)	(*iv*)
(*d*)	(*iii*)	(*i*)	(*ii*)	(*iv*)

46. NAAC is an autonomous institution under the aegis of:

(*a*) ICSSR

(*b*) CSIR

(*c*) AICTE

(*d*) UGC

47. National Council for Women's Education was established in:

(*a*) 1958

(*b*) 1976

(*c*) 1989

(*d*) 2000

48. Which one of the following is not situated in New Delhi?

(*a*) Indian Council of Cultural Relations

(*b*) Indian Council of Scientific Research

(*c*) National Council of Educational Research and Training

(*d*) Indian Institute of Advanced Studies

49. Autonomy in higher education implies freedom in:

(*a*) Administration

(*b*) Policy-making

(*c*) Finance

(*d*) Curriculum development

50. Match List-I with List-II and select the correct answer from the code given below:

	List-I (Institutions)	List-II (Locations)
A	Dr. Hari Singh Gour University	(*i*) Mumbai
B	S.N.D.T. University	(*ii*) Baroda
C	M.S. University	(*iii*) Jodhpur
D	J.N. Vyas University	(*iv*) Sagar

Codes:

	A	B	C	D
(*a*)	(*iv*)	(*i*)	(*ii*)	(*iii*)
(*b*)	(*i*)	(*ii*)	(*vi*)	(*iv*)
(*c*)	(*iii*)	(*i*)	(*ii*)	(*iv*)
(*d*)	(*ii*)	(*iv*)	(*i*)	(*iii*)

ANSWERS

1. (*b*)	**2.** (*b*)	**3.** (*b*)	**4.** (*d*)	**5.** (*c*)	**6.** (*c*)	**7.** (*b*)	**8.** (*b*)	**9.** (*a*)	**10.** (*b*)
11. (*c*)	**12.** (*b*)	**13.** (*a*)	**14.** (*a*)	**15.** (*a*)	**16.** (*d*)	**17.** (*b*)	**18.** (*c*)	**19.** (*a*)	**20.** (*b*)
21. (*c*)	**22.** (*c*)	**23.** (*c*)	**24.** (*c*)	**25.** (*b*)	**26.** (*a*)	**27.** (*b*)	**28.** (*c*)	**29.** (*a*)	**30.** (*d*)
31. (*c*)	**32.** (*b*)	**33.** (*a*)	**34.** (*a*)	**35.** (*c*)	**36.** (*b*)	**37.** (*b*)	**38.** (*b*)	**39.** (*a*)	**40.** (*a*)
41. (*)	**42.** (*a*)	**43.** (*a*)	**44.** (*c*)	**45.** (*b*)	**46.** (*d*)	**47.** (*a*)	**48.** (*d*)	**49.** (*d*)	**50.** (*a*)

■■

Solved Paper 2007 (December)

UGC NET

PAPER-I

Note : This paper contains **Fifty (50)** multiple choice questions, each question carrying **two** (2) marks.

1. Verbal guidance is least effective in the learning of:
(*a*) Aptitudes (*b*) Skills
(*c*) Attitudes (*d*) Relationship

2. Which is the most important aspect of the teacher's role in learning?
(*a*) The development of insight into what constitutes an adequate performance
(*b*) The development of insight into what constitutes the pitfalls and dangers to be avoided
(*c*) The provision of encouragement and moral support
(*d*) The provision of continuous diagnostic and remedial help

3. The most appropriate purpose of learning is:
(*a*) personal adjustment
(*b*) modification of behaviour
(*c*) social and political awareness
(*d*) preparing oneself for employment

4. The students who keep on asking questions in the class should be:
(*a*) encouraged to find answer independently
(*b*) advised to meet the teacher after the class
(*c*) encouraged to continue questioning
(*d*) advised not to disturb during the lecture

5. Maximum participation of students is possible in teaching through:
(*a*) discussion method (*b*) lecture method
(*c*) audio-visual aids (*d*) text book method

6. Generalised conclusion on the basis of a sample is technically known as:
(*a*) Data analysis and interpretation
(*b*) Parameter inference
(*c*) Statistical inference
(*d*) All of the above

7. The experimental study is based on:
(*a*) The manipulation of variables
(*b*) Conceptual parameters
(*c*) Replication of research
(*d*) Survey of literature

8. The main characteristic of scientific research is:
(*a*) empirical (*b*) theoretical
(*c*) experimental (*d*) all of the above

9. Authenticity of a research finding is its:
(*a*) Originality (*b*) Validity
(*c*) Objectivity (*d*) All of the above

10. Which technique is generally followed when the population is finite?
(*a*) Area Sampling Technique
(*b*) Purposive Sampling Technique
(*c*) Systematic Sampling Technique
(*d*) None of the above

Direction (Q. 11-15) : *Read the following passage and answer them :*

Gandhi's overall social and environmental philosophy is based on what human beings need rather than what they want. His early introduction to the teachings of Jains, Theosophists, Christian sermons, Ruskin and Tolstoy, and most significantly the Bhagavad Gita, were to have profound impact on the development of Gandhi's holistic thinking on humanity, nature and their ecological interrelation. His deep concern for the disadvantaged, the poor and rural population created an ambience for an alternative social thinking that was at once far-sighted, local and immediate. For Gandhi was acutely aware that the demands generated by the need to feed and sustain human life, compounded by the growing industrialization of India, far outstripped the finite resources of nature. This might nowadays appear naive or commonplace, but such pronouncements were as rare as they were heretical a century ago. Gandhi was also concerned about the destruction, under colonial and modernist designs, of the existing infrastructures which had more potential for keeping a community flourishing within ecologically-sensitive traditional patterns of subsistence, especially in the rural areas, than did the incoming Western alternatives based on nature-blind technology and the enslavement of human spirit and energies.

Perhaps the moral principle for which Gandhi is best known is that of active non-violence, derived from the traditional moral restraint of not injuring another being. The most refined expression of this value is in the great epic of the Mahabharata, (c. 100 BCE to 200 CE), where moral development proceeds through placing constraints on the liberties, desires and acquisitiveness endemic to human life. One's action is judged in terms of consequences and the impact it is likely to have on another. Jainas had generalized this principle to include all sentient creatures and biocommunities alike. Advanced Jaina monks and nuns will sweep their path to avoid harming insects and even bacteria. Non-injury is a non-negotiable universal prescription.

11. Which one of the following have a profound impact on the development of Gandhi's holistic thinking on humanity, nature and their ecological interrelations?

(*a*) Jain teachings (*b*) Christian sermons
(*c*) Bhagavad Gita (*d*) Ruskin and Tolstoy

12. Gandhi's overall social and environmental philosophy is based on human beings':

(*a*) need (*b*) desire
(*c*) wealth (*d*) welfare

13. Gandhiji's deep concern for the disadvantaged, the poor and rural population created an ambience for an alternative:

(*a*) rural policy (*b*) social thinking
(*c*) urban policy (*d*) economic thinking

14. Colonial policy and modernisation led to the destruction of:

(*a*) major industrial infrastructure
(*b*) irrigation infrastructure
(*c*) urban infrastructure
(*d*) rural infrastructure

15. Gandhi's active non-violence is derived from:

(*a*) Moral restraint of not injuring another being
(*b*) Having liberties, desires and acquisitiveness
(*c*) Freedom of action
(*d*) Nature-blind technology and enslavement of human spirit and energies

16. DTH service was started in the year:

(*a*) 2000 (*b*) 2002
(*c*) 2004 (*d*) 2006

17. National Press day is celebrated on:

(*a*) 16th November (*b*) 19th November
(*c*) 21th November (*d*) 30th November

18. The total number of members in the Press Council of India are:

(*a*) 28 (*b*) 14
(*c*) 17 (*d*) 20

19. The right to impart and receive information is guaranteed in the Constitution of India by Article:

(*a*) 19 (2) (*a*) (*b*) 19(16)
(*c*) 19(2) (*d*) 19(1) (*a*)

20. Use of radio for higher education is based on the presumption of:

(*a*) Enriching curriculum based instruction
(*b*) Replacing teacher in the long run
(*c*) Everybody having access to a radio set
(*d*) Other means of instruction getting outdated

21. Find out the number which should come at the place of question mark which will complete the following series: 5, 4, 9, 17, 35, ? = 139

(*a*) 149 (*b*) 79
(*c*) 49 (*d*) 69

Direction (Q. 22-24) : are based on the following diagram in which there are three interlocking circles I, S and P, where circle I stands for Indians, circle S for Scientists and circle P for Politicians. Different regions in the figure are lettered from a to f

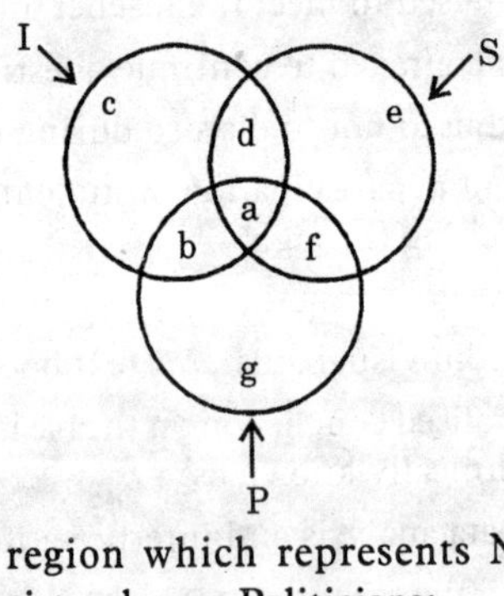

22. The region which represents Non-Indian Scientists who are Politicians:

(*a*) f (*b*) d
(*c*) a (*d*) c

23. The region which represents Indians who are neither Scientists nor Politicians:

(*a*) g (*b*) c
(*c*) f (*d*) a

24. The region which represents Politicians who are Indians as well as Scientists:

(*a*) b (*b*) c
(*c*) a (*d*) d

25. Which number is missing in the following series?

2, 5, 10, 17, 26, 37, 50, ?

(*a*) 63 (*b*) 65
(*c*) 67 (*d*) 69

26. The function of measurement includes:

(*a*) Prognosis (*b*) Diagnosis
(*c*) Prediction (*d*) All of the above

27. Logical arguments are based on:

(*a*) Scientific reasoning
(*b*) Customary reasoning
(*c*) Mathematical reasoning
(*d*) Syllogistic reasoning

28. Insert the missing number: 4 : 17 : : 7 : ?

(*a*) 48 (*b*) 49
(*c*) 50 (*d*) 51

29. Choose the odd word:

(*a*) Nun (*b*) Knight
(*c*) Monk (*d*) Priest

30. Choose the number which is different from others in the group:

(*a*) 49 (*b*) 63
(*c*) 77 (*d*) 81

31. Probability sampling implies:

(*a*) Stratified Random Sampling
(*b*) Systematic Random Sampling
(*c*) Simple Random Sampling
(*d*) All of the above

32. Insert the missing number:

36/62, 39/63, 43/61, 48/64, ?

(*a*) 51/65 (*b*) 56/60
(*c*) 54/65 (*d*) 33/60

33. At what time between 3 and 4 O'clock will the hands of a watch point in opposite directions?

(*a*) 40 minutes past three
(*c*) 50 minutes past three
(*b*) 45 minutes past three
(*d*) 55 minutes past three

34. Mary has three children. What is the probability that none of the three children is a boy?

(*a*) 1/2 (*b*) 1/3
(*c*) 3/4 (*d*) 1

35. If the radius of a circle is increased by 50 per cent. Its area is increased by:

(*a*) 125 per cent (*b*) 100 per cent
(*c*) 75 per cent (*d*) 50 per cent

36. CD ROM stands for:

(*a*) Computer Disk Read Only Memory
(*b*) Compact Disk Read Over Memory
(*c*) Compact Disk Read Only Memory
(*d*) Computer Disk Read Over Memory

37. The 'brain' of a computer which keeps peripherals under its control is called:

(*a*) Common Power Unit
(*b*) Common Processing Unit
(*c*) Central Power Unit
(*d*) Central Processing Unit

38. Data can be saved on backing storage medium known as :

(*a*) Compact Disk Recordable
(*b*) Computer Disk Rewritable
(*c*) Compact Disk Rewritable
(*d*) Computer Data Rewritable

39. RAM means:

(*a*) Random Access Memory
(*b*) Rigid Access Memory
(*c*) Rapid Access Memory
(*d*) Revolving Access Memory

40. www represents:

(*a*) who what and where
(*b*) weird wide web
(*c*) word wide web
(*d*) world wide web

41. Deforestation during the recent decades has led to:

(*a*) Soil erosion (*b*) Landslides

(*c*) Loss of bio-diversity (*d*) All the above

42. Which one of the following natural hazards is responsible for causing highest human disaster?

(*a*) Earthquakes (*b*) Snow-storms

(*c*) Volcanic eruptions (*d*) Tsunami

43. Which one of the following is appropriate for natural hazard mitigation?

(*a*) International AID

(*b*) Timely Warning System

(*c*) Rehabilitation

(*d*) Community Participation

44. Slums in metro-city are the result of:

(*a*) Rural to urban migration

(*b*) Poverty of the city-scape

(*c*) Lack of urban infrastructure

(*d*) Urban-governance

45. The great Indian Bustard bird is found in:

(*a*) Thar Desert of India

(*b*) Coastal regions of India

(*c*) Temperate Forests in the Himalaya

(*d*) Tarai zones of the Himalayan Foot

46. The first Indian Satellite for serving the educational sector is known as:

(*a*) SATEDU (*b*) INSAT - B

(*c*) EDUSAT (*d*) INSAT-C

47. Exclusive educational channel of IGNOU is known as:

(*a*) GyanDarshan (*b*) Cyan Vani

(*c*) DoorDarshan (*d*) Prasar Bharati

48. The head quarter of Mahatma Gandhi Antarrashtriya Hindi Vishwavidyalaya is situated in:

(*a*) Sevagram

(*b*) New Delhi

(*c*) Wardha

(*d*) Ahmedabad

49. Match List - I with List - II and select the correct answer using the codes given below:

List-I (Institutes)	**List-II (Locations)**
A. Central Institute of English	(i) Chitrakoot and Foreign Languages
B. Gramodaya Vishwavidyalaya	(ii) Hyderabad
C. Central Institute of Higher Tibetan Studies	(iii) New Delhi
D. IGNOU	(iv) Dharmasala

Codes :

	A	B	C	D
(*a*)	(ii)	(i)	(iv)	(iii)
(*b*)	(iv)	(iii)	(ii)	(i)
(*c*)	(iii)	(iv)	(i)	(ii)
(*d*)	(i)	(ii)	(iv)	(iii)

50. The aim of vocationalization of education is:

(*a*) preparing students for a vocation along with knowledge

(*b*) converting liberal education into vocational education

(*c*) giving more importance to vocational than general education

(*d*) making liberal education job-oriented

ANSWERS

1. (*b*)	**2.** (*a*)	**3.** (*b*)	**4.** (*a*)	**5.** (*a*)	**6.** (*a*)	**7.** (*a*)	**8.** (*d*)	**9.** (*c*)	**10.** (*c*)
11. (*c*)	**12.** (*a*)	**13.** (*b*)	**14.** (*d*)	**15.** (*a*)	**16.** (*c*)	**17.** (*a*)	**18.** (*a*)	**19.** (*d*)	**20.** (*c*)
21. (*d*)	**22.** (*a*)	**23.** (*b*)	**24.** (*c*)	**25.** (*b*)	**26.** (*d*)	**27.** (*d*)	**28.** (*c*)	**29.** (*b*)	**30.** (*d*)
31. (*d*)	**32.** (*c*)	**33.** (*c*)	**34.** (*)	**35.** (*a*)	**36.** (*c*)	**37.** (*d*)	**38.** (*c*)	**39.** (*a*)	**40.** (*d*)
41. (*d*)	**42.** (*d*)	**43.** (*b*)	**44.** (*a*)	**45.** (*a*)	**46.** (*c*)	**47.** (*a*)	**48.** (*c*)	**49.** (*a*)	**50.** (*d*)

■■

Solved Paper 2007 (June)

UGC NET

PAPER-I

Note : This paper contains **Fifty (50)** multiple choice questions, each question carrying **two (2)** marks.

1. Teacher uses visual-aids to make learning:
   (*a*) simple
   (*b*) more knowledgeable
   (*c*) quicker
   (*d*) interesting
2. The teacher's role at the higher educational level is to:
   (*a*) provide information to students
   (*b*) promote self-learning in students
   (*c*) encourage healthy competition among students
   (*d*) help students to solve their personal problems
3. Which one of the following teachers would you like the most:
   (*a*) punctual
   (*b*) having research aptitude
   (*c*) loving and having high idealistic philosophy
   (*d*) who often amuses his students
4. Micro teaching is most effective for the student-teacher:
   (*a*) during the practice-teaching
   (*b*) after the practice-teaching
   (*c*) before the practice-teaching
   (*d*) none of the above
5. Which is the least important factor in teaching?
   (*a*) punishing the students
   (*b*) maintaining discipline in the class
   (*c*) lecturing in impressive way
   (*d*) drawing sketches and diagrams on the black-board
6. To test null hypothesis, a researcher uses:
   (*a*) t test (*b*) ANOVA
   (*c*) X^2 (*d*) factorial analysis
7. A research problem is feasible only when:
   (*a*) it has utility and relevance
   (*b*) it is researchable
   (*c*) it is new and adds something to knowledge
   (*d*) all the above
8. Bibliography given in a research report:
   (*a*) shows vast knowledge of the researcher
   (*b*) helps those interested in further research
   (*c*) has no relevance to research
   (*d*) all the above
9. Fundamental research reflects the ability to:
   (*a*) Synthesize new ideals
   (*b*) Expound new principles
   (*c*) Evaluate the existing material concerning research
   (*d*) Study the existing literature regarding various topics
10. The study in which the investigators attempt to trace an effect is known as:
   (*a*) Survey Research
   (*b*) 'Ex-post Facto' Research
   (*c*) Historical Research
   (*d*) Summative Research

Direction (Qs. 11 - 15) : *Read the following passage and answer them :*

All political systems need to mediate the relationship between private wealth and public power. Those that fail risk a dysfunctional government captured by wealthy interests. Corruption is one symptom of such failure with private willingness-to-pay trumping public goals. Private individuals and business firms pay to get routine services and to get to the head of the bureaucratic queue. They pay to limit their taxes, avoid costly regulations, obtain contracts at inflated prices and get concessions and privatised firms at low prices. If corruption is endemic, public officials - both bureaucrats and elected officials - may redesign programmes and propose public projects with few public benefits and many opportunities for private profit. Of course, corruption, in the sense of bribes, pay-offs and kickbacks, is only one type of government failure. Efforts to promote 'good governance' must be broader than anti-corruption campaigns. Governments may be honest but inefficient because no one has an incentive to work productively, and narrow elites may capture the state and exert excess influence on policy. Bribery may induce the lazy to work hard and permit those not in the inner circle of cronies to obtain benefits. However, even in such cases, corruption cannot be confined to 'functional' areas. It will be a temptation whenever private benefits are positive. It may be a reasonable response to a harsh reality but, over time, it can facilitate a spiral into an even worse situation.

11. The governments which fail to focus on the relationship between private wealth and public power are likely to become:

(*a*) Functional

(*b*) Dysfunctional

(*c*) Normal functioning

(*d*) Good governance

12. One important symptom of bad governance is:

(*a*) Corruption

(*b*) High taxes

(*c*) Complicated rules and regulations

(*d*) High prices

13. When corruption is rampant, public officials always aim at many opportunities for:

(*a*) Public benefits

(*b*) Public profit

(*c*) Private profit

(*d*) Corporate gains

14. Productivity linked incentives to public/private officials is one of the indicatives for:

(*a*) Efficient government

(*b*) Bad governance

(*c*) Inefficient government

(*d*) Corruption

15. The spiralling corruption can only be contained by promoting:

(*a*) Private profit

(*b*) Anti-corruption campaign

(*c*) Good governance

(*d*) Pay-offs and kick backs

16. Press Council of India is located at:

(*a*) Chennai (*b*) Mumbai

(*c*) Kolkata (*d*) Delhi

17. Adjusting the photo for publication by cutting is technically known as:

(*a*) Photo cutting

(*b*) Photo bleeding

(*c*) Photo cropping

(*d*) Photo adjustment

18. Feed-back of a message comes from:

(*a*) Satellite

(*b*) Media

(*c*) Audience

(*d*) Communicator

19. Collection of information in advance before designing communication strategy is known as:

(*a*) Feed-back

(*b*) Feed-forward

(*c*) Research study

(*d*) Opinion poll

20. The aspect ratio of TV screen is:

(*a*) 4:3

(*b*) 4:2

(*c*) 3:5

(*d*) 2:3

21. Which is the number that comes next in the sequence?

9, 8, 8, 8, 7, 8, 6,

(*a*) 5 (*b*) 6

(*c*) 8 (*d*) 4

22. If in a certain language TRIVANDRUM is coded as 2 5 9 5 3 5 4 7 5 8, how would MADRAS be coded?

(*a*) 834536 (*b*) 834538

(*c*) 834530 (*d*) 834539

23. The question to be answered by factorial analysis of the quantitative data does not explain one of the following:

(*a*) Is 'X' related to 'Y'?

(*b*) How is 'X' related to 'Y'?

(*c*) How does 'X' affect the dependent variable 'Y' at different levels of another independent variable 'K' or 'M'?

(*d*) How is 'X' by 'K' related to 'M'?

24. January 12, 1980 was Saturday, what day was January 12, 1979:

(*a*) Saturday (*b*) Friday

(*c*) Sunday (*d*) Thursday

25. How many Mondays are there in a particular month of a particular year, if the month ends on Wednesday?

(*a*) 5 (*b*) 4

(*c*) 3 (*d*) None of the above

26. From the given four statements, select the two which cannot be true but yet both can be false.

Choose the right pair:

(*i*) All men are mortal

(*ii*) Some men are mortal

(*iii*) No man is mortal

(*iv*) Some men are not mortal

(*a*) (*i*) and (*ii*)

(*b*) (*iii*) and (*iv*)

(*c*) (*i*) and (*iii*)

(*d*) (*ii*) and (*iv*)

27. A Syllogism must have:

(*a*) Three terms (*b*) Four terms

(*c*) Six terms (*d*) Five terms

28. Copula is that part of proposition which denotes the relationship between:

(*a*) Subject and predicate

(*b*) Known and unknown

(*c*) Major premise and minor premise

(*d*) Subject and object

29. "E" denotes:

(*a*) Universal Negative Proposition

(*b*) Particular Affirmative Proposition

(*c*) Universal Affirmative Proposition

(*d*) Particular Negative Proposition

30. 'A' is the father of 'C, and 'D' is the son of 'B'. 'E' is the brother of 'A'. If 'C is the sister of 'D', how is 'B' related to 'E'?

(*a*) daughter (*b*) husband

(*c*) sister-in-law (*d*) brother-in-law

31. Which of the following methods will you choose to prepare choropleth map of India showing urban density of population:

(*a*) Quartiles (*b*) Quintiles

(*c*) Mean and SD (*d*) Break - point

32. Which of the following methods is best suited to show on a map the types of crops being grown in a region?

(*a*) Choropleth (*b*) Chorochromatic

(*c*) Choroschematic (*d*) Isopleth

33. A ratio represents the relation between:

(*a*) Part and Part (*b*) Part and Whole

(*c*) Whole and Whole (*d*) All of the above

34. Out of four numbers, the average of the first three numbers is thrice the fourth number. If the average of the four numbers is 5, the fourth number is:

(*a*) 4.5 (*b*) 5

(*c*) 2 (*d*) 4

35. Circle graphs are used to show:

(*a*) How various sections share in the whole?

(*b*) How various parts are related to the whole?

(*c*) How one whole is related to other wholes

(*d*) How one part is related to other parts?

36. On the keyboard of computer each character has an "ASCII" value which stands for:

(*a*) American Stock Code for Information Interchange

(*b*) American Standard Code for Information Interchange

(*c*) African Standard Code for Information Interchange

(*d*) Adaptable Standard Code for Information Change

37. Which part of the Central Processing Unit (CPU) performs calculation and makes decisions:

(*a*) Arithematic Logic Unit

(*b*) Alternating Logic Unit

(*c*) Alternate Local Unit

(*d*) American Logic Unit

38. "Dpi" stands for:

(*a*) Dots per inch

(*b*) Digits per unit

(*c*) Dots pixel inch

(*d*) Diagrams per inch

39. The process of laying out a document with text, graphics, headlines and photographs is involved in

(*a*) Deck Top Publishing

(*b*) Desk Top Printing

(*c*) Desk Top Publishing

(*d*) Deck Top Printing

40. Transfer of data from one application to another line is known as:

(*a*) Dynamic Disk Exchange

(*b*) Dodgy Data Exchange

(*c*) Dogmatic Data Exchange

(*d*) Dynamic Data Exchange

41. Tsunami occurs due to:

(*a*) Mild earthquakes and landslides in the oceans

(*b*) Strong earthquakes and landslides in the oceans

(*c*) Strong earthquakes and landslides in mountains

(*d*) Strong earthquakes and landslides in deserts

42. Which of the natural hazards have big effect on Indian people each year?

(*a*) Cyclones (*b*) Floods

(*c*) Earthquakes (*d*) Landslides

43. Comparative Environment Impact Assessment study is to be conducted for:

(*a*) the whole year

(*b*) three seasons excluding monsoon

(*c*) any three seasons

(*d*) the worst season

44. Sea level rise results primarily due to:

(*a*) Heavy rainfall

(*b*) Melting of glaciers

(*c*) Submarine volcanism

(*d*) Seafloor spreading

45. The plume rise in a coal based power plant depends on:

(*i*) Buoyancy

(*ii*) Atmospheric stability

(*iii*) Momentum of exhaust gases

Identify the correct code:

(*a*) (*i*) and (*ii*) only

(*b*) (ii) and (*iii*) only

(*c*) (i) and (*iii*) only

(*d*) (*i*), (*ii*) and (*iii*)

46. Value education makes a student:

(*a*) Good citizen

(*b*) Successful businessman

(*c*) Popular teacher

(*d*) Efficient manager

47. Networking of libraries through electronic media is known as:

(*a*) Inflibnet (*b*) Libinfnet

(*c*) Internet (*d*) HTML

48. The University which telecasts interactive educational programmes through its own channel is:

(*a*) B. R. Ambedkar Open University, Hyderabad

(*b*) I.G.N.O.U.

(*c*) University of Pune

(*d*) Annamalai University

49. The Government established the University Grants Commission by an Act of Parliament in the year:

(*a*) 1980 (*b*) 1948

(*c*) 1950 (*d*) 1956

50. Universities having central campus for imparting education are called:

(*a*) Central Universities

(*b*) Deemed Universities

(*c*) Residential Universities

(*d*) Open Universities

ANSWERS

1. (*d*)	**2.** (*b*)	**3.** (*b*)	**4.** (*a*)	**5.** (*a*)	**6.** (*b*)	**7.** (*d*)	**8.** (*b*)	**9.** (*b*)	**10.** (*b*)
11. (*b*)	**12.** (*a*)	**13.** (*c*)	**14.** (*a*)	**15.** (*a*)	**16.** (*d*)	**17.** (*c*)	**18.** (*a*)	**19.** (*d*)	**20.** (*a*)
21. (*c*)	**22.** (*a*)	**23.** (*d*)	**24.** (*b*)	**25.** (*b*)	**26.** (*d*)	**27.** (*b*)	**28.** (*a*)	**29.** (*a*)	**30.** (*c*)
31. (*a*)	**32.** (*a*)	**33.** (*d*)	**34.** (*c*)	**35.** (*b*)	**36.** (*b*)	**37.** (*a*)	**38.** (*a*)	**39.** (*c*)	**40.** (*d*)
41. (*b*)	**42.** (*b*)	**43.** (*a*)	**44.** (*b*)	**45.** (*b*)	**46.** (*a*)	**47.** (*a*)	**48.** (*b*)	**49.** (*d*)	**50.** (*a*)

Solved Paper 2006 (December)

UGC NET

PAPER-I

Note : This paper contains **Fifty (50)** multiple choice questions, each question carrying **two (2)** marks.

1. Which of the following is not instructional material?
   (*a*) Over Head Projector
   (*b*) Audio Casset
   (*c*) Printed Material
   (*d*) Transparency
2. Which of the following statement is not correct?
   (*a*) Lecture Method can develop reasoning
   (*b*) Lecture Method can develop knowledge
   (*c*) Lecture Method is one way process
   (*d*) During Lecture Method students are passive
3. The main objective of teaching at Higher Education Level is:
   (*a*) To prepare students to pass examination
   (*b*) To develop the capacity to take decisions
   (*c*) To give new information
   (*d*) To motivate students to ask questions during lecture
4. Which of the following statement is correct?
   (*a*) Reliability ensures validity
   (*b*) Validity ensures reliability
   (*c*) Reliability and validity are independent of each other
   (*d*) Reliability does not depend on objectivity
5. Which of the following indicates evaluation?
   (*a*) Ram got 45 marks out of 200
   (*b*) Mohan got 38 percent marks in English
   (*c*) Shyam got First Division in final examination
   (*d*) All the above
6. Research can be conducted by a person who:
   (*a*) has studied research methodology
   (*b*) holds a postgraduate degree
   (*c*) possesses thinking and reasoning ability
   (*d*) is a hard worker
7. Which of the following statements is correct?
   (*a*) Objectives of research are stated in first chapter of the thesis
   (*b*) Researcher must possess analytical ability
   (*c*) Variability is the source of problem
   (*d*) All the above
8. Which of the following is not the Method of Research?
   (*a*) Observation (*b*) Historical
   (*c*) Survey (*d*) Philosophical
9. Research can be classified as:
   (*a*) Basic, Applied and Action Research
   (*b*) Quantitative and Qualitative Research
   (*c*) Philosophical, Historical, Survey and Experimental Research
   (*d*) All the above
10. The first step of research is:
   (*a*) Selecting a problem
   (*b*) Searching a problem
   (*c*) Finding a problem
   (*d*) Identifying a problem

Directions Q. (11 – 15) : *Read the following passage and answer the question.*

After almost three decades of contemplating Swarovski-encrusted navels on increasing flat abs, the Mumbai film industry is on a discovery of India and itself. With budgets of over 30 crore each, four soon to be released movies by premier directors are exploring the idea of who we are and redefining who the other is. It is a fundamental question which the bling-bling, glam-sham and disham-disham tends to avoid. It is also a question which binds an audience when the lights go dim and the projector rolls: as a nation, who are we? As a people, where are we going?

The Germans coined a word for it, zeitgeist, which perhaps Yash Chopra would not care to pronounce. But at 72, he remains the person who can best capture it. After being the first to project the diasporic Indian on screen in Lamhe in 1991, he has returned to his roots in a new movie. Veer Zaara, set in 1986, where Pakistan, the traditional other, the part that got away, is the lover and the saviour. In Subhash Ghai's Kisna, set in 1947, the other is the English woman. She is not a memsahib, but a mehbooba. In Ketan Mehta's The Rising, the East India Englishman is not the evil oppressor of countless cardboard characterisations, which span the spectrum from Jewel in the Crown to Kranti, but an honourable friend.

This is Manoj Kumar's Desh Ki dharti with a difference: there is culture, not contentious politics; balle balle, not bombs: no dooriyan (distance), only nazdeekiyan (closeness).

All four films are heralding a new hero and heroine. The new hero is fallible and vulnerable, committed to his dharma, but also not afraid of failure - less of a boy and more of a man. He even has a grown up name: Veer Pratap Singh in Veer-Zaara and Mohan Bhargav in Swades. The new heroine is not a babe, but often a bebe, dressed in traditional Punjabi clothes, often with the stereotypical body type as well, as in Bride and Prejudice of Gurinder Chadha.

11. Which word Yash Chopra would not be able to pronounce?

(*a*) Bling + bling (*b*) Zeitgeist
(*c*) Montaz (*d*) Dooriyan

12. Who made Lamhe in 1991?

(*a*) Subhash Ghai (*b*) Yash Chopra
(*c*) Aditya Chopra (*d*) Sakti Samanta

13. Which movie is associated with Manoj Kumar?

(*a*) Jewel in the Crown
(*b*) Kisna
(*c*) Zaara
(*d*) Desh Ki dharti

14. Which is the latest film by Yash Chopra?

(*a*) Deewar
(*b*) Kabhi Kabhi
(*c*) Dilwale Dulhaniya Le Jayenge
(*d*) Veer Zaara

15. Which is the dress of the heroine in Veer-Zaara?

(*a*) Traditional Gujarati Clothes
(*b*) Traditional Bengali Clothes
(*c*) Traditional Punjabi Clothes
(*d*) Traditional Madras Clothes

16. Which one of the following can be termed as verbal communication?

(*a*) Prof. Sharma delivered the lecture in the class room.
(*b*) Signal at the cross-road changed from green to orange.
(*c*) The child was crying to attract the attention of the mother.
(*d*) Dipak wrote a letter for leave application.

17. Which is the 24 hours English Business news channel in India?

(*a*) Zee News (*b*) NDTV 24×7
(*c*) CNBC (*d*) India News

18. Consider the following statements in communication:

(*i*) Hema Malini is the Chairperson of the Children's Film Society, India.
(*ii*) Yash Chopra is the Chairman of the Central Board of Film Certification of India.
(*iii*) Sharmila Tagore is the Chairperson of National Film Development Corporation.
(*iv*) Dilip Kumar, Raj Kapoor and Preeti Zinta have all been recipients of Dada Saheb Phalke Award.

Which of the statements given above is/are correct?

(*a*) (*i*) and (*iii*) (*b*) (*ii*) and (*iii*)
(*c*) (*iv*) only (*d*) (*iii*) only

19. Which of the following pair is not correctly matched?

(*a*) N. Ram: The Hindu

(*b*) Barkha Dutt : Zee News

(*c*) Pranay Roy: NDTV 24×7

(*d*) Prabhu Chawla: Aaj tak

20. "Because you deserve to know" is the punchline used by:

(*a*) The Times of India

(*b*) The Hindu

(*c*) Indian Express

(*d*) Hindustan Times

21. In the sequence of numbers 8, 24, 12, X, 18, 54 the missing number X is:

(*a*) 26 (*b*) 24

(*c*) 36 (*d*) 32

22. If A stands for 5, B for 6, C for 7, D for 8 and so on, then the following numbers stand for 17, 19, 20, 9 and 8:

(*a*) PLANE (*b*) MOPED

(*c*) MOTOR (*d*) TONGA

23. The letters in the first set have certain relationship. On the basis of this relationship, what is the right choice for the second set?

AST : BRU : : NQV : ?

(*a*) ORW (*b*) MPU

(*c*) MRW (*d*) OPW

24. In a certain code, PAN is written as 31 and PAR as 35. In this code PAT is written as:

(*a*) 30 (*b*) 37

(*c*) 38 (*d*) 39

25. The sides of a triangle are in the ratio of 1/2 : 1/3 : 1/4. If its perimeter is 52 cm, the length of the smallest side is:

(*a*) 9 cm

(*b*) 10 cm

(*c*) 11 cm

(*d*) 12 cm

26. Which one of the following statements is completely non-sensical?

(*a*) He was a bachelor, but he married recently.

(*b*) He is a bachelor, but he married recently.

(*c*) When he married, he was not a bachelor.

(*d*) When he was a bachelor, he was not married.

27. Which of the following statements are mutually contradictory?

(*i*) All flowers are not fragrant.

(*ii*) Most flowers are not fragrant.

(*iii*) None of the flowers is fragrant.

(*iv*) Most flowers are fragrant.

Choose the correct answer from the code given below:

Code:

(*a*) (*i*) and (*ii*)

(*b*) (*i*) and (*iii*)

(*c*) (*ii*) and (*iii*)

(*d*) (*iii*) and (*iv*)

28. Which of the following statements say the same thing?

(*i*) "I am a teacher" (said by Arvind)

(*ii*) "I am a teacher" (said by Binod)

(*iii*) "My son is a teacher" (said by Binod's father)

(*iv*) "My brother is a teacher" (said by Binod's sister)

(*v*) "My brother is a teacher" (said by Binod's only sister)

(*vi*) "My sole enemy is a teacher" (said by Binod's only enemy)

Choose the correct answer from the code given below:

Codes :

(*a*) (*i*) and (*ii*)

(*b*) (*ii*), (*iii*), (*iv*) and (*v*)

(*c*) (*ii*) and (vi)

(*d*) (*v*) and (vi)

29. Which of the following are correct ways of arguing?

(*i*) There can be no second husband without a second wife.

(*ii*) Anil is a friend of Bob, Bob is a friend of Raj, hence Anil is a friend of Raj.

(*iii*) A is equal to B, B is equal to C, hence A is equal to C.

(*iv*) If everyone is a liar, then we cannot prove it.

Choose the correct answer from the code given below:

Code:

(*a*) (*iii*) and (*iv*)

(*b*) (*i*), (*iii*) and (*iv*)

(*c*) (*ii*), (*iii*) and (*iv*)

(*d*) (*i*), (*ii*), (*iii*) and (*iv*)

30. Which of the following statement/s are ALWAYS FALSE?

(*i*) The sun will not rise in the East some day.

(*ii*) A wooden table is not a table.

(*iii*) Delhi city will be drowned under water.

(*iv*) Cars run on water as fuel. Choose the correct answer from the code given below:

Code:

(*a*) (*i*), (*iii*) and (*iv*) (*b*) Only (*iii*)

(*c*) (*i*), (*ii*) and (*iii*) (*d*) (*ii*) alone

Directions Q. (31 – 33) : *Study the following graph and answer question numbers.*

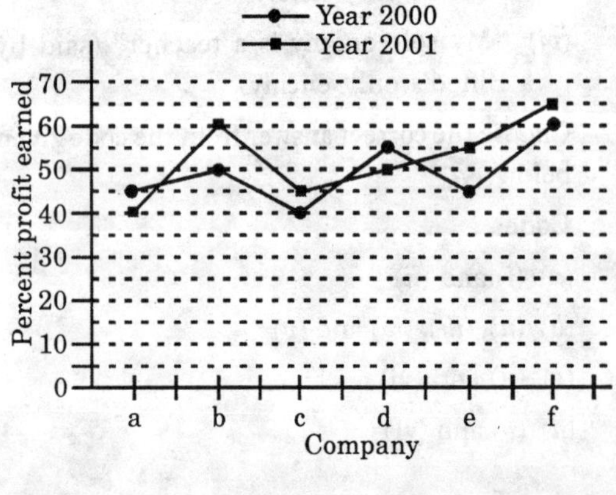

31. In the year 2000, which of the following Companies earned maximum percent profit?

(*a*) a (*b*) b

(*c*) d (*d*) f

32. In the year 2001, which of the following Companies earned minimum percent profit?

(*a*) a (*b*) c

(*c*) d (*d*) e

33. In the years 2000 and 2001, which of the following Companies earned maximum average percent profit?

(*a*) f (*b*) e

(*c*) d (*d*) b

34. Human Development Report for 'each' of the year at global level has been published by:

(*a*) UNDP (*b*) WTO

(*c*) IMF (*d*) World Bank

35. The number of students in four classes A, B, C, D and their respective mean marks obtained by each of the class are given below:

	Class A	Class B	Class C	Class D
Number of students	10	40	30	20
Arithmetic mean	20	30	50	15

The combined mean of the marks of four classes together will be:

(*a*) 32 (*b*) 50

(*c*) 20 (*d*) 15

36. LAN stands for:

(*a*) Local And National

(*b*) Local Area Network

(*c*) Large Area Network

(*d*) Live Area Network

37. Which of the following statement is correct?

(*a*) Modem is a software

(*b*) Modem helps in stabilizing the voltage

(*c*) Modem is the operating system

(*d*) Modem converts the analog signal into digital signal and vice-versa

38. Which of the following is the appropriate definition of a computer?

(*a*) Computer is a machine that can process information.

(*b*) Computer is an electronic device that can store, retrieve and process both qualitative and quantitative data quickly and accurately.

(*c*) Computer is an electronic device that can store, retrieve and quickly process only quantitative data.

(*d*) Computer is a machine that can store, retrieve and process quickly and accurately only qualitative information

39. Information and Communication Technology includes:

(*a*) On line learning

(*b*) Learning through the use of EDUSAT

(*c*) Web Based Learning

(*d*) All the above

40. Which of the following is the appropriate format of URL of e-mail?

(*a*) www_mail.com

(*b*) www@mail.com

(*c*) WWW@mail.com

(*d*) www.mail.com

41. The most significant impact of volcanic eruption has been felt in the form of:

(*a*) change in weather

(*b*) sinking of islands

(*c*) loss of vegetation

(*d*) extinction of animals

42. With absorption and decomposition of CO_2 in ocean water beyond desired level, there will be:

(*a*) decrease in temperature

(*b*) increase in salinity

(*c*) growth of phytoplankton

(*d*) rise in sea level

43. Arrange column II in proper sequence so as to match it with column I and choose the correct answer from the code given below:

Column I Water Quality	Column II pH Value
A. Neutral	(*i*) 5
B. Moderately acidic	(*ii*) 7
C. Alkaline	(*iii*) 4
D. Injurious	(*iv*) 8

Code:

	A	B	C	D
(*a*)	(*ii*)	(*iii*)	(*i*)	(*iv*)
(*b*)	(*i*)	(*iii*)	(*ii*)	(*iv*)
(*c*)	(*ii*)	(*i*)	(*iv*)	(*iii*)
(*d*)	(*iv*)	(*ii*)	(*iii*)	(*i*)

44. The maximum emission of pollutants from fuel sources in India is caused by:

(*a*) Coal

(*b*) Firewood

(*c*) Refuse burning

(*d*) Vegetable waste product

45. The urbanisation process accounts for the wind in the urban centres during nights to remain:

(*a*) faster than that in rural areas

(*b*) slower than that in rural areas

(*c*) the same as that in rural areas

(*d*) cooler than that in rural areas

46. The University Grants Commission was constituted on the recommendation of:

(*a*) Dr. Sarvapalli Radhakrishnan Commission

(*b*) Mudaliar Commission

(*c*) Sargent Commission

(*d*) Kothari Commission

47. Which one of the following Articles of the Constitution of India safeguards the rights of Minorities to establish and run educational institutions of their own liking?

(*a*) Article 19 (*b*) Article 29

(*c*) Article 30 (*d*) Article 31

48. Match List - I (Institutions) with List - II (Functions) and select the correct answer by using the code given below:

List - I (Institutions)	List - II (Functions)
A. Parliament	(*i*) Formulation of Budget
B. C & A.G.	(*ii*) Enactment of Budget
C. Ministry of Finance	(*iii*) Implementation of Budget
D. Executing Departments	(*iv*) Legality of expenditure
	(*v*) Justification of Income

Code:

	A	B	C	D
(*a*)	(*iii*)	(*iv*)	(*ii*)	(*i*)
(*b*)	(*ii*)	(*iv*)	(*i*)	(*iii*)
(*c*)	(*v*)	(*iii*)	(*iv*)	(*ii*)
(*d*)	(*iv*)	(*ii*)	(*iii*)	(*v*)

49. Foundation training to the newly recruited IAS (Probationers) is imparted by:

(*a*) Indian Institute of Public Administration

(*b*) Administrative Staff College of India

(*c*) L.B.S. National Academy of Administration

(*d*) Centre for Advanced Studies

50. Electoral disputes arising out of Presidential and Vice-Presidential Elections are settled by:

(*a*) Election Commission of India

(*b*) Joint Committee of Parliament

(*c*) Supreme Court of India

(*d*) Central Election Tribunal

ANSWERS

1. (*d*)	**2.** (*a*)	**3.** (*b*)	**4.** (*c*)	**5.** (*d*)	**6.** (*a*)	**7.** (*d*)	**8.** (*a*)	**9.** (*d*)	**10.** (*d*)
11. (*b*)	**12.** (*b*)	**13.** (*d*)	**14.** (*d*)	**15.** (*c*)	**16.** (*a*)	**17.** (*c*)	**18.** (*b*)	**19.** (*b*)	**20.** (*d*)
21. (*c*)	**22.** (*b*)	**23.** (*d*)	**24.** (*b*)	**25.** (*d*)	**26.** (*b*)	**27.** (*d*)	**28.** (*b*)	**29.** (*a*)	**30.** (*a*)
31. (*d*)	**32.** (*a*)	**33.** (*a*)	**34.** (*a*)	**35.** (*a*)	**36.** (*b*)	**37.** (*d*)	**38.** (*b*)	**39.** (*d*)	**40.** (*b*)
41. (*a*)	**42.** (*c*)	**43.** (*a*)	**44.** (*a*)	**45.** (*a*)	**46.** (*a*)	**47.** (*c*)	**48.** (*b*)	**49.** (*c*)	**50.** (*c*)

Solved Paper 2006 (June)

UGC NET

PAPER-I

Note : This paper contains **Fifty (50)** multiple choice questions, each question carrying **two (2)** marks.

1. Which of the following comprise teaching skill?

(*a*) Black Board writing

(*b*) Questioning

(*c*) Explaining

(*d*) All the above

2. Which of the following statements is most appropriate?

(*a*) Teachers can teach.

(*b*) Teachers help can create in a student a desire to learn.

(*c*) Lecture Method can be used for developing thinking.

(*d*) Teachers are born.

3. The first Indian chronicler of Indian history was:

(*a*) Megasthanese (*b*) Fahiyan

(*c*) Huan Tsang (*d*) Kalhan

4. Which of the following statements is correct?

(*a*) Syllabus is a part of curriculum.

(*b*) Syllabus is an annexure to curriculum.

(*c*) Curriculum is the same in all educational institutions affiliated to a particular university.

(*d*) Syllabus is not the same in all educational institutions affiliated to a particular university.

5. Which of the two given options is of the level of understanding?

(I) Define noun.

(II) Define noun in your own words.

(*a*) Only I (*b*) Only II

(*c*) Both I and II (*d*) Neither I nor II

6. Which of the following options are the main tasks of research in modern society?

I. to keep pace with the advancement in knowledge.

II. to discover new things.

III. to write a critique on the earlier writings.

IV. to systematically examine and critically analyse the investigations/sources with objectivity.

(*a*) IV, II and I

(*b*) I, II and III

(*c*) I and III

(*d*) II, III and IV

7. Match List-I (Interviews) with List-II (Meaning) and select the correct answer from the code given below:

List - I (*Interviews*)	**List - II** (*Meaning*)
A. structured interviews	(*i*) greater flexibility approach
B. Unstructured interviews	(*ii*) attention on the questions to be answered
C. Focused interviews	(*iii*) individual life experience
D. Clinical interviews	(*iv*) Pre determined question
	(*v*) non-directive

Code:

	A	B	C	D
(*a*)	(*iv*)	(*i*)	(*ii*)	(*iii*)
(*b*)	(*ii*)	(*iv*)	(*i*)	(*iii*)
(*c*)	(*v*)	(*ii*)	(*iv*)	(*i*)
(*d*)	(*i*)	(*iii*)	(*v*)	(*iv*)

8. What do you consider as the main aim of inter disciplinary research?
   (*a*) To bring out holistic approach to research.
   (*b*) To reduce the emphasis of single subject in research domain.
   (*c*) To over simplify the problem of research.
   (*d*) To create a new trend in research methodology.

9. One of the aims of the scientific method in research is to:
   (*a*) improve data interpretation
   (*b*) eliminate spurious relations
   (*c*) confirm triangulation
   (*d*) introduce new variables

10. The depth of any research can be judged by:
   (*a*) title of the research.
   (*b*) objectives of the research.
   (*c*) total expenditure on the research.
   (*d*) duration of the research.

(Directions Q. (11 – 15) : Read the following passage and answer the questions.

The superintendence, direction and control of preparation of electoral rolls for, and the conduct of, elections to Parliament and State Legislatures and elections to the offices of the President and the Vice - President of India are vested in the Election Commission of India. It is an independent constitutional authority.

Independence of the Election Commission and its insulation from executive interference is ensured by a specific provision under Article 324 (5) of the constitution that the chief Election Commissioner shall not be removed from his office except in like manner and on like grounds as a Judge of the Supreme Court and conditions of his service shall not be varied to his disadvantage after his appointment.

In C.W.P. No. 4912 of 1998 (Kushra Bharat Vs. Union of India and others), the Delhi High Court directed that information relating to Government dues owed by the candidates to the departments dealing with Government accommodation, electricity, water, telephone and transport etc. and any other dues should be furnished by the candidates and this information should be published by the election authorities under the commission.

11. The text of the passage reflects or raises certain questions:
   (*a*) The authority of the commission cannot be challenged.
   (*b*) This would help in stopping the criminalization of Indian politics.
   (*c*) This would reduce substantially the number of contesting candidates.
   (*d*) This would ensure fair and free elections.

12. According to the passage, the Election Commission is an independent constitutional authority. This is under Article No.
   (*a*) 324 (*b*) 356
   (*c*) 246 (*d*) 161

13. Independence of the Commission means:
   (*a*) have a constitutional status.
   (*b*) have legislative powers.
   (*c*) have judicial powers.
   (*d*) have political powers.

14. Fair and free election means:
   (*a*) transparency
   (*b*) to maintain law and order
   (*c*) regional considerations
   (*d*) role for pressure groups

15. The Chief Election Commissioner can be removed from his office under Article :
   (*a*) 125 (*b*) 352
   (*c*) 226 (*d*) 324

16. The function of mass communication of supplying information regarding the processes, issues, events and societal developments is known as:
   (*a*) content supply
   (*b*) surveillance
   (*c*) gratification
   (*d*) correlation

17. The science of the study of feedback systems in humans, animals and machines is known as:

(*a*) cybernetics

(*b*) reverse communication

(*c*) selectivity study

(*d*) response analysis

18. Networked media exist in inter-connected:

(*a*) social environments

(*b*) economic environments

(*c*) political environments

(*d*) technological environments

19. The combination of computing, telecommunications and media in a digital atmosphere is referred to as:

(*a*) online communication

(*b*) integrated media

(*c*) digital combine

(*d*) convergence

20. A dialogue between a human-being and a computer programme that occurs simultaneously in various forms is described as:

(*a*) man-machine speak

(*b*) binary chat

(*c*) digital talk

(*d*) interactivity

21. Insert the missing number:

16/32, 15 /33, 17/31, 14/34 ?

(*a*) 19/35 (*b*) 19/30

(*c*) 18/35 (*d*) 18/30

22. Monday falls on 20th March 1995. What was the day on 3rd November 1994?

(*a*) Thursday (*b*) Sunday

(*c*) Tuesday (*d*) Saturday

23. The average of four consecutive even numbers is 27. The largest of these numbers is:

(*a*) 36 (*b*) 32

(*c*) 30 (*d*) 28

24. In a certain code, FHQK means GIRL. How will WOMEN be written in the same code?

(*a*) VNLDM (*b*) FHQKN

(*c*) XPNFO (*d*) VLNDM

25. At what time between 4 and 5 O'clock will the hands of a watch point in opposite directions?

(*a*) 45 min. past 4

(*b*) 40 min. past 4

(*c*) 50 4/11 min. past 4

(*d*) 54 6/11 min. past 4

26. Which of the following conclusions is logically valid based on statement given below?

Statement : Most teachers are hard working.

Conclusions :

(I) Some teachers are hard working.

(II) Some teachers are not hard working.

(*a*) Only (I) is implied

(*b*) Only (II) is implied

(*c*) Both (I) and (II) are implied

(*d*) Neither (I) nor (II) is implied

27. Who among the following can be asked to make a statement in Indian Parliament?

(*a*) Any MLA

(*b*) Chief of Army Staff

(*c*) Solicitor General of India

(*d*) Mayor of Delhi

28. Which of the following conclusions is logically valid based on statement given below?

Statement : Most of the Indian states existed before independence.

Conclusions:

(I) Some Indian States existed before independence.

(II) All Indian States did not exist before independence.

(*a*) only (I) is implied

(*b*) only (II) is implied

(*c*) Both (I) and (II) are implied

(*d*) Neither (I) nor (II) is implied

29. Water is always involved with landslides. This is because it:

(*a*) reduces the shear strength of rocks

(*b*) increases the weight of the overburden

(*c*) enhances chemical weathering

(*d*) is a universal solvent

30. Given below are two statements (A) and (B) followed by two conclusions (*i*) and (*ii*). Considering the statements to be true, indicate which of the following conclusions logically follow from the given statements by selecting one of the four response alternatives given below the conclusion :

Statements:

(A) all businessmen are wealthy.

(A) all wealthy people are hard working.

Conclusions:

(*i*) All businessmen are hard working.

(*ii*) All hardly working people are not wealthy

(*a*) Only (*i*) follows

(*b*) Only (*ii*) follows

(*c*) Only (*i*) and (*ii*) follows

(*d*) Neither (*i*) nor (*ii*) follows

31. Using websites to pour out one's grievances is called:

(*a*) cyber venting (*b*) cyber ranting

(*c*) web hate (*d*) web plea

32. In web search, finding a large number of documents with very little relevant information is termed:

(*a*) poor recall

(*b*) web crawl

(*c*) poor precision rate

(*d*) poor web response

33. The concept of connect intelligence is derived from:

(*a*) virtual reality

(*b*) fuzzy logic

(*c*) Bluetooth technology

(*d*) value added networks

34. Use of an ordinary telephone as an Internet applicance is called:

(*a*) voice net (*b*) voice telephone

(*c*) voice line (*d*) voice portal

35. Video transmission over the Internet that looks like delayed livecasting is called:

(*a*) virtual video

(*b*) direct broadcast

(*c*) video shift

(*d*) real-time video

36. Which is the smallest North-east State in India?

(*a*) Tripura

(*b*) Meghalaya

(*c*) Mizoram

(*d*) Manipur

37. Tamilnadu coastal belt has drinking water shortage due to:

(*a*) high evaporation

(*b*) sea water flooding due to tsunami

(*c*) over exploitation of ground water by tube wells

(*d*) seepage of sea water

38. While all rivers of Peninsular India flow into the Bay of Bengal, Narmada and Tapti flow into the Arabian Sea because these two rivers:

(*a*) Follow the slope of these rift valleys

(*b*) The general slope of the Indian peninsula is from east to west

(*c*) The Indian peninsula north of the Satpura ranges, is tilted towards the west

(*d*) The Indian peninsula south of the satpura ranges is tilted towards east

39. Soils in the Mahanadi delta are less fertile than those in the Godavari delta because of:

(*a*) erosion of top soils by annual floods

(*b*) inundation of land by sea water

(*c*) traditional agriculture practices

(*d*) the derivation of alluvial soil from red-soil hinterland

40. Which of the following institutions in the field of education is set up by the MHRD Government of India?

(*a*) Indian council of world Affair, New Delhi

(*b*) Mythic Society, Bangalore

(*c*) National Bal Bhavan, New Delhi

(*d*) India International Centre, New Delhi

41. Assertion (A) : Aerosols have potential for modifying climate

Reason (R) : Aerosols interact with both short waves and radiation

(*a*) Both (A) and (R) are true, and (R) is the correct explanation of (A)

(*b*) Both (A) and (R) are true, but (R) is not the correct explanation of (A)

(*c*) (A) is true, but (R) is false

(*d*) (A) is false, but (R) is true

42. 'SITE' stands for:

(*a*) System for International technology and Engineering

(*b*) Satellite Instructional Television Experiment

(*c*) South Indian Trade Estate

(*d*) State Institute of Technology and Engineering

43. What is the name of the Research station established by the Indian Government for 'Conducting Research' at Antarctic?

(*a*) Dakshin Gangotri

(*b*) Yamunotri

(*c*) Uttari Gangotri

(*d*) None of the above

44. Ministry of Human Resource Development (HRD) includes:

(*a*) Department of Elementary Education and Literacy

(*b*) Department of Secondary Education and Higher Education

(*c*) Department of Women and Child Development

(*d*) All the above

45. Parliament can legislate on matters listed in the State list:

(*a*) With the prior permission of the President.

(*b*) Only after the constitution is amended suitably.

(*c*) In case of inconsistency among State legislatures.

(*d*) At the request of two or more States.

Directions Q. (46 – 50) : *The following pie chart indicates the expenditure of a country on various sports during a particular year. Study the pie chart and answer it.*

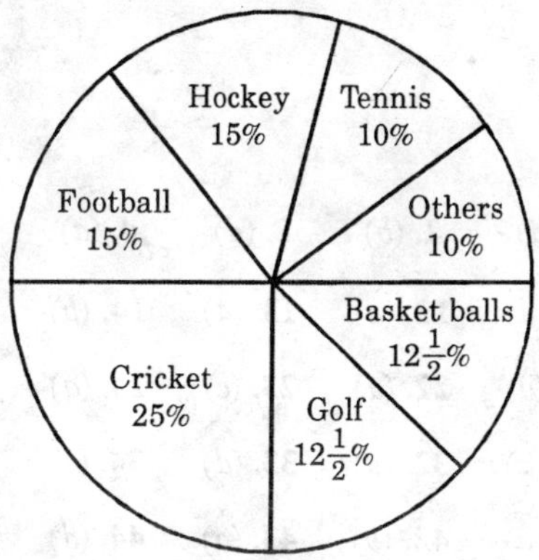

46. The ratio of the total expenditure on football to that of expenditure on hockey is:

(*a*) 1 : 15 (*b*) 1 : 1

(*c*) 15 : 1 (*d*) 3 : 20

47. if the total expenditure on sports during the year was ₹ 1,20,000,00 how much was spent on basket ball?

(*a*) ₹ 9,50,000

(*b*) ₹ 10,00,000

(*c*) ₹ 12,00,000

(*d*) ₹ 15,00,000

48. The chart shows that the most popular game of the country is :

(*a*) Hockey

(*b*) Football

(*c*) Cricket

(*d*) Tennis

49. Out of the following country's expenditure is the same on :

(a) Hockey and Tennis
(b) Golf and Basket ball
(c) Cricket and Football
(d) Hockey and Golf

50. If the total expenditure on sport during the year was ₹ 1,50,00,000 the expenditure on cricket and hockey together was:

(a) ₹ 60,00,000 (b) ₹ 50,00,000
(c) ₹ 37,50,000 (d) ₹ 25,00,000

ANSWERS

1. (d)	**2.** (b)	**3.** (d)	**4.** (a)	**5.** (b)	**6.** (a)	**7.** (a)	**8.** (a)	**9.** (b)	**10.** (b)
11. (d)	**12.** (a)	**13.** (a)	**14.** (b)	**15.** (d)	**16.** (a)	**17.** (a)	**18.** (d)	**19.** (d)	**20.** (d)
21. (d)	**22.** (a)	**23.** (c)	**24.** (a)	**25.** (d)	**26.** (c)	**27.** (c)	**28.** (b)	**29.** (b)	**30.** (a)
31. (a)	**32.** (a)	**33.** (d)	**34.** (c)	**35.** (d)	**36.** (a)	**37.** (d)	**38.** (a)	**39.** (a)	**40.** (c)
41. (a)	**42.** (b)	**43.** (a)	**44.** (d)	**45.** (d)	**46.** (b)	**47.** (d)	**48.** (c)	**49.** (b)	**50.** (a)

Solved Paper 2005 (December)

UGC NET

PAPER-I

Note : This paper contains **Fifty (50)** multiple choice questions, each question carrying **two (2)** marks.

1. Team teaching has the potential to develop :
   (*a*) Competitive spirit
   (*b*) Cooperation
   (*c*) The habit of supplementing the teaching of each other
   (*d*) Highlighting the gaps in each other's teaching
2. Which of the following is the most important characteristic of Open Book Examination system ?
   (*a*) Students become serious.
   (*b*) It improves attendance in the classroom.
   (*c*) It reduces examination anxiety amongst students.
   (*d*) It compels students to think.
3. Which of the following methods of teaching encourages the use of maximum senses ?
   (*a*) Problem-solving method
   (*b*) Laboratory method
   (*c*) Self-study method
   (*d*) Team teaching method
4. Which of the following statement is correct ?
   (*a*) Communicator should have fine senses
   (*b*) Communicator should have tolerance power
   (*c*) Communicator should be soft spoken
   (*d*) Communicator should have good personality
5. An effective teacher is one who can :
   (*a*) control the class
   (*b*) give more information in less time
   (*c*) motivate students to learn
   (*d*) correct the assignments carefully
6. One of the following is not a quality of researcher:
   (*a*) Unison with that of which he is in search
   (*b*) He must be of alert mind
   (*c*) Keenness in enquiry
   (*d*) His assertion to outstrip the evidence
7. A satisfactory statistical quantitative method should not possess one of the following qualities :
   (*a*) Appropriateness
   (*b*) Measurability
   (*c*) Comparability
   (*d*) Flexibility
8. Books and records are the primary sources of data in :
   (*a*) historical research
   (*b*) participatory research
   (*c*) clinical research
   (*d*) laboratory research
9. Which of the following statement is correct ?
   (*a*) objectives should be pin-pointed
   (*b*) objectives can be written in statement or question form
   (*c*) another word for problem is variable
   (*d*) all the above
10. The important pre-requisites of a researcher in sciences, social sciences and humanities are :
    (*a*) laboratory skills, records, supervisor, topic
    (*b*) Supervisor, topic, critical analysis, patience
    (*c*) archives, supervisor, topic, flexibility in thinking
    (*d*) topic, supervisor, good temperament, pre-conceived notions

Direction (Q. 11 - 15) : *Read the following passage and answer the questions :*

Knowledge creation in many cases requires creativity and idea generation. This is especially important in generating alternative decision support solutions. Some people believe that an individual's creative ability stems primarily from personality traits such as inventiveness, independence, individuality, enthusiasm, and flexibility. However, several studies have found that creativity is not so much a function of individual traits as was once believed, and that individual creativity can be learned and improved. This understanding has led innovative companies to recognise that the key to fostering creativity may be the development of an idea-nurturing work environment. Idea-generation methods and techniques, to be used by individuals or in groups, are consequently being developed. Manual methods for supporting idea generation, such as brainstorming in a group, can be very successful in certain situations. However, in other situations, such an approach is either not economically feasible or not possible. For example, manual methods in group creativity sessions will not work or will not be effective when : (1) there is no time to conduct a proper idea-generation session; (2) there is a poor facilitator (or no facilitator at all); (3) it is too expensive to conduct an idea-generation session; (4) the subject matter is too sensitive for a face-to-face session; or (5) there are not enough participants, the mix of participants is not optimal, or there is no climate for idea generation. In such cases, computerised idea-generation methods have been tried, with frequent success.

Idea-generation software is designed to help stimulate a single user or a group to produce new ideas, options and choices. The user does all the work, but the software encourages and pushes, something like a personal trainer. Although idea-generation software is still relatively new, there are several packages on the market. Various approaches are used by idea-generating software to increase the flow of ideas to the user. Idea Fisher, for example, has an associate lexicon of the English language that cross-references words and phrases. These associative links, based on analogies and metaphors, make it easy for the user to be fed words related to a given theme. Some software packages use questions to prompt the user towards new, unexplored patterns of thought. This helps users to break out of cyclical thinking patterns, conquer mental blocks, or deal with bouts of procrastination.

11. The author, in this passage has focussed on

(*a*) knowledge creation

(*b*) idea-generation

(*c*) creativity

(*d*) individual traits

12. Fostering creativity needs an environment of

(*a*) decision support systems

(*b*) idea-nurturing

(*c*) decision support solutions

(*d*) alternative individual factors

13. Manual methods for the support of idea-generation, in certain occasions,

(*a*) are alternatively effective

(*b*) can be less expensive

(*c*) do not need a facilitator

(*d*) require a mix of optimal participants

14. Idea-generation software works as if it is a :

(*a*) stimulant

(*b*) knowledge package

(*c*) user-friendly trainer

(*d*) climate creator

15. Mental blocks, bouts of procrastination and cyclical thinking patterns can be won when :

(*a*) innovative companies employ electronic thinking methods

(*b*) idea-generation software prompts questions

(*c*) manual methods are removed

(*d*) individuals acquire a neutral attitude towards the software

16. Level C of the effectiveness of communication is defined as :

(*a*) channel noise (*b*) semantic noise

(*c*) psychological noise (*d*) source noise

17. Recording a television programme on a VCR is an example of :

(*a*) time-shifting

(*b*) content reference

(*c*) mechanical clarity

(*d*) media synchronisation

18. A good communicator is the one who offers to his audience :

(*a*) plentiful of information

(*b*) a good amount of statistics

(*c*) concise proof

(*d*) repetition of facts

19. The largest number of newspapers in India is published from the state of :

(*a*) Kerala

(*b*) Maharashtra

(*c*) West Bengal

(*d*) Uttar Pradesh

20. Insert the missing number :

8 24 12 ? 18 54

(*a*) 26 (*b*) 24

(*c*) 36 (*d*) 32

21. January 1, 1995 was Sunday. What day of the week lies on January 1, 1996 ?

(*a*) Sunday (*b*) Monday

(*c*) Saturday (*d*) None of these

22. The sum of a positive number and its reciprocal is twice the difference of the number and its reciprocal. The number is :

(*a*) $\sqrt{2}$ (*b*) $\frac{1}{\sqrt{2}}$

(*c*) $\sqrt{3}$ (*d*) $\frac{1}{\sqrt{3}}$

23. In a certain code, ROUNDS is written as RONUDS. How will PLEASE will be written in the same code :

(*a*) LPAESE (*b*) PLAESE

(*c*) LPAEES (*d*) PL A SEE

24. At what time between 5.30 and 6.00 will the hands of an clock be at right angles ?

(*a*) $43\frac{5}{11}$ min. past 5

(*b*) $43\frac{7}{11}$ min. past 5

(*c*) 40 min. past 5

(*d*) 45 min past 5

25. Statements : I. All students are ambitious

II. All ambitious persons are hard working

Conclusions : (*i*) All students are hard-working

(*ii*) All hardly working people are not ambitious

Which of the following is correct ?

(*a*) Only (*i*) is correct

(*b*) Only (*ii*) is correct

(*c*) Both (*i*) and (*ii*) are correct

(*d*) Neither (*i*) nor (*ii*) is correct

26. Statement : Most students are intelligent

Conclusions : (*i*) Some students are intelligent

(*ii*) All students are not intelligent

Which of the following is implied ?

(*a*) Only (*i*) is implied

(*b*) Only (*ii*) is implied

(*c*) Both (*i*) and (*ii*) are implied

(*d*) Neither (*i*) nor (*ii*) is implied

27. Statement : Most labourers are poor

Conclusions : (*i*)Some labourers are poor

(*ii*) All labourers are not poor

Which of the following is implied ?

(*a*) Only (*i*) is implied

(*b*) Only (*ii*) is implied

(*c*) Both (*i*) and (*ii*) are implied

(*d*) Neither (*i*) nor (*ii*) is implied

28. Line access and avoidance of collision are the main functions of :

(*a*) the CPU

(*b*) the monitor

(*c*) network protocols

(*d*) wide area networks

29. In the hypermedia database, information bits are stored in the form of :

(*a*) signals

(*b*) cubes

(*c*) nodes

(*d*) symbols

30. Communications bandwidth that has the highest capacity and is used by microwave, cable and fibre optics lines is known as :

(*a*) hyper-link

(*b*) broadband

(*c*) bus width

(*d*) carrier wave

31. An electronic bill board that has a short text or graphical advertising message is referred to as:

(*a*) bulletin

(*b*) strap

(*c*) bridge line

(*d*) banner

32. Which of the following is not the characteristic of a computer ?

(*a*) computer is an electrical machine

(*b*) computer cannot think at its own

(*c*) computer processes information error free

(*d*) computer can hold data for any length of time

33. Bitumen is obtained from :

(*a*) Forests and Plants

(*b*) Kerosene oil

(*c*) Crude oil

(*d*) underground mines

34. Malaria is caused by :

(*a*) bacterial infection

(*b*) viral infection

(*c*) parasitic infection

(*d*) fungal infection

35. The cloudy nights are warmer compared to clear nights (without clouds) during winter days. This is because :

(*a*) clouds radiate heat towards the earth

(*b*) clouds prevent cold wave from the sky, descend on earth

(*c*) clouds prevent escaping of the heat radiation from the earth

(*d*) clouds being at great heights from earth absorb heat from the sun and send towards the earth

36. Largest soil group of India is :

(*a*) Red soil

(*c*) Sandy soil

(*b*) Black soil

(*d*) Mountain soil

37. Main pollutant of the Indian coastal water is :

(*a*) oil spill

(*b*) municipal sewage

(*c*) industrial effluents

(*d*) aerosols

38. Human ear is most sensitive to noise in the following frequency ranges

(*a*) 1 – 2 KHz

(*b*) 100 – 500 Hz

(*c*) 10 – 12 KHz

(*d*) 13 – 16 KHz

39. Which species of chromium is toxic in water :

(*a*) Cr + 2

(*b*) Cr + 3

(*c*) Cr + 6

(*d*) Cr is non-toxic element

40. Match List - I (Dams) with List - II (River) in the following

List - I (Dams)	List - II (River)
A. Bhakra	(*i*) Krishna
B. Nagarjunasagar	(*ii*) Damodar
C. Panchet	(*iii*) Sutlej
D. Hirakud	(*iv*) Bhagirathi
E. Tehri	(*v*) Mahanadi

Codes :

	A	B	C	D	E
(*a*)	*v*	*iii*	*iv*	*ii*	*i*
(*b*)	*iii*	*i*	*ii*	*v*	*iv*
(*c*)	*i*	*ii*	*iv*	*iii*	*v*
(*d*)	*ii*	*iii*	*iv*	*i*	*v*

41. A negative reaction to a mediated communication is described as :

(*a*) flak

(*b*) fragmented feedback

(*c*) passive response

(*d*) non-conformity

42. The launch of satellite channel by IGNOU on 26th January 2003 for technological education for the growth and development of distance education is :

(*a*) Eklavya channel

(*c*) Rajrishi channel

(*b*) Gyandarshan channel

(*d*) None of these

43. Match List - I with List-II and select the correct answer from the code given below :

List -I (Institutions)	List -II (Locations)
A. The Indian Council of Historical Reasearch (ICHR)	(i) Shimla
B. The Indian Institute of Advanced Studies (IIAS)	(*ii*) New Delhi
C. The Indian Council of Philosophical Research (ICPR)	(*iii*) Banglore
D. The Central Institute of Coastal Engineering for fisheries	(*iv*) Lucknow

Codes :

	A	B	C	D
(*a*)	*ii*	*i*	*iv*	*iii*
(*b*)	*i*	*ii*	*iii*	*iv*
(c)	*ii*	*iv*	*i*	*iii*
(*d*)	*iv*	*iii*	*ii*	*i*

44. Which of the following is not a Fundamental Right ?

(*a*) Right to equality

(*b*) Right against exploitation

(*c*) Right to freedom of speech and expression

(*d*) Right of free compulsory education of all children upto the age of 14

45. The Lok - Sabha can be dissolved before the expiry of its normal five year term by

(*a*) The Prime Minister

(*b*) The Speaker of Lok Sabha

(*c*) The President on the recommendation of the Prime Minister

(*d*) None of the above

Direction (Q. 46 – 50) : *Study the following graph carefully and answer the questions.*

EXPORT OF TINS

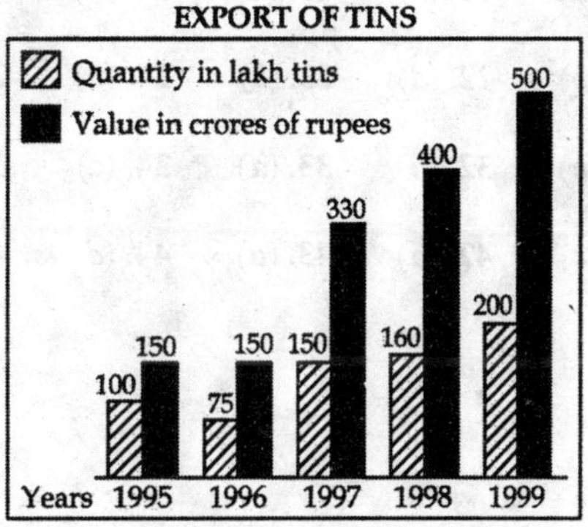

46. In which year the value per tin was minimum?

(*a*) 1995 (*b*) 1996

(*c*) 1998 (*d*) 1999

47. What was the difference between the tins exported in 1997 and 1998 ?

(*a*) 10 (*b*) 1000

(*c*) 100000 (*d*) 1000000

48. What was the approximate percentage increase in export value from 1995 to 1999 ?

(*a*) 350

(*b*) 330.3

(*c*) 433.3

(*d*) None of these

49. What was the percentage drop in export quantity from 1995 to 1996 ?

(*a*) 75

(*b*) 50

(*c*) 25

(*d*) None of these

50. If in 1998, the tins were exported at the same rate per tin as that in 1997, what would be the value (in crores of rupees) of export in 1998 ?

(*a*) 400

(*b*) 375

(*c*) 352

(*d*) 330

ANSWERS

1. (*c*)	**2.** (*d*)	**3.** (*b*)	**4.** (*a*)	**5.** (*c*)	**6.** (*d*)	**7.** (*d*)	**8.** (*a*)	**9.** (*a*)	**10.** (*b*)
11. (*a*)	**12.** (*b*)	**13.** (*a*)	**14.** (*a*)	**15.** (*b*)	**16.** (*a*)	**17.** (*d*)	**18.** (*a*)	**19.** (*d*)	**20.** (*c*)
21. (*b*)	**22.** (*d*)	**23.** (*b*)	**24.** (*b*)	**25.** (*c*)	**26.** (*b*)	**27.** (*b*)	**28.** (*c*)	**29.** (*a*)	**30.** (*b*)
31. (*b*)	**32.** (*a*)	**33.** (*d*)	**34.** (*c*)	**35.** (*c*)	**36.** (*a*)	**37.** (*c*)	**38.** (*d*)	**39.** (*c*)	**40.** (*b*)
41. (*c*)	**42.** (*a*)	**43.** (*a*)	**44.** (*d*)	**45.** (*c*)	**46.** (*a*)	**47.** (*a*)	**48.** (*d*)	**49.** (*c*)	**50.** (*c*)

Solved Paper 2004 (December)

UGC NET

PAPER-I

Note : This paper contains **Fifty (50)** multiple choice questions, each question carrying **two** (2) marks.

1. Discussion Method can be used when :
   (*a*) The topic is very difficult
   (*b*) The topic is easy
   (*c*) The topic is difficult
   (*d*) All the above

2. Which of the following is a teaching aid ?
   (*a*) Working Model of Wind Mill
   (*b*) Tape Recorder
   (*c*) 16 mm Film Projector
   (*d*) All the above

3. The main aim of teaching is :
   (*a*) To develop only reasoning
   (*b*) To develop only thinking
   (*c*) Both (*a*) and (*b*)
   (*d*) To give information

4. The quality of teaching is reflected :
   (*a*) By the attendance of students in the class
   (*b*) By the pass percentage of students
   (*c*) By the quality of questions asked by students
   (*d*) By the duration of silence maintained in the class

5. The present annual examination system :
   (*a*) promotes rote learning
   (*b*) does not promote good study habits
   (*c*) does not encourage students to be regular in class
   (*d*) All the above

6. A college wants to give training in use of Statistical Package for Social Sciences (SPSS) to researchers. For this the college should organise :
   (*a*) Conference (*b*) Seminar
   (*c*) Workshop (*d*) Lecture

7. Which of the following is NOT the characteristic of a research ?
   (*a*) Research is systematic
   (*b*) Research is not a process
   (*c*) Research is problem oriented
   (*d*) Research is not passive

8. Which of the following statement is correct ?
   (*a*) Discoveries are researches
   (*b*) Researches lead to discovery
   (*c*) Invention and Research are related
   (*d*) None of the above

9. Which of the following statement is correct ?
   (*a*) In research, objectives can be worded in question form
   (*b*) In research, objectives can be worded in statement form
   (*c*) Objectives are to be stated in Chapter I of the Thesis
   (*d*) All the above

10. Match List A with List B and choose the correct answer from the code given below :

List A	List B
A. Historical Method	(*i*) Past events
B. Survey Method	(*ii*) Vision
C. Philosophical Method	(*iii*) Present events
D. Experimental Method	(*iv*) Exceptional cases
	(*v*) Future action

Code :

	A	B	C	D
(a)	(i)	(iii)	(ii)	(v)
(b)	(i)	(ii)	(iv)	(v)
(c)	(i)	(iv)	(ii)	(v)
(d)	(i)	(ii)	(iii)	(iv)

Directions Q. (11 – 15) : *Read the following passage and answer the question.*

Each day at the Shantiniketan School starts with the Saraswati Vandana. When painting competitions are held in the school, images of Hindu gods and goddesses are most common. Sanskrit is a favourite subject of many a student. Nothing new about it except that the 1,200 - odd students studying in the Hindu - run school are Muslims.

In 1983, when Ranchodbhai Kiri started Shantiniketan in the all - Muslim Juhapura area of Ahmedabad in Gujarat, only 20 percent of the students were Muslims. But when riots involving the Muslims of Juhapura and the Hindus of nearby Jivrajpark -Vejalpur affected the locality, Hindus started migrating. Today, all the students are Muslims and the school is an unparalled example of harmony. In the 2002, when a section of inflamed Muslims wanted the school closed, the parents of the students stood like a wall behind it. Shantiniketan's principal says, "We never thought of moving the school out of the area because of the love and affection of the local Muslims. Indeed they value the high standard of education which we have set." Such is the reputation of the school that some of the local Muslim strongmen accused of involvement in communal riots are willing to protect the school during the riots.

The parents of Shantiniketan's students believe that it's the best school when it comes to the quality of the teaching. A large number of students have gone for both graduation and post graduation studies. Significantly, the only Muslim teacher in the 40 - member teaching staff, Husena Mansuri, teaches Sanskrit. Infact, she is so happy at the school that she recently declined the principalship of another Muslim - run school.

Some of the students' entries in a recent school painting competition mere truly moving. One drew a picture of Bharat Mata with a mosque and temple, while another portrayed a boy tying rakhi to his sister. Trully, Shantiniketan is a beacon of hope that, despite the provocations from both communities, Hindus and Muslims can live side-by-side with mutual respect.

11. How the Shantiniketan school starts the day ?

(a) National anthem
(b) Prayer
(c) Saraswati Vandana
(d) Puja

12. Write the subject which is preferred by most of the students

(a) Hindi (b) English
(c) Sanskrit (d) Gujarati

13. Who protects the school during the riot times?

(a) Local Muslims (b) Hindus
(c) Politicians (d) Christians

14. Who is the teacher of Sanskrit ?

(a) Ranchodbhai Kiri
(b) Manisha Vakil
(c) Husena Mansuri
(d) Husena Khatoon

15. What is the hope despite the communal riots?

(a) Hindus and Muslims cannot live side by side
(b) Hindus and Muslims can live side by side
(c) Only Hindus can live
(d) Only Muslims can live

16. Match List I with List II and choose the correct answer using the codes given below :

List I (Distinguished Ladies)	**List II** (Area of work)
A. Jhumpa Lahiri	(i) Journalist
B. Barkha Dutt	(ii) Novel Writing
C. Aparna Sen	(iii) Film Actress
D. Smita Patil	(iv) Film Director

Code :

	A	B	C	D
(a)	(iv)	(iii)	(ii)	(i)
(b)	(ii)	(i)	(iv)	(iii)
(c)	(iv)	(i)	(iii)	(ii)
(d)	(ii)	(iii)	(iv)	(i)

17. Which of the following pair is not correctly matched ?

(*a*) Aajtak - 24 hours news channel
(*b*) F.M. Stations - Radio
(*c*) National Geography channel - Television
(*d*) Vir Sanghvi - India Today

18. Which is the oldest soap opera telecasted in India ?

(*a*) Kahani Ghar Ghar Ki
(*b*) Buniad
(*c*) Humlog
(*d*) Saas bhi Kabhi Bahu Thee

19. Which satellite channel uses the adline, "Knowing is everything" ?

(*a*) BBC World (*b*) Star
(*c*) Sony (*d*) Zee

20. Which is the "First made in India" Kids channel of television ?

(*a*) Cartoon Network
(*b*) Walt Disney
(*c*) United Home Entertainment's Hungama TV
(*d*) Nick Jr.

21. The letters in the first set have certain relationships. On the basis of the relationship which is the right choice for the second set ?

BF : GK : : LP : ?

(*a*) JK (*b*) QW
(*c*) VW (*d*) RQ

22. If the BLOOD is coded as 24113 and BRUST as 20678, then code for ROBUST is :

(*a*) 620781 (*b*) 012678
(*c*) 678102 (*d*) 610732

23. A bag contains an equal number of one rupee, 50 paise and 25 paise coins. If the total amount in the bag is ₹ 35, how many coins of each type are there ?

(*a*) 15 (*b*) 18
(*c*) 20 (*d*) 25

24. In the sequence of numbers

$\frac{2}{3}, \frac{4}{7}, X, \frac{11}{21}, \frac{16}{31}$

the missing number X is :

(*a*) $\frac{8}{10}$ (*b*) $\frac{6}{10}$
(*c*) $\frac{5}{10}$ (*d*) $\frac{7}{10}$

25. If A stands for 5 , B for 6, C for 7, D for 8, and so on, what do the following numbers stand for: 22, 25, 8, 22 and 5 ?

(*a*) PRIYA (*b*) NEEMA
(*c*) MEENA (*d*) RUDRA

26. Which of the following statements are always true ?

A. A wooden table is a table
B. Now, it is raining or not raining
C. The sun rises in the East every day
D. A chicken comes out of a hen's egg

Choose the correct answer from the code given below :

Code :

(*a*) (A) and (C) (*b*) (A), (C) and (D)
(*c*) (A) and (B) (*d*) (B) and (C)

27. Which of the following statements are mutually inconsistent ?

A. Mostly poets are not egoistic
B. Mostly poets are humble
C. Some poets are egoistic
D. Some poets are not non - egoistic

Choose the correct answer from the code given below :

Code :

(*a*) (A) and (D) (*b*) (B) and (C)
(*c*) (A) and (C) (*d*) (C) and (D)

28. Which of the following statements is/are absolutely impossible ?

A. A woman giving birth to her own grandchild
B. A man attending his own funeral
C. The Sun not rising in the East some day
D. Cars running without petrol

Choose the correct answer from the code given below :

Code :

(*a*) (A) and (B) (*b*) (C) and (D)
(*c*) (B) (*d*) (A)

29. Which of the following are incorrect ways of arguing ?

A. If horses are cows, and if cows are sheep, then all horses must be sheep.

B. If top actors are famous, and Shah Rukh Khan is famous, then Shah Rukh Khan is a top actor

C. Lata is the second sister of Raju, hence Raju is the second brother of Lata

D. A is not equal to B, but B is equal to C, hence A is equal to C.

Choose the correct answer from the code given below :

Code :

(*a*) (A), (B) and (C) (*b*) (A), (C) and (D)

(*c*) (B), (C) and (D) (*d*) (A), (B) and (D)

30. Which of the following statements say the same thing ?

A. "I am clever" (said by Rama)

B. "I am clever" (said by Raju)

C. "My son is clever" (said by Rama's father)

D. "My brother is clever" (said by Rama's sister)

E. "My brother is clever" (said by Rama's only sister)

F. "My sole enemy is clever" (said by Rama's only enemy)

Choose the correct answer from the code given below :

Code :

(*a*) (A), (C), (D), (E) and (F)

(*b*) (A) and (B)

(*c*) (D) and (E)

(*d*) (A) and (F)

Directions Q. (31 – 33) : *Study the following graph and answer Question.*

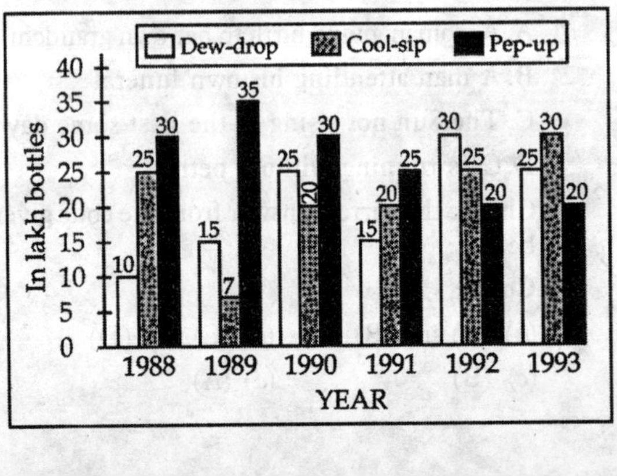

31. In which year was the sale of 'Pep - up' the maximum ?

(*a*) 1990 (*b*) 1992

(*c*) 1993 (*d*) None of the above

32. In the case of which soft drink was the average annual sale maximum during the period 1988 - 1993.

(*a*) Pep - up only

(*b*) Cool - sip only

(*c*) Cool - sip and Dew - drop

(*d*) Pep - up and Dew - drop

33. What was the approximate percent drop in the sale of Pep - up in 1990 over its sale in 1989 ?

(*a*) 5 (*b*) 12

(*c*) 14 (*d*) 20

34. The "Report on Currency and Finance" for each of the financial year in India is published by:

(*a*) Reserve Bank of India

(*b*) Ministry of Finance

(*c*) Planning Commission

(*d*) Central Statistical Organisation

35. The number of students in two classes A and B and the respective "mean" of the marks obtained by each of the class are given in the following table :

	Class A	Class B
Number of Students	20	80
Arithmatic Mean	10	20

The combined "mean" of the marks of the two classes will be :

(*a*) 18 (*b*) 15

(*c*) 10 (*d*) 20

36. ICT stands for :

(*a*) International Communication Technology

(*b*) Intera Common Terminology

(*c*) Information and Communication Technology

(*d*) Inter connected Terminals

37. Which of the following statement is NOT correct ?

(*a*) Computer is capable of processing only digital signal

(*b*) Computer is capable of analysing both quantitative and qualitative data

(*c*) Appropriate software is required for processing the data

(*d*) Computer is capable of processing digital as well as analog signals

38. Which of the following is the appropriate definition of Information Technology ?

(*a*) Information Technology refers to the use of hardware and software for processing information

(*b*) Information Technology refers to the use of hardware and software for distribution of useful information

(*c*) Information Technology refers to the use of hardware and software for storage, retrieval, processing and distributing information of many kinds.

(*d*) Information Technology refers to the use of principles of Physical sciences and Social sciences for processing of information of many kinds.

39. Which of the following statement is correct ?

(*a*) Virus improves the speed of processing information through computer

(*b*) Internet does not allow the virus to spread

(*c*) Virus is a part of software

(*d*) Virus is an operating system

40. Which of the following is correct statement ?

(*a*) Computers can be used for diagnosing the difficulty of a student in learning a subject

(*b*) Psychological testing can be done with the help of computer provided a software is available

(*c*) A set of instructions is called a programme

(*d*) All the above

41. Global warning during winter becomes more pronounced at the :

(*a*) Equator

(*b*) Poles

(*c*) Tropic of Cancer

(*d*) Tropic of Capricorn

42. In the study of man - environment interaction, the statement of Miss Semple that "the humans are solely the product of their environment", is :

(*a*) An opinion

(*b*) A prejudice

(*c*) A fact

(*d*) A widely accepted phenomenon

43. In analysis of man - environment relationship Pragmatic Possibilism implies that :

(*a*) There is no limit for man to exploit resources of earth

(*b*) There are limited possibilities to explore earth's resources

(*c*) The man has to watch and assess the situation and then go ahead with resource utilization

(*d*) The man has to keep in mind only his basic needs while planning to harness the potential of resourceful earth

44. Arrange Column II in proper sequence so as to match it with Column I and choose the correct answer from the code given below :

Column I (Activity)	**Column II** (Noise level)
A. Hearing	(*i*) 30 dB
B. Whispering	(*ii*) 1 dB
C. Interference with sleep	(*iii*) 60 dB
D. Normal talk	(*iv*) 30 - 50 dB

Code :

	A	**B**	**C**	**D**
(*a*)	(*i*)	(*ii*)	(*iii*)	(*iv*)
(*b*)	(*ii*)	(*i*)	(*iv*)	(*iii*)
(*c*)	(*iv*)	(*ii*)	(*iii*)	(*i*)
(*d*)	(*iii*)	(*i*)	(*ii*)	(*iv*)

45. The maximum loss of forest lands in India is caused by :

(*a*) River valley projects

(*b*) Industries

(*c*) Means of transportation

(*d*) Agriculture

46. In which year the University Grants Commission was established ?

(*a*) 1948

(*b*) 1944

(*c*) 1953

(*d*) 1960

47. Another name of Basic Education or Nai Talim is :

(*a*) Compulsory Education

(*b*) New Education Policy

(*c*) Wardha Education Plan

(*d*) Sarva Shikshya Abhiyan

48. The Idea of 'Democratic Decentralisation' in India was popularised by :

(*a*) A.D. Gorwala Committee, 1951

(*b*) Paul H. Appleby Committee, 1953

(*c*) B.R. Mehta Committee, 1957

(*d*) Ashok Mehta Committee, 1978

49. In India, a political party is recognised as a National or Regional Party by the :

(*a*) President of India

(*b*) Election Commission of India

(*c*) Law ministry in consultation with the Law Commission of India

(*d*) Union Parliament in consultation with the State Legislatures

50. Which of the following factors is/are responsible for the increase of the role of Government in Developing Countries ?

A. Economic Planning

B. Rising expectation of People

C. Privatisation

D. Emergence of the concept of Welfare State

Select the most appropriate answer from the code given below :

Code :

(*a*) (A) and (D) (*b*) (A), (B) and (D)

(*c*) Only (C) (*d*) Only (D)

ANSWERS

1. (*c*)	**2.** (*d*)	**3.** (*c*)	**4.** (*c*)	**5.** (*d*)	**6.** (*c*)	**7.** (*b*)	**8.** (*b*)	**9.** (*c*)	**10.** (*b*)
11. (*c*)	**12.** (*c*)	**13.** (*a*)	**14.** (*c*)	**15.** (*b*)	**16.** (*b*)	**17.** (*d*)	**18.** (*c*)	**19.** (*a*)	**20.** (*c*)
21. (*b*)	**22.** (*b*)	**23.** (*c*)	**24.** (*d*)	**25.** (*d*)	**26.** (*b*)	**27.** (*a*)	**28.** (*a*)	**29.** (*b*)	**30.** (*a*)
31. (*d*)	**32.** (*a*)	**33.** (*c*)	**34.** (*a*)	**35.** (*b*)	**36.** (*c*)	**37.** (*a*)	**38.** (*c*)	**39.** (*c*)	**40.** (*d*)
41. (*d*)	**42.** (*c*)	**43.** (*c*)	**44.** (*b*)	**45.** (*a*)	**46.** (*c*)	**47.** (*c*)	**48.** (*c*)	**49.** (*b*)	**50.** (*a*)